Scottish Island Hopping

Scottish Island Hopping

A Guide for the Independent Traveller

Compiled and researched by
Hubert Andrew, Hugh Andrew, Douglas Fraser,
Robert Alan Jamieson, Duncan McLean, Kathryn MacLean,
Alison Munro and Marion Sinclair

Polygon
Edinburgh

© Polygon 1994

Published by Polygon
22 George Square
Edinburgh

Set in Melior
by Koinonia, Manchester and
printed and bound in Great Britain
by Page Bros. Ltd, Norwich

A British Library Cataloguing In
Publication Data Record is available

ISBN 0 74866164 6

General Editor: Marion Sinclair
Assistant Editor: Alison Munro
Production: Pamela O'Connor
Publicity: Kathryn MacLean
Maps: Baynefield Cartographics Ltd
Cover design: Fionna Robson

Contents

Acknowledgements

The contributors would like to thank the following for their help while compiling the guide:

Archie Bevan, Stromness

Caledonian MacBrayne

Joanna Campbell

Louise Fortune, Eday

Sam Harcus, Westray

Jimmy Henderson

Brian Howell

Davie Kirkpatrick

John Lindsay

Joan Mackay

Nan MacLean

David Martin

Robert Miller

Helen Templeton

Jean Whittaker, Tiree

Notes on the contributors

SHETLAND
Robert Alan Jamieson, novelist and poet, was born and brought up in Shetland.

ORKNEY
Duncan McLean, novelist, was born in Aberdeenshire and now lives in Orkney.

SKYE and OUTER HEBRIDES
Douglas Fraser is Highlands and Islands Correspondent for the *Scotsman* newspaper.

INNER HEBRIDES and ISLANDS OF THE CLYDE
Hubert Andrew is a vet, now retired, living in Argyll.

Hugh Andrew is a publisher and freelance rep.

Kathryn MacLean lives in Edinburgh and has family ties with Mull.

Alison Munro is the only contributor to cycle the length of the Western Isles against the prevailing wind.

Marion Sinclair was brought up on Barra.

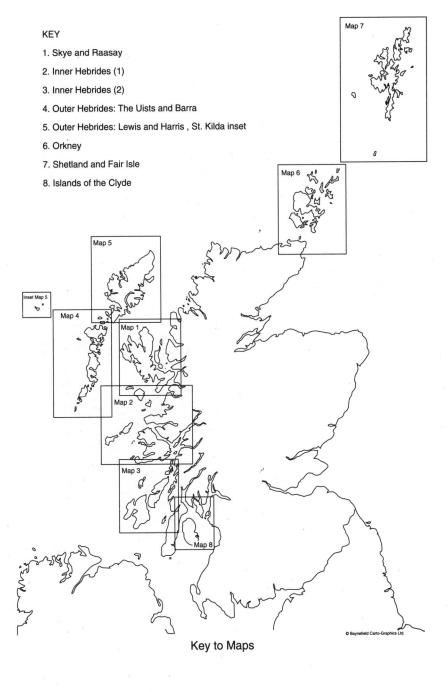

KEY

1. Skye and Raasay

2. Inner Hebrides (1)

3. Inner Hebrides (2)

4. Outer Hebrides: The Uists and Barra

5. Outer Hebrides: Lewis and Harris , St. Kilda inset

6. Orkney

7. Shetland and Fair Isle

8. Islands of the Clyde

Map 7

Map 6

Map 5

Inset Map 5

Map 4

Map 1

Map 2

Map 3

Map 8

© Baynefield Carto-Graphics Ltd.

Key to Maps

1. Skye and Raasay

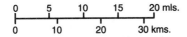

2. Inner Hebrides (1)

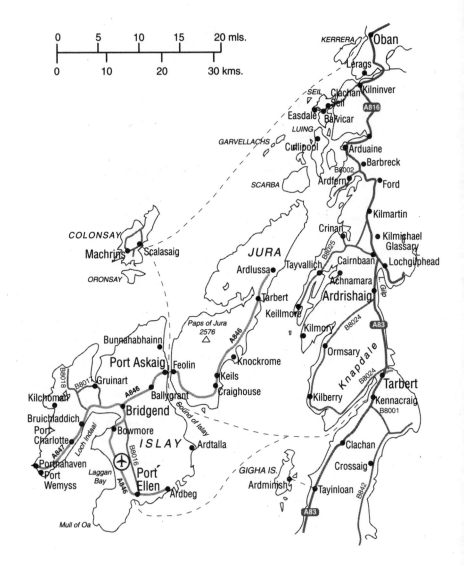

3. Inner Hebrides (2)

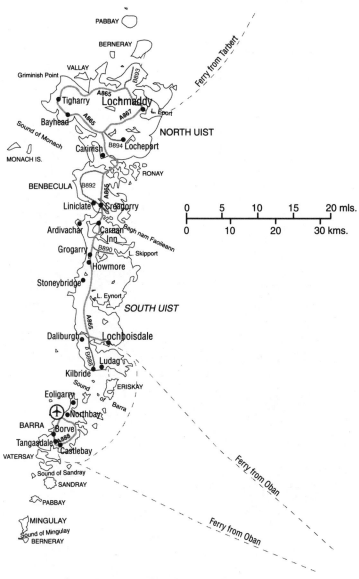

4. Outer Hebrides: The Uists and Barra

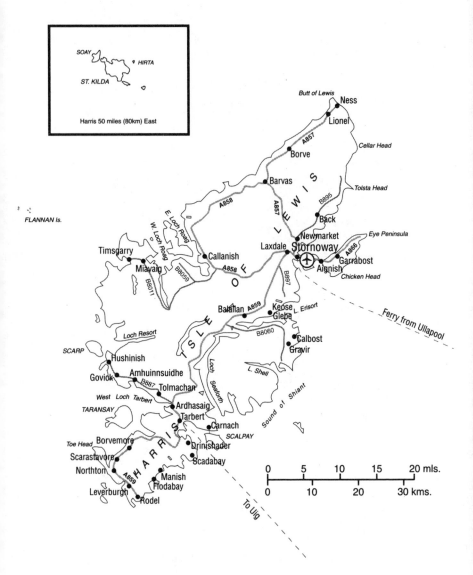

5. Outer Hebrides: Lewis and Harris

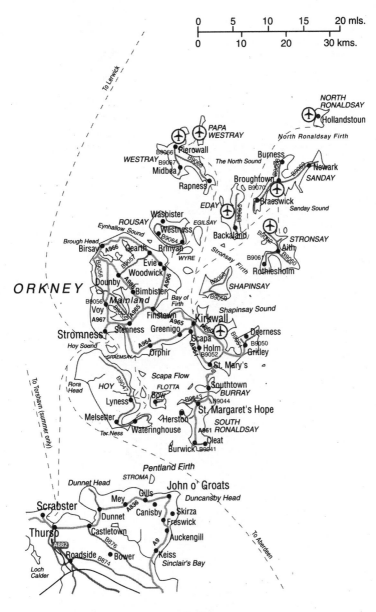

6. Orkney

7. Shetland & Fair Isle

8. Islands of the Clyde

Introduction

Scotland's islands remains a final frontier on the edge of what was once was
the known world – warmed, watered
and walloped by the continuous, rest-
less attentions of the North Atlantic.
Their unique cultures and wild,
unspoilt, often breathtaking scenery
have long attracted travellers. Today,
they still do. For although this is not
quite the land that time forgot, it is a
place where time is slowed and
distorted. Priorities are re-ordered.
Perspective is renewed. Here, the inter-
play of land, sea, light, weather and
people creates and re-creates the possibilities for an endless journey of
delights and surprises. Although
having some of the oldest rocks and
human habitation in the world, the
islands remain a frontier for undiscov-
ered or long forgotten lifestyles, for the
soul of Scotland, and for Europe's last
great wilderness.

Many travellers want to distance themselves from their usual lives – in the
cliché, to get away from it all. They
savour the quiet thrill of escaping by
boat, and take time to enjoy the peace
and the islands' rugged scenery. For the
motorist or cyclist, there is hardly a
road that does not offer great views. For
those wanting to walk, climb, fish or
take to the water, all are quiet and easily
reached. And for those days when the
views aren't all they might be, there is
the attraction of a peat fire, a good book
and a dram of Islay single malt whisky.

But the islands are not only a place to
escape. They are a place to be welcomed
and to learn about the people's unique
culture. For the Scottish islands have
been visited and settled by prehistoric
farmers, later by monks and Vikings. To
the Hebridean west, they maintained
the Gaelic language and culture of their
Celtic heritage. Bitter clan feuds were
pursued. Huge numbers of people were
cleared off the land and sent to Canada
and America, because landowners
found sheep farming more economical.
To the north, they were being deeply
influenced by more than a thousand
years of Viking domination and trading.
Island people farmed the thin, rocky
soil, cut peat from the earth for fuel, and
harvested birds from the sea cliffs. They
took to the sea: to plunder the rich fishing banks, to provide the backbone for
Britain's navies and to extract the black
gold of the North Sea oil boom.

Such a past has moulded people with a
variety of subtly distinct cultures on
each island, combining their past, their
traditions, their strong church adher-
ence and their language and dialects.
Scottish islanders value their communities, their land and the sea in a way
long forgotten in more developed areas.
Crofting – the small-scale system of
part-time farming found only in the
Highlands and Islands – is not the only
lesson held in trust for a world outside
which has re-discovered the importance of protecting the environment.

So island-hopping in Scotland provides
a wealth of natural contrasts and
beauty, combined with rich and diverse
island cultures. The two come together
in some of the great experiences and
attractions. Climb the mountains of
Skye's Cuillin range. Marvel at the slen-
der sea stack of Orkney's Old Man of
Hoy. Or land by scheduled plane on the
cockle beach, when the tide is out at
Barra. Visit the prehistoric remains of
Skara Brae in Orkney, the Mousa broch
on Shetland or the mysterious Callanish stone circle on Lewis. Walk the holy
turf of Iona to see its ancient abbey and
vibrant modern religious community.
Wind-surf in world-class conditions off
the beach at Tiree. Thrill to Shetland's
festival of fire, Up Helly Aa, in which a
Viking longboat is ceremonially
burned. Or sample Islay's superb whiskies after a tour of its distilleries.

Those who visit Scotland's islands almost
always want to come back for more. But
there is a big risk. As many of today's
newer islanders will testify, the danger
is that you may refuse to go home again.

Where to stay

The islands offer a wide range of accommodation – from Victorian stone-built hotels with open fires and local food, to isolated youth hostels and camping grounds on deserted beaches. Whatever your preference (or budget) most islands can accommodate you. We have included details of some hotels, Bed and Breakfasts and self-catering cottages and would like to emphasise that this is only a small selection of the accommodation available. Omission does not imply any criticism. Hotels range from expensive luxury lodges to basic guest house accommodation. On most of the smaller islands, the hotel and particularly its bar, forms the hub of community life – bike hire, cheque encashment and good advice is handed out with the drams and pints. Contact the Scottish Tourist Board for a full listing of recommended hotels.

Guest houses and bed and breakfast places vary in quality and style. You could stick to the Scottish Tourist Board recommended places where you can be guaranteed clean, warm rooms and enormous cooked breakfasts but bear in mind that some B&B owners have chosen not to participate and *pay for* the scheme; not to be 'commended' does not imply service of a lesser quality. Most will return from the islands with tales of wonderful welcomes by their B&B hosts, of home-made bread and freshly-laid eggs at breakfast, but there's no rule of thumb to discovering the 'perfect B&B'. But wherever you go you'll find B&B hosts endlessly helpful, able to dry the wettest, muddiest clothes, and provide hot baths and stacks of towels at the drop of a hat.

SYHA hostels on the islands are the usual mixture of comfortable heated places with showers, and bare converted schoolhouses with outside cold-water washrooms. Bedding is provided but you should bring your own sheet sleeping bag. Small stores are usually found at most hostels and all have cooking facilities. Most hostels close over the winter so check with the SYHA before you go. The SYHA hostels are relatively limited and often at a distance from each other, so it can be difficult for budget travellers to move from hostel to hostel without using alternative accommodation. Private hostels and bunk houses are beginning to plug these gaps – see 'Useful addresses and phone numbers' or contact the local Tourist Information Centres for full details. A must for all romantics travelling in the Western Isles are the Gatliff Hebridean Hostels – traditional thatched blackhouses in beautiful settings. Although a few of the hostels have been excellently refurbished in recent years, a Gatliff hostel experience is never a comfortable one – if you survive the midges and the midnight deluges as the thatch fails to keep out summer storms, then sharing two tiny rooms with fifteen unwashed bodies will make your stay memorable. Cheap and basic, you'll need to bring your own sleeping bag and food.

The best way to appreciate island tranquillity is to camp. Campsites with facilities are fairly scarce and expensive, but free camping is allowed in most places. Make sure you ask permission at the nearest house before you make camp, and be scrupulous about taking your rubbish away with you when you leave. Some landowners will ask a small fee for staying on their land. Caravanners beware – most roads are single-track with passing places and you may experience restrictions on some ferry services. If camping or caravanning, bring some midge repellent.

Booking accommodation

It is always safest to book ahead (and essential on Tiree), but you can usually find somewhere to stay on the larger islands in season. To book, either contact the establishment direct, or go through a local Tourist Information Centre or your own travel agent. The Tourist Information Centres operate a

Book-A-Bed-Ahead (BABA) service which allows you to book accommodation a day or so in advance, or further ahead, as you travel. Simply visit any TIC and pay a small fee. The SYHA operates a fax booking system in some of the larger hostels, or you can book by post or phone. Self-catering accommodation should always be booked well in advance as many people return to the same cottages year after year. Again, contact the STB or the landlord direct.

Climate and what to pack

Be warned – the Scottish islands bear little resemblance to the Greek islands. Be prepared for constantly changing weather and temperatures, for rain, wind and breathtakingly clear warm days when the air hums with peace and pollen-gathering. The best months to island-hop are May and June, when the winds drop and the machair is ablaze with wild flowers. Between May and September it's generally warm, but make sure you have a sweater and waterproof just in case. From October to April take more substantial clothing – although it rarely snows in the islands, winters can be unpleasantly windy, wet and cold. Island-hopping from October to Easter is definitely not recommended unless you want to get away from all other tourists. Most visitor attractions, restaurants, cafes, B&Bs bus and ferry services are either closed or on restricted service during the winter months, with the islands coming back to life at Easter. Although you can buy most things you need, specialist shops are scarce and goods can be more expensive. If you have particular medical or photographic requirements, it's safest to bring your own pills or films. Cyclists – you should always carry basic spare equipment as the nearest cycle repair outlet may be on the next island.

Useful addresses and phone numbers

The Scottish Tourist Board
Central Information
23 Ravelston Terrace
EDINBURGH
EH3 4EU
☎031-332 2433 (written and telephone enquiries only)
☎0891 666465 (24 hour info. line)

The Scottish Tourist Board (London)
19 Cockspur Street
Trafalgar Square
LONDON
SW1Y 5BL
☎071-930 8661/2/3

Scottish Youth Hostels Association
7 Glebe Crescent
STIRLING
FK8 2JA
☎0786 451181
Fax: 0786 450198

Gatliff Hebridean Hostels Trust
Membership details from:
Lynn and Richard Genner
45 Godwinsway
Stamford Bridge
YORK
YO4 1DA

Independent Backpackers Hostels –
Scotland
Contact: The Secretary
13 Lower Breakish
ISLE OF SKYE
IV42 8QA
(send SAE for reply)

Caledonian MacBrayne
The Ferry Terminal
GOUROCK
PA19 1QP
☎0475 33755
Fax: 0475 37607
(Ask for their special deals, 'Island Hopscotch' and 'Island Rover', which enable you to take in several islands at a time for more advantageous prices.)

The National Trust for Scotland
5 Charlotte Square
EDINBURGH
EH2 4DU
☎031 226 5922
Fax: 031 243 9501

Food and local specialities

The type of cooking you will find in the islands will not differ much from that found on mainland Scotland so it's worth seeking out a hotel which offers local produce and local dishes. The 'Taste of Scotland' scheme ensures that the dishes are Scottish in conception and use Scottish ingredients. Look out for the sign.

Otherwise you might like to try the seafood: the cold waters of the West and Northern coasts provide an ideal habitat for lobster, crab, mussels, oysters and scallops. (Barra specialises in cockles.) Traditional island fish dishes include herring in oatmeal and salt mackerel, the latter rarely found in restaurants. You'll come across the ubiquitous breaded haddock time and time again.

For meat-eaters, the local lamb is particularly good as the island method of farming usually involves an organic approach to rearing sheep. If the sheep graze near the coast, it's even better, as the flavour of the lamb will be slightly salty and tender (much appreciated by the French).

You'll find local cheeses in Arran and Orkney, and the latter islands are famed for their oatcakes.

The more traditional island dishes may not appeal to the majority of travellers, offering such delicacies as sheep's head broth, cormorant, guga (the young of the solan goose, highly prized in Lewis) and various confections using oatmeal. (You will not be offered these dishes in restaurants, in any case.) There is no doubt though that the islanders' diet of seventy years ago, involving lots of fresh fish, oatmeal and potatoes, low in cholesterol and animal fats, was very healthy and provided a clue to the longevity of much of the population. Nowadays, sadly, the menace of processed foods has reached the islands so don't expect to find gourmet, healthy-option meals wherever you go. If you do, they'll be expensive.

One last thing: the chips (french fries) served on the Caledonian MacBrayne ferries are astonishingly good! Not quite reason enough to island hop but still ...

Shopping and souvenirs

Most Scottish souvenirs are kitschy and fun if you like that sort of thing, tacky if you don't – the crafts found in the islands are slightly less so. (See the piece on *Crafts on Orkney* for more detailed information.) Traditionally, though, you can expect to find knitwear, especially in Shetland; tweed articles from the Western Isles; Celtic jewellery from Orkney and Mull; Chessmen from Lewis (a very classy souvenir); provisions from Arran and teatowels from everywhere. Whisky is readily available especially from the distilleries in Skye, Orkney, Islay and Jura. You will also want to bring home pebbles and shells (à la *Local Hero*).

For more conventional shopping, opening times vary and you may have some trouble finding exotic ingredients if you're self-catering and fancy making a Thai curry with some local fish.

Placename derivations

Most of the placenames in the islands will come from Gaelic and the Norse. In the case of the Hebrides, both influences will be apparent as the islands were under Norse rule for some time. Listed below are some of the most common words or elements:

Gaelic

aber: mouth of a river
achadh/ach: field
aird/ard: height
baile: town, village
beag/beg: small
beinn/ben: hill, mountain
caolas/kyle: a strait
carn: heap of stones
ceann/ken: headland
cille/kil: church
clach: stone
cladach: beach
coire/corrie: hollow
cnoc/knock: hill
creag/craig: rock
druim/drum: ridge or back
dubh: black
dun: fort
eilean: island
fada: long
machar: a sandy plain by the sea
mór: big
rubha/ru: point
sgeir/skerry: sea, rock
strath: valley
struth: stream
tigh/tay: house
tobar: well
uisge/esk: water

Norse

ay/ey: island
bost: settlement
holm: islet
hope: haven or bay
lax: salmon
ness: headland
ob/uig/voe: bay
papa: priest
shader: shieling
vik/wick: village or creek

Crofting

Crofting is a system of small-scale agriculture practised in the Highlands and Islands; around 18,000 crofts are registered in Scotland but unlike farming, crofting rarely provides an adequate income. A lot of crofters therefore supplement their income with a bit of fishing and other jobs. The land is mainly of poorer quality than that of a mainland farm – it's often inadequately drained and infertile, and supports some sheep, some cattle and vegetable growing. Normally a croft would have a crofthouse on it though not necessarily. In addition, each crofter usually has a share of a part of the land for the common grazing of his or her animals.

The history of crofting is tied up with the (still) emotive issue of the Highland Clearances in which landlords 'cleared' their land of people to replace them with sheep or deer. The many ruined crofthouses and townships, especially in the Hebrides, testify to cleared areas but not all emigration was forced. The land could not always support a community in the 19th century, particularly following the potato famine of the 1850s. To many Highlanders, however, the folk-memory of the evictions and the burning of the houses of their ancestors still remains clear in the mind.

Crofts were created in the late 18th and early 19th centuries by parcelling off the land into strips. Following the Clearances, and given the poor nature of the land people were left with, unrest began to grow in the 1870s resulting in land raids. This led to the landmark Crofters Act of 1886 which gave all crofters security of tenure and the right to pass on their tenancy to a member of their family. A further act in 1976 gave the crofter the right to purchase his croft but as yet, in the islands at least, there has been no rush to buy as the croft status gives certain advantages and access to the subsidies coming from local government and the EEC. These subsidies enable crofters to improve the quality of the soil, to fence their land and upgrade their crofthouses.

Gaelic

It's estimated there are around 80,000 Gaelic speakers in Scotland today (just over 1.5% of the population), mainly concentrated in the Western Isles, Skye, and in the Glasgow and Edinburgh areas where there's a lot of expatriate Gaels.

The language has been in decline this century, not helped by schooling in the islands which was done in English and where the speaking of Gaelic in the classroom, and often the playground, was frowned upon. Recently, though, there has been an upsurge of interest and pride in the language with the introduction of Gaelic-medium education, and a government allocation of some £9 million to provide television and radio programmes in Gaelic. This has resulted in the first Gaelic soap, Machair, set in a fictional college on Lewis. The future of the language, according to most Gaels, looks brighter than it's done for years.

Bibliography

The following list is a very small selection of the books on and about the islands of Scotland. Some other books are recommended within the texts of the individual islands.

General Non-Fiction

Margaret Bennett: *Scottish Customs from the Cradle to the Grave*
Michael Brander: *The Essential Guide to Scots Whisky*
Christopher Carrell (ed.): *As an Fhearann (From the Land)*
David Craig: *On the Crofters Trail*
J. Crumley and Colin Baxter: *St Kilda*
Derek Cooper: *The Road to Mingulay*
— *Hebridean Connections*
Kathleen Cory: *Tracing Your Scottish Ancestry*
Iain Fraser Grigor: *Mightier Than a Lord*
John Gifford: *The Highlands and Islands* (Building of Scotland series)
Finlay J. MacDonald: *Crowdie and Cream*
— *Crotal and White*
— *The Corncrake and the Lysander*
Cailean Maclean and James Hunter: *Skye, the Island*
James Shaw Grant: *Discovering Lewis and Harris*

James Hunter: *The Making of the Crofting Community*
Margaret Fay Shaw: *Folksongs and Folklore of South Uist*
T.C. Smout: *A History of the Scottish People, 1560–1830*
D.S. Thomson: *An Introduction to Gaelic Poetry*
D.S. Thomson (ed.): *A Companion to Gaelic Scotland*

Fiction and Folktales

A. Bruford and D.A. MacDonald: *Scottish Traditional Tales*
J.F. Campbell: *Popular Tales of the West Highlands*
R.A. Jamieson: *Thin Wealth* (Shetland)
Anything by George Mackay Brown (Orkney)
Compton Mackenzie: *Whisky Galore* (Outer Hebrides)
Gavin Maxwell: *Ring of Bright Water*

Poetry

Angus Peter Campbell: *The Greatest Gift* (Outer Hebrides)
R.A. Jamieson: *Shoormal* (Shetland)
Sorley MacLean: *Spring Tide and Neap Tide* (Inner Hebrides)
Aonghas MacNeacail: *Rock and Water* (Inner Hebrides)
Iain Crichton Smith: *Collected Poems* (Outer Hebrides)
Ian Stephen: *Malin, Hebrides, Minches* (Outer Hebrides)

Activities

Scottish Youth Hostel Association Handbook
Scottish Mountaineering Trust: *The Islands of Scotland including Skye*
—, *Scrambler's Guide to the Black Cuillin*
Roderick Wilkinson: *Fishing the Western Isles*

Music

Traditional
Traditional island sounds can be heard at a *ceilidh,* if you're lucky, and will

usually consist of accordion, fiddle, harp or pipe music, and singing, either accompanied with music or not. (Gaelic singers are usually unaccompanied.) Styles of song to listen out for are *puirt-a-beul* (in English, mouth music) which are usually very fast and where the singer is trying to make the sound of musical instruments to accompany dance, and waulking songs which are rhythmic, rousing songs where one singer will sing the verses and others join in for the chorus; these songs were used to accompany work – in this case, on the tweed. The subject matter of Gaelic song follow traditional patterns: love, war, exile and longing, and praise for the singer's native island. Ceilidhs (the word means 'visit' in Gaelic) normally took place in houses; these days the action has moved to hotels and community halls.

Modern

(Most of the singers and groups mentioned below are available on cassette or CD.)

Shetland is particularly renowned for its fiddle tunes. Look out for anything by Aly Bain or Tom Anderson.

Orkney has a resident composer, Peter Maxwell Davies, whose classical compositions are world-famous. Often works in collaboration with local writers.

Gaelic groups include Runrig (folk/rock), Capercaillie (folk), Mactalla (folk), Mouth Music (avant-garde 'world music') and Na h-Oganaich (mainly traditional singing). Singers worth a listen include Flora MacNeil, Isobel MacAskill, Christine Primrose, Catherine Ann MacPhee, Anne Lorne Gillies, Calum Kennedy, Talitha Mackenzie, Mairi MacInnes, Arthur MacCormick and the MacDonald sisters.

Skye and the Inner Hebrides

Skye

Saucy Mary was one of Skye's early tourism entrepreneurs. At the time when the islands belonged to the Norse kings, this Viking princess resided in Castle Moil at Kyleakin, overlooking the kilometre-wide strait to the mainland at Kyle of Lochalsh. Across the narrows she had placed a chain, and any boat wishing to get past had to pay a toll.

Almost a millennium later, and the principle remains the same. If you want to cross the strait from bank to bank, Caledonian MacBrayne's pontoon-style ferries will take you at a price. But Saucy Mary would be particularly full of ADmiration for a project to build a bridge 'over the sea to Skye' which will cost even more than the ferry. The building programme has gone ahead in the teeth of local opposition, arguing the bridge will damage the delicate environment and otter sanctuary in which Gavin Maxwell wrote *Ring of Bright Water*. Critics say it will cost too much and deserves government subsidy, and the tourist industry is concerned that a large chunk of concrete spanning the kyles will seriously compromise Skye's valued status as an island.

For many island-hoppers – particularly the lazy or time-limited variety – the Isle of Skye provides all the island experience they feel they need. Among its many attractions is the fact that one doesn't need to risk seasickness to get there. On one island can be found a wide variety of rock types, soil types, vegetation and wildlife. It has, by widespread agreement, the most impressive and challenging mountains in the British Isles. There are good, modern services for the visitor, with lots to do and particularly strong photography potential.

Skye measures, at maximum, seventy-five km north to south and forty km east to west. But it is deeply indented by sea lochs and extended by long peninsulas leaving it, with a bit of imagination, something like the ungainly shape of a lobster. This means that no point in the island is more than five miles from the sea. So the roads around its various districts and headlands, each with its own character, rarely fail to provide great vistas of mountain and sea.

Well, that's not quite true. They actually fail to do so quite often, because the downside of Skye is its weather. Not for nothing was the name Skye derived from the Norse 'skuy' meaning cloud. In Gaelic, it is nicknamed *Eilean a' Cheo*, the isle of mist. Having fifteen Munros (mountains over 3,000 feet, or 910 metre), the battle between warm and cold air is joined with depressing regularity over the roughly 7,000 droukit residents of the island. A further, minor drawback is the absence of good beaches. Go to the Outer Hebrides for the best of them.

But the most obvious weakness of Skye is that the rest of the world has discovered it before you. The unspoilt nature of so many other islands has been lost on Skye, where tourism and incomers have, controversially, brought in their money and their attitudes. To islanders, these are known, in the language of British imperialism, as 'white settlers': those who spend only a few weeks a year on holiday in their island homes, the flaky craftsfolk and those with south-east English accents, the ageing hippies running seaweed-and-tofu-bake restaurants. Even the Hindu mystic Sri Chinmoy has made his mark. On the old tower hill above Portree harbour is a plaque placed by his organisation praising Skye for its 'sense of vastness, majesty and harmony, qualities which touch the heart and bring forward a sense of oneness and inner peace'.

This is not so for the young people who have been unable to compete with incomers' spending power in purchasing homes, effectively driving people from the island with the same amoral economic arguments used in the 18th and 19th centuries about land clear-ances for sheep. And islanders have often lost the lead role in community affairs; perhaps because of their reti-cence, perhaps because of the incomer's assertiveness. For the short-term visi-tor, it can be hard work getting to meet a genuine Skye-person. The tourist in-dustry can appear to be almost entirely run by settlers – most of them hospi-table and providing a fine service, but not exactly the Real MacLeod of the island life which people visit Skye to see and meet. If all else fails, Skye folk can be viewed in what has become one of their native habitats – the Co-op supermarket in Portree. And remember that, as a tourist/visitor, you are not an impartial observer, but have a long-term effect on changing the nature and the culture of Skye.

The history of Skye is a colourful one and one of the most attractive parts of the visitors' experience. Shaped by its turbulent geological past, people settled more than 4,000 years ago in coastal areas. Skeabost and the east of Loch Snizort Beag have some of the best remains, and the finest of the Pictish brochs is above Struan at the mouth of Loch Harport. Columba is thought to have visited in 585 AD, and lived for a while on an island monastery in what is now a drained area to the north-west of Trotternish, known as Chalum Chille Cashel. Given the widely varied fertil-ity of Skye soil, this was another area to be settled early, and is still known as the Granary of Skye. The Norse had control of the island from the 8th century until the middle of the 13th, at which point John MacDonald of Islay took the title of Lord of the Isles with Skye as his administrative centre. For centuries, there was bitter feuding between the clans on the islands. The Mackinnons, to the east, were relatively peaceful. But the battles for land and power were between the MacLeods of Dunvegan and Harris, the MacLeods of Lewis and Waternish and the MacDonalds of Sleat, who also owned much of Trot-

ternish in the north of Skye. They sank their differences in protection of Charles Edward Stewart, or Bonnie Prince Charlie, the Young Pretender to the British throne, who in 1745 and 1746 led a dismally unsuccessful mili-tary challenge to the monarchy.

Part of Charlie's travels included time spent on Skye – hence the song: 'Speed bonny boat, like a bird on the wing, ... carrying the lad who was born to be king, over the sea to Skye...' This may lose some of its mystique for those coming across the narrows at Kyleakin. In fact, the would-be king eschewed the Wallace Arnold 'Misty Island' coach-tour option, and landed in Skye on the north-west coast of the northern Trot-ternish peninsula. Following the rout of the clan forces at the Battle of Culloden, near Inverness, he had become a fugi-tive with a £30,000 government reward for his capture. Those familiar with the story will be well-versed in what seem like interminable ramblings and intrigues as he sought a boat to take him to the European continent. Having evaded capture in the Outer Hebrides, he was bundled out of Benbecula on a small boat across the Minch to Skye, disguised as Betty Burke, the Irish maidservant to the Uist-born, Edin-burgh-educated Flora Macdonald. (One would have thought the Jacobite enter-prise was miserable enough for the clansmen without the lead character having to appear in drag.)

He first sought refuge in Monkstadt House, Trotternish, where the occu-pant, a Jacobite sympathiser, happened also to have government troops visiting. So the duo abruptly changed their plans, and set off for Portree, where they parted company in MacNab's Inn, now the Royal Hotel. The Young Pretender (so named because his father had tried a similar escapade in 1715) went to Raasay, then returned to Skye at the coast north of Portree, near the Storr on east Trotternish. Disguised again, this time under the name of Lewie Caw, he then walked south across the island to Elgol on the west side. He was feasted in a cave by the chief of the Clan Mackinnon, who also arranged for the would-be monarch to return next day to the mainland near Mallaig. Flora Macdonald, then aged twenty-four, was imprisoned in London for her part in the escape, but was soon released to become a society heroine and then to return to Skye. All these activities on Skye took the prince only one week, from 29 June to 4 July 1746. But that does not stop it being used extensively by today's tourist industry to milk the romantic mythology which accompanies his story.

The next key area in Skye history was its leading role in the Crofters' Revolt of the 1880s. Between 1840 and 1888, almost 30,000 people were forced to leave Skye to make way for landlords' sheep farming and sporting estates. It was a massive exodus, when one considers that only about 7,500 people live on the island today. A combination of rising anger, Protestant church assertiveness, and several years of poor harvest and poor fishing led to the start of crofter revolts in Lewis in 1874. In 1882, Skye crofters in the area known as Braes, south of Portree and bordering the narrows of Raasay, were told their grazing rights on Ben Lee were being withdrawn in favour of the landlord. They withheld rent and put their sheep on the hillside. When sheriff's officers were sent to evict the crofters, the court papers were burned, provoking the Inverness-shire sheriff to send a force of fifty Glasgow policemen to serve summonses. After a long stand-off, during which many of the crofting men had gone to join the fishing fleet, the police moved in at the rainy daybreak of 19 April. They arrested several men, but the crofters had prepared an ambush for them on their return up the road to Portree. After showering the police with rocks, a hand-to-hand battle ensued, and the police returned to Portree with only five prisoners. Skye was seething at the news, and the government despatched ships and marines to the island in fear of further unrest. This incident, along with a simi-lar revolt by Skye crofters in the north-west township of Glendale, led to a Royal Commission, under Lord Napier, to look into their complaints. It reported, in 1883, 'a state of misery, of wrong-doing, and of patient long-suffering, without parallel in the history of our country'. And in 1886, legislation provided substantial safeguards for crofting rights which remain in place today, under the Crofters' Commission. The Battle of the Braes, incidentally, is sometimes referred to as the last battle on British soil – unless you count the Ulster Troubles, the 1984 Miners' Strike and the 1990 Poll Tax Riot in London.

Island-hopping on Skye requires dividing the island into different segments, as there is plenty to keep anyone busy here for a week – even a fugitive prince. The southern peninsula of Sleat (pronounced Slate) seems as good a place to start as any – either landing at Armadale on the ferry from the mainland port of Mallaig, or on the turn-off on the road at Broadford. The peninsula mixes some of the oldest rocks on Skye (and in the world) with a lush, green, east coast, full of oak and beech trees, as well as the more common fir and birch, and carpets of colourful flowers from spring to autumn. Sleat is known as the garden of Skye, the kind of place where a mainlander might feel at home. And sure enough, they do, in large numbers. 'Garden!' scorns one of them. 'It would be if it weren't for all the rabbits.'

One of the incomers is Sir Iain Noble, an Edinburgh merchant banker, who owns the northern part of the peninsula and is an activist in the rejuvenation of the Gaelic language. He was instrumental in setting up the independent Gaelic college called Sabhal Mór Ostaig (pronounced sawal-more-ostack: from Gaelic and Norse, meaning 'big barn of the east bay') towards the south of Sleat. In the converted farmstead, visitors can do short courses in Gaelic, music or culture, and full-time students learn about business, computing and the media in the island's native tongue. Sir

Iain lives in Isleornsay, a beautiful settlement, where he runs a well-rated hotel, a shop and art gallery. This village also has the unusual distinction of being the location, in 1820, of Skye's first public toilet. But it has stuck longer than it should with some of the hygiene practices of that time. After a recent campaign centred on Isleornsay, its water supply is now properly filtered. But be careful of some of Skye's other townships in mid-summer, when the water has a special protein-filled crunchiness from the microscopic bugs in it.

Across from Isleornsay, on the other bank of Loch na Dal, is the Kinloch Lodge Hotel, run by the chief of the MacDonald Clan and his wife, a renowned cook and cookery writer. There is a good, short coastal walk nearby. Death duties forced the Mac-Donald Clan to sell much of its property, but the Clan Donald Lands Trust, subscribed by American members of the clan, still owns 20,000 acres of the south of Sleat. The trust is most notable for its award-winning Clan Donald Centre, near the Armadale ferry terminal. This is clan headquarters to an estimated three million MacDonalds worldwide, rewarding short visits to see its relics or eat in its converted 1822 stables restaurant. It also offers ranger-guided walks through extensive 19th-century woodland and gardens, and requiring longer visits to study its archives of clan and Skye history. The library is in a restored wing of the large Armadale Castle built in 1815-19, but burned down a few years later. The centre is also responsible for selling permits to some of the local fishing; on Loch Dhughaill, for instance.

Also on the east coast is the ruin of 14th-century Knock Castle, which got into its sad state of disrepair through stone being taken to build nearby Knock House. The castle was to guard the Sound of Sleat and Kyle narrows for the MacDonald clan, and is famed both for Mary of the Castle, a gallant woman who fought off a siege by the MacLeods,

and for a female ghost who can be kept content if supplied with large amounts of milk.

Armadale has a range of craft shops, and is home to the Skye Yacht Club, while further south, the road runs through more dense townships on the most fertile land. You can walk the two miles down a dirt track to the lighthouse at the Point of Sleat, with views across to Rum, though local residents are not exactly welcoming if you wish to share their rural idyll.

A winding and very steep road extends across central Sleat to make a loop round part of its west coast, which looks very different in character to the east and is one of many parts of the island from which the Cuillin mountains can look spectacular. At Toskavaig is the stumpy ruin of Dunscaith Castle, which again is more interesting for its legend than its present-day reality. This is where Scathac the Wise, Queen of Skye, with one hundred warriors, taught the art of war to Cuchulainn, the 3rd-century Irish hero and supporter of Ossian. Tarskavaig, further south, was the base for the MacDonald clan until the early 1600s.

At the north end of the Sleat peninsula is the forested area which used to be the main link with the mainland. A winding road still leads to the ferry crossing at Kylerhea to Glendale. Until 1906, up to 8,000 cattle used to be swum across here at slack tide before their journey down the drove roads on the way to the Lowland and English markets. Near the ferry terminal is an otter sanctuary run by the Forestry Commission. Visitors can walk two kilometres to the hide, in a converted lighthouse, and watch for these elusive relatives of the weasel. Or they can just enjoy the view. The north coast of that peninsula is far better known to travellers, as that is the main road from Kyleakin. Some travellers only stop briefly in Kyleakin before returning to the mainland, to tell the folks back home they have been 'over the sea to Skye'. But it is not a town on which to gain an impression of the island. In fact, it has nothing much to recommend it, other than ample parking space. This is where Saucy Mary used to exact her toll – strangely, one of three women to be associated with three ruined castles in the area, and there are more further north.

From Kyleakin to Broadford, the road passes the little-used airstrip, and Broadford itself, the second largest township on the island, is a straggly arrangement of B & Bs, a hotel, a few shops, a large garage, and a shingle beach on which fossils can be found. The women at the conspicuous tourist office are more helpful than most in their profession. The village has a privately-run environmental centre and, of all things, a serpentarium. It is also home, on a characterless industrial estate, to the *West Highland Free Press*. Since 1972, this has been a radical weekly newspaper serving the north-west Highlands and Islands, maintaining a strong disregard for the sensibilities of landlords and regarded as essential reading for locals. But the best advice for visiting Broadford is to keep moving on.

Turning off at Broadford Hotel, a narrow minor road winds to the west and leads to Elgol. On a good day, this high road offers tremendous views to the island of Rum, and and the village of Elgol itself looks out to the Cuillins. Indeed, a small boat leaves from there in reasonable weather to take people into Loch Coruisk, and the heart of the mountains. (It was near here that Prince Charles was entertained in a cave by the Mackinnons.) On the road, at Kilmarie, is the start of a very tough walk into the Cuillin and on the other side of Loch Slapin is a large marble quarry and a 7th-century chapel, associated with St Columba. One word of warning though: there is supposed to be a goblin called Ludag along this road. According to the writings of Hugh Miller, he can be seen at dusk taking immense hops on his one leg, wrapped in rags and with a hollowed eye. 'He has dealt heavy blows,

it is said, on the cheeks of benighted travellers.' Don't say you weren't warned, when you go for treatment at Broadford's cottage hospital.

The main road north out of Broadford passes by Luib, where a local tourism entrepreneur, Peter MacAskill, has one of his mildly eccentric thatched museums. This one, allegedly linked to Bonnie Prince Charlie, is a simple affair to show the lifestyle of a traditional Skye crofter in the early part of the 20th century. Further on is Sconser, with a golf course, the ferry terminal for Raasay and a fierce wind tunnel contrived by the surrounding mountains. The road then winds round Loch Sligachan (of which more later) and through the commercial forestry of Glen Varragill to Skye's main settlement.

The Highlands and Islands have few beautiful towns, but Portree must rate among them – not least for its setting around a steeply banked harbour and with mountain views to north and south. Less beautiful is its secondary school, on the road south and serving all of Skye, which has variously been described – and not only by pupils – as resembling Alcatraz, a Soviet canning factory and Stalag 17. Although home to only around 1,600 people, a wide variety of services are available in the town, including the only places you will find cash dispensers and a shop which contrives to sell fish and chips, tropical fish and pet food at adjacent counters. Included in its restaurants is Gandhi's, Stevie's Kitchen, the Bistro, Ben Tianavaig, the Granary, and Portree House.

On wet days in summer, Portree is full of disgruntled tourists with Pacamacs and waterproof hairnets to preserve their perms. They would do well to visit the nearby, all-weather Aros Heritage Centre. Meaning home, it opened in 1993, and has relatively expensive entrance fees, but houses several displays in the vogue approach to cultural interpretation for tourists, including Gaelic culture since 1745, the clearances, emigration and the crofters' revolt, and, of course, the ubiquitous Bonnie Prince Charlie. There are foreign-language commentaries available from headsets.

North out of Portree, past the camp-site, leads to one of the most bizarre geological phenomena in Britain. Almost the full length of the Trotternish peninsula is shaped by the heavy weight of volcanic basalt pressing down on the softer Jurassic sedimentary rocks – sandstone, limestone and shale – and creating a thirty-kilometre landslide which continues to move imperceptibly today. The result is a ridge running up the east side, clearly visible from the road with outlandish rocky outcrops where pinnacles of the harder rock survived the ice-age, but the surrounding soft rock was eroded. The ascent over the full length of the ridge is more than 2,300 metres. Near the south is the Old Man of Storr, fifty metres high, with a large overhang and not climbed until 1955. It makes a magnificent sight just past the lochs which, from 1952, have supplied Skye's hydro-electric water supply. Near there is a rock where the Clan MacQueen is said to have raised the devil using an ancient ceremony called *Taghairm*, which involved the roasting of live cats. This is one part of island tradition which has not been commercially interpreted for tourists – yet.

The road north, on the east coast of Trotternish, passes Lealt Gorge, with its short slippery walk, and on to Loch Mealt, a rich freshwater habitat. On the other side of the road are the Mealt Falls and Kilt Rock. This high cliff-face, with views across to Rona and Torridon on the mainland, is formed again from volcanic basalt, from which the softer sedimentary rock has been eroded. It got its name from the crystalline structure creating long pleats in the rock, and the stripes of rock near the base.

The village of Staffin is built on one of the more conspicuous pieces of landslide, with dark volcanic ash forming its beach. This is a fertile area, with relatively intensive crofting. It is also said to have a Spanish galleon sunk in its bay, and, as a result, people of Spanish descent living in the local community. The road heading across the peninsula from the village heads into the hills and, although holding out the prospect of spotting a golden eagle, it threatens to become rather dull – until, that is, you turn a hairpin bend and suddenly encounter a breathtaking view of the Quiraing, the best example of Trotternish's bizarre rock formations. A half day scrambling on potentially rather dangerous scree will take you across the features on this landscape, known as the Prison, the Needle (another stack rising forty metres) and the Table. According to a previous guidebook (published 1967), the needle 'stands like a billiard table of the Titans on an emerald carpet of lush grass in the middle of a great amphitheatre of black shattered cliffs'. Why don't they write like that any more?

Towards the north end of Trotternish is Flodigarry House Hotel and a nearby hostel. It was in the former that Flora Macdonald and her husband lived the early part of their married life, with the first five of their seven children. Sitting at the front of the hotel at dusk, enjoying a dram of the local Talisker whisky, while looking south over the contorted landscape, it is not hard to see, at least with a wee bit of imagination, why the north of Skye has a disproportionately large folklore in fairy stories. If they exist, it will certainly be in this kind of terrain. The hotel is warmly recommended for its excellent service.

On the north-west coast of Trotternish is another of Skye's fine examples of precariously-perched and ruined castles. Near another country house hotel, this is Duntulm, once a stronghold of the MacDonalds of Sleat, but deserted, it is said in tragic circumstances. A nurse of one of the chief's infant children dropped it from a window onto the rock below. One legend says the place was cursed as the family left it in 1732: another that the clan chief took revenge by setting the hapless nurse adrift on an open boat full of holes. Although a precarious walk (don't carry children, in case the curse story is true), it is not hard to see from the views to Harris why a clan chief would wish to build a castle on the promontory. It offers strong defences against your MacLeod enemies, and good potential for interpretative tourist development in more peaceful times.

The fertile land on the west coast, the Granary of Skye, has connections with St Columba and the landing from Benbecula of Bonnie Prince Charlie which were mentioned before, while in the cemetery at Kilmuir is the grave of Flora Macdonald, who died in 1790. This is near one of the more impressive cultural museums on Skye – a collection of thatched cottages on an exposed hillside with displays of crofting life, crofting implements, fossils, spinning, a smithy, the educational tradition, the clearances and the inevitable peat fire.

A steep, but strikingly picturesque descent into Uig bay shows this, one of the main townships on Skye, to be a scattered community. The ferry terminal, linking Skye with Tarbert on Harris and Lochmaddy on North Uist, is surrounded   by car parks and an unpretty industrial estate. To get to more useful services, like a hotel, hostel or bike hire, takes a trek of three kilometres round the bay. Further south still, the standing stones of Kensaleyre are supposed to have been the pot-stand of local giants.

This is where the seventy-km road round Trotternish meets the road out of Portree to the island's west coast and Dunvegan. At Skeabost is a crenellated white confection of a hotel which puts up guests for golfing and excellent salmon fishing on the River Snizort – at a price. Further on is the township of Edinbane, with a large pottery, and the base of the Waternish, or Vaternish peninsula. This is one of the shorter

detours, but worth it for yet more great high-level views from the road, across the sea lochs and over to the Harris hills. The village of Stein was the site of an 18th-century bid to set up a fishing industry to benefit the MacLeod estates, but it failed, apparently through the high cost of salt. You can still arrange sea-fishing trips from the harbour there. Ask at the inn, which is the oldest licensed premises on Skye, perhaps going as far back as 1648. An Ipswich lawyer recently had plans to develop it and build a marina, but faced fierce local protest. He withdrew, and it is now run with less grandiose plans and the warm welcome of a Stirlingshire landlord.

The road branches near a broch, still standing to a height of about two metres, with one branch going to Geary, still a community of God-fearing Skye people. The other branch leads to the lone church at Trumpan, site of one of the worst atrocities of the islands' clan rivalries. The MacDonalds of Uist were seeking revenge for a massacre on Eigg. A group of them barred the doors, while a gathering of MacLeods were at worship, and set fire to the building. It is said that only one woman escaped as the burning thatch roof came down on the congregation, and she raised the alarm. The MacLeods came, with their magical Fairy Flag, and massacred the MacDonald force before the tide had risen sufficiently for the expeditionary force to put to sea again.

In the graveyard at Trumpan, Lady Grange is buried, renowned for ill-treatment at the behest of her husband. When she threatened to divulge his Jacobite plotting, ahead of the 1745 rising, he exiled her to the remote St Kilda islands and left her there for seven years. The Fairy Bridge, at the turn-off to the Waternish peninsula, has, as one might expect, yet more fairy stories associated with it. This is also the point at which islanders gathered from surrounding townships both for gospel meetings during the 19th-century revival and for the agitation against landlords and clearances. From there, the road descends to the main western township of Dunvegan and its castle.

This is perched on a rock overlooking a sea-loch. But unlike the derelict stumps of former fortresses, Dunvegan Castle has been turned into a Hebridean stately home. Though the basis of the castle which can be seen today is 15th-century, much of the architecture dates from the 19th century, and the defences have been turned into a landscaped garden. This is the seat of the chief of the Clan MacLeod, and has been since around 1200, making it the Scottish castle which has had the longest continuous occupancy by one family.

Inside are elegant rooms and furnishings, weapons and hunting trophies, with the main attractions including the Dunvegan Cup, from which each new chief has to prove his worthiness by drinking a large measure of claret. The best legend concerns the Fairy Flag, which was given to the MacLeod chief by his fairy lover when they had to part at Fairy Bridge. Or, an alternative version is that the fairy lover returned to the castle and put the silk flag over their sleeping child. Either way, the same fairy endowed the flag with the magical property of saving the MacLeods when the clan's survival is threatened – but only three times. It has been used twice already, once following the massacre at Trumpan Church, and it can still be seen hanging, ominously awaiting the time when it can give the MacLeods one last escape. Those who refuse to believe in fairies might be more easily persuaded by the theories that the flag was connected with the Crusades, and that it was made on the Mediterranean island of Rhodes during the 7th century.

The current owner, John MacLeod of MacLeod, has been in charge since 1965, but is limited in the time he can spend at his castle. As a trained actor and classical baritone, the opportunity to ply his trade is somewhat limited on the Duirinish peninsula and environs,

so he lives in London and organises an annual arts festival in which he performs. Yet even at that distance, he runs a formidable marketing exercise, with castle visits, restaurants, seal island tours and one of the better class of gift shops on Skye – selling, of course, recordings of the MacLeod himself in performance. There is, it seems, little sign that the Fairy Flag will be required to bail out the finances of his estate.

On the landward side of the castle there are walking opportunities in the mixed woodland. You can also go to the so-called coral beaches on the east side of the mouth of Loch Dunvegan. The town, or village, has a couple of hotels, a police station, a nearby campsite, petrol, B&Bs and the Giant MacAskill Museum. The same Peter MacAskill who started the Luib crofthouse has created an exhibit which celebrates the life and times of the world's largest pathological giant, Angus MacAskill (1825-63), whose 2.36 metre (7 feet 9 inch) frame earned him celebrity and a job in a freak show. He was born in Berneray, in the Sound of Harris, and there is no evidence that he ever visited Dunvegan. But tourists do, and that's good enough for the giant's distant descendant, Peter, to put on one of his eccentric displays for the paying public. The high point is a model of the big man, fashioned, using traditional crofting methods, from fibre-glass and styrofoam.

The Duirinish peninsula, the most westerly part of Skye, is yet another characterful detour from the visitor, though its attraction to settlers has earned parts of it the disparaging monicker of Little England. Mr MacAskill's museum empire extends to a 19th-century croft display at Colbost, complete with illicit whisky still. Its neighbour is the highly-rated *Three Chimneys Restaurant*, the menu of which features a marmalade pudding which has become one of Skye's modern legends.

At the north end of Duirinish is Mac-Crimmon country, the spiritual home of bagpiping. This is the land given to the MacCrimmon family when they became official pipers to the chiefs of the MacLeods around 1500. In Boreraig, the family ran the leading Scottish piping college for more than 250 years, specialising in building up the corpus of ceol mór, or 'the big music'. Their talent – and here comes another of Skye's tales – was derived from a fairy who taught one of the young MacCrimmons to play on a magical, silver chanter. The college was closed, it seems, because the silver chanter was lost. Or, more plausibly, the MacLeod chief wanted his land back and the MacCrimmons had to leave for North Carolina in the 1770s. There they backed the wrong side in the American Revolution, and had to leave for Canada. The full story, and a lot more about piping, is explained at the Skye Piping Centre in Galtrigall.

The Duirinish roads extend to the spectacular sweep of sea and 300-metre sheer cliffs at Neist Point, where self-catering lighthouse cottages are suitable only for those with a head for heights. Coastal and cliff walking to the south leads to villages which were cleared by landlords and their residents sent across the Atlantic. The village of Lorgill was cleared on 4 August 1830, after its people had been told either to go to Canada or prison, with the old being sent to the poorhouse.

Before leaving the peninsula, stop at Glendale. This dispersed community of Free Presbyterians and settlers was the site of one of the crofters' risings in 1882, which led first to gunboats appearing in Loch Dunvegan and then, happily, to land rights reform four years later. One of Glendale's attractions today is a toy museum now in its eighth year, where a Wigan-born collector enthuses boyishly in his front room about his vast collection of childhood memorabilia. Exhibits include a doll manufactured around 1894 and a jigsaw from 1863. Great for children of all ages.

The west coast road south of Dunvegan passes the inlets and peninsulas of Loch Bracadale, with its reminders of prehistoric and Norse settlements. On the other side of Loch Harport is the Talisker whisky distillery (the only one on Skye), which has tours available – and the malt whisky itself, of course. From near there, a narrow road takes you down towards Glen Brittle, and the dark mountains which have drawn the attention and so dominated the landscape from viewpoints all over the rest of the island. These are the Cuillin, the most rugged, majestic and revered of British mountain ranges, topped by a twelve-km sawtooth ridge and very often a swirling cauldron of angry cloud. They were formed from gabbro, a coarse and very hard crystalline rock, which is strikingly different from the granite and scree of the Red Hills or Red Cuillin on the east coast between Portree and Broadford.

At the tourist office, they refuse to give advice on climbing in the Cuillin. Such an activity is only for those with the experience to know they can and should get their information from more specialised sources. It requires quality equipment and ability with some tough rocks and scrambling. And even for those with all the recommended attire, their compass may be rendered useless by the strong magnetism of the rock.

There are three ways to approach the mountains. Glen Brittle, with a hostel, busy campsite and one of Skye's few sandy bays, is the approach from the west. To get into Loch Coruisk, in the heart of the mountains, requires a tough walk even by taking the coastal route. Elgol, already mentioned, at the end of a road from Broadford, also has a difficult walk in, or the easier option of a boat trip, with wild camping and a bothy at Coruisk. But the most common approach is from the hotel at Sligachan, on the road between Broadford and Portree, where the *Seumas* Bar is full of day-glo, fleecy tops, and a sense of shared adventure round a roaring fire. From there, the view shows some of the less demanding peaks, and the most impressive low-level walk takes you thirteen km down Glen Sligachan to the coast at Camusunary. Or with an ascent, this can divert into the Loch Coruisk basin. For the experienced, one of the best routes onto the peaks is to start at Sligachan and climb to the nearest visible peak, Bruach na Frithe, 958 metres above Sligachan's sea-level. This takes you onto the main Cuillin ridge, but as that includes more than thirty rock peaks, including eleven Munros and nine lesser Tops, the effort may only just have started. More common is to start in Glen Brittle and climb the highest peak, Sgurr Alasdair, at 992 metres. The views, on an island where each new turn can be breathtaking, are unrivalled.

How to get there

Until the Skye Bridge is open, crossing from Kyle of Lochalsh to Kyleakin, Cal-Mac will continue to run its two shuttle ferries. These take only five minutes to cross, and although there is a fee for cars, passengers travel free. (CalMac: ☎0599 4482). Be prepared, in summer, for queues at either side. Further south on the narrows is the Glenelg-Kylerhea crossing, which has a six-car, privately-run ferry operation, running less regularly between 9am and 8pm (☎0599 81302).

The other Cal-Mac ferry from the mainland is between Mallaig and Armadale on Sleat. This takes half an hour, and runs four times a day (CalMac: ☎04714 248).

Getting to Mallaig is a very different journey from that to Kyle of Lochalsh, with a train from Glasgow or a winding road up through Glenfinnan and Arisaig. Kyle of Lochalsh's train service comes through Inverness (Kyle rail station: ☎0599 4439). There are also direct bus services to Skye, via Kyle, from Glasgow, Edinburgh and Inverness. Returning to Glasgow from Portree takes 6 hours 30 minutes and buses leave five times a day, the last one at 2.20pm (Skye-ways coaches: ☎0599-

4328, Citylink ☎041-332 9191).

Skye is also linked by Cal-Mac ferries with the Outer Hebrides. The Hebridean Isles runs a triangular route between Uig on Trotternish, Tarbert, Harris, and Lochmaddy on North Uist (CalMac: ☎047 042 219). Day trips by coach on Harris and Lewis are available.

Getting around

The main roads on Skye are very good quality, the side-roads often being single-track. Cycling is good, though hilly, and on the main roads traffic tends to move past you very fast. The bus service on the island is good on the main roads connecting Uig, Dunvegan, Portree and Broadford with Kyleakin. Service buses centre round Somerled Square, Portree (Highland Omnibuses ☎0463 33371 and Clan Coaches ☎0599 4328).

Post buses meander down the back routes daily. Tourist coaches leave Kyleakin Monday to Friday for a five-hour whisk round the island, or are less hurried from Portree to Trotternish or Dunvegan Castle (Highland Buses, ☎0478 612622).

Car hire
Ewen MacRae Garage, Portree ☎0478 2554/72002).
Taxis
Waterloo Taxis, Broadford: ☎0471 822630: MacRob, Portree: ☎0471 822343, Gus's, Portree: ☎0471 613000/612074, Ardvasar Taxis, Armadale on Sleat: ☎04714 361.
Bicycle Hire
Skye Bikes is next to Kyleakin pier. In Broadford, there is Donaldson's in Elgol Rd (☎0471 822270) and in Portree, Island Cycles, at the Green (☎0470 572284). At Dunvegan, there is cycle hire and repairing near the Giant MacAskill museum, on ☎0470 572310.

Accommodation

There are numerous hotels and bed and breakfasts all over the island. It is very tourist-oriented. Among the classier ones are the Skeabost House Hotel

(☎047 032 202) and Flodigarry House Hotel (☎047 052 203) near Staffin. In Portree, the Cuillin Hills Hotel (☎0478 2003) is in relative peace and quiet; the Bosville Hotel comes recommended (☎0478 2846); and Sleat has two well-rated hotels in Eilean Iarmain (☎04713 332) and Kinloch Lodge, run by the chief of the MacDonald clan (☎04713 214).

Hostels

Skye is well-supplied with hostels and bunk-houses. Scottish Youth Hostels have establishments in Broadford, Glen Brittle, Armadale and Uig.
Independent Hostels (there are seven in Skye): Skye Backpackers, Kyleakin (☎0599 4510); Fossil Bothy, Breakish (☎0471 822644); Blaven Bunkhouse, Strathaird (☎0471 822397); Croft Bunk-house and Bothy, Portnalong (☎0478 640254); Skyewalker Independent Hostel, Portnalong (☎0478 640250); Dun Flodigarry Hostel, Staffin (☎0470 552212) and Glen Hinnisdal Bunk-house (☎047 042 293). Many 'book-a-bed ahead' scheme; check at individual hostels.

Campsites

Edinbane, Glenbrittle on the north side of Portree, Sligachan, Staffin and Uig. With permission, you can camp outside the sites, except in Glen Brittle.

Where to eat

There are, again, a large number of restaurants, bars, guest houses and hotels. The food can be very variable. Among those included in the 'Taste of Scotland' programme are: Ardvasar Hotel, just south of Armadale pier; Atholl House Hotel, Dunvegan; Flodi-garry House Hotel near Staffin; Harlosh House, south of Dunvegan with good views of the Cuillin; Hotel Eilean Iarmain, in Isleornsay, Sleat; Ord House, on the west coast of Sleat; Skea-bost House Hotel and Ullinish Lodge Hotel on Loch Bracadale, again with tremendous views of the lochs and the Cuillin. The Three Chimneys Restaurant at Colbost is the best of the stand-alone eateries, where the seafood spectacular costs £60 for two (☎047 081

258), and there is good seafood also at Seagull Restaurant, Breakish, near Broadford. Vegetarians go to Ben Tianavaig Bistro, in Portree, bookings advised on ☎0478 2152.

Bars and Music

In the evening, most hotels have bars, and there are very few separate pubs outside Portree. In the town, the Cale-donian is recommended for hip young ravers, the Pier and Tangadale hotels for the best local crack. Live music can be found at irregular intervals almost anywhere, though the hotel in Edin-bane (south Waternish) tries to be more regular than most with its ceilidh dances. Also watch for events at the Gathering Hall, Portree, and An Tuire-ann, a bohemian art gallery, perfor-mance space and restaurant on the north-west side of Portree (open Tue-Sun 10-5).

Things to do and see

Outdoor activities are very varied, but Skye specialises in climbing, hillwalk-ing and fishing. For walking in the Cuillin, see above, or pay for expertise from Pinnacle Ridge Mountain Guiding (☎04714 239). There are guides pub-lished to walks in other parts of the island. Particularly good are the Storr and Quiraing in Trotternish, the area north of Flodigarry, and the central and south coastal routes in Duirinish.

Outdoor centres include Whitewater Activities, Uig (kayaking, windsurfing, walking, archery), and Wild Explorer Holidays, in Broadford (☎0471 822487) with its own accommodation and nature-watching programmes. Pony trekking at Uig Hotel (☎047 042 205). Hebridean Diving Services, at Stein on Waternish, has boat charter, equipment and accommodation, but only for those with underwater experience.

Fishing permits are available from a range of sources. Try Jansport, in central Portree for north-west Skye, the Clan Donald Centre for Sleat. The bigger hotels have permits, as do the tourist offices for some rivers and lochs. Skeabost House has fishing coaching with an expert ghillie. Seal-viewing cruises from Kyleakin pier (☎0599 4641) and from Portree ☎047 482 272). Nine-hole golf courses are at Sconser (£8 day ticket) and Skeabost House Hotel (£6 day ticket). Young kids might like Hillcroft Open Farm, on the Portree-Bracadale road, where they can meet Pugwash, the saddleback pig, and Domino, the pygmy goat.

Indoor activities

When it rains, and it does, there are swimming pools at Camanachd Square, Portree (until 9pm, Mon-Thur, shorter hours on Fri and Sat, ☎0478-2655) and across the narrows at Kyle of Lochalsh. The Aros Centre, one mile south of Portree, has a wide range of displays (☎0478 613649), and there are crofthouse displays in Luib (on the Broadford-Portree road), Colbost in Duirinish (all week, 9.30-6), and the best of them is near Kilmuir in northern Trotternish (Mon-Sat, 9.30-5.30). A whisky distillery tour is on free offer round the Talisker stills and mash tubs next to Loch Harport (Mon-Fri 9.30-4). The Skye Piping Centre is at Galtrigall in North Duirinish. There is Dunvegan Castle, though that is at its best in fine weather (☎047 022 206). The Clan Donald Centre, near Armadale, has displays on island history, but is also best when you can take in the nature trails in dry weather (☎04714 305/227). And the Glendale Toy Museum is worth a trip, with or without children (☎047 081 240). There's a games room at Sligachan Hotel and at Edinbane village hall. Remember little is open on a Sunday, so plan ahead.

Events and festivals

There is a Skye Folk Festival, based in Portree in late July, and Dunvegan arts festival in August. Highland Games are at Portree in early August, specialising in the bagpiping competition.

Tourist information offices

In Portree, open all year round, 9am-8pm. The office may seem hard to find up a stair in Meall House, on the hill to the south of the harbour (☎0478 2137). In Broadford, it's easier to spot, in the main bay-front car park (☎0471 822361). There is an information desk at the Cal-Mac office by Uig pier (☎047 042 404), and full details about Skye from the Kyle of Lochalsh office perched above the ferry waiting area (☎0599 4276).

Craft shops and souvenirs

These are numerous, with many workshops open to the public and shops where a wider range of items is on offer. Portree has a selection of Skye produce, and a wide range of choice can also be found at the nearby Aros Centre, Dunvegan Castle and near Armadale pier.

Mountain rescue: ☎0478 2888.

Weather forecast: ☎0898 500441 (premium prices for calls).

Raasay

There is a notion that Skye exists to shelter Raasay from the worst of the North Atlantic weather. Raasay's complementary role seems to be an antidote to the fast roads and touristic excesses of Skye. And, to add to this symbiotic relationship, one of Raasay's main attractions is the perspective it can give you of Skye, particularly the views to the Red Hills of the Cuillin and to the Storr at the north end. It was this view that must have provoked Dr Johnson, during his Hebridean travels with Boswell in 1773, to dance a Highland Reel on the top of Dun Caan, the highest hill at 443m – and this after an open-air breakfast of cold mutton, bread, cheese, brandy and punch.

Dr Johnson clearly enjoyed himself on Raasay, being generously entertained by the clan chief of the MacLeods of Raasay. 'We found nothing but civility, elegance and plenty,' he wrote. 'Such a seat of hospitality, amidst the winds and waters, fills the imagination with a delightful contrariety of images.'

It would take a lot of imagination to feel as enthusiastic about Raasay now. Much of it is eerily quiet, its 150-strong population cornered in the south-east at Inverarish and Churchton townships. Even they can seem deserted much of the time. Visitors can expect to be welcomed only by an elderly sheepdog basking in the sun, eyeing strangers warily and acknowledging them with a desultory thump of the tail.

The island itself is long and thin, twenty km by four km, much of it made of gneiss rock with some of the oldest plant fossils found anywhere. It combines bare rock with clumped grass and heath, and lush, varied woodland near the main settlements. On the east side, facing towards the mainland Applecross peninsula, there are high cliffs.

The MacLeods of Raasay – linked to those of Dunvegan but keen to impress their independence – built an eyrie-like fortress, Brochel Castle, probably in the 15th century. It is now a ruin requiring a scramble up to the top of the volcanic plug on which it sits towards the north end of the island. Along with the island of South Rona just to the north, this MacLeod domain became notorious in the 16th century for its piracy of passing ships trading on the west coast of Scotland. (South Rona and Scalpay, to north and south of Raasay, are all but deserted and cannot be reached by scheduled ferry.)

The clan gave whole-hearted backing to the Jacobite cause in the 1745 uprising, and sheltered Bonnie Prince Charlie for two days – and, it was written, two uncomfortable nights on a bed of heather – before he was returned to Skye. As punishment for that support, government troops moved onto Raasay soon after and burned all 300 homes

then on the island, sank the boats, and slaughtered 280 cows and 700 sheep. The MacLeods had recovered sufficiently by 1773 to welcome Johnson and Boswell in what has since been extended to become Raasay House, on a bay towards the north end of the main settlements. And in the next century, the clan chief was conspicuous for his attempts to alleviate the poverty and famine which led to clearances from other islands. But the costs to the chief were such that he had to sell the island in 1843 and left for Canada. The new, somewhat less enlightened owner, George Rainy, forbade young people to marry unless they also emigrated. Within ten years, twelve townships had been cleared, and Rainy's son went on to develop the island as a sporting estate.

In 1893, Raasay was at the centre of the rift within the Free Church of Scotland over a doctrinal question concerning the notion of salvation, and it remains strongly identified with the small minority who left to form the Free Presbyterian Church. That gives it one of the most austere outlooks of any community in the Hebrides, the Free Presbyterian church building occupying a sight above Churchton Bay which no-one can ignore. The Free Church is relegated to the woods on the outskirts of the settlement, while a prominent sign at the children's playpark says it is most certainly not to be used on a Sunday.

In 1912, the mining company Baird and Co. bought the island for its iron deposits, and worked them until 1919, using German prisoners-of-war as labourers. The workings can still be seen, and the depot above the present-day pier. The company also built two incongruous rows of miners' terraced houses at Inverarish, which remain home to the bulk of the population. Also in that decade, thirty-six of Raasay's men went to fight in the First World War, and as they left from the gathering place at the clock tower near Borodale House, the clock stopped. Only fourteen men returned, and the clock has never worked since. That is not only symbolic of the war, but of an island which time seems to have forgotten. Little changes and little moves.

That is one of the attractions for the island-hopper, along with Raasay's birdlife, forest walks and plants. Raasay House in 1984 was re-opened as an outdoor centre, having fallen into derelict neglect. The day-glo leggings and tops of the rock climbers contrast starkly with the rather dour islanders. The centre's courses include rock-climbing, canoeing, sailing and windsurfing, but you won't need one of their guides for the walking opportunities. These include climbing Dun Caan or covering the east coast of the island. Near the outdoor centre (Raasay House) is St Moluag's chapel, which was built around the 13th century, and a Pictish stone at the foot of the splendidly-named Temptation Hill.

But one of the most popular attractions on the island is a very special road. It was built by Calum MacLeod, who lived at the northerly township of Torran on the north side of Loch Arnish. The council refused to build a road to his home, but Calum believed the only way the seven families in Torran would stay there would be if their homes could be reached by road. So, in 1966, he bought a booklet on road-building for four shillings and set to work. The three-kilometre track took him more than ten years, two wheelbarrows, six picks, six shovels, four spades and five hammers. But it came too late. By the time he had finished, only he and his wife remained in Torran. And in 1988, he died, having already passed into Highlands and Islands folklore. These Raasay folk are made of stern and determined stuff.

Lastly, Raasay is home to one of Gaeldom's greatest poets, Sorley MacLean (born 1911). His poetry explores the desolation of Gaelic culture and the problematic nature of its renewal; the haunting, incantatory verse is well worth seeking out in the various bilingual editions of his work.

How to get there

There is a car ferry from Skye to Raasay, run by CalMac. During summer, it runs at least six times a day from the village of Sconser, which is roughly mid-way between Broadford and Portree on Skye. No Sunday sailings. The pier at Suisinish, on Raasay, is about two km from the main township of Inverarish. For ferry information, contact Portree (☎0478 612075).

Getting around

If you don't take a car across, it's a long hike to the north end, but an easy walk round the south. Don't rely on hitching a lift, as the roads are very quiet. The outdoor centre hires two bikes. No petrol is for sale on the island.

Accommodation

Isle of Raasay Hotel (☎0478 62222) and Churchton House (☎0478 62260). The youth hostel is set well apart, and five km from the pier. The outdoor centre (☎0478 62266) in Raasay House is residential, offering long or day courses, and it has a cafe.

Things to do and see

The outdoor centre has lots of them, with staff and equipment. Or walk (see above), watch the birdlife and see the plants. The centre also has permits for loch trout fishing. The hotel can organise sea angling. The village hall, part of Raasay House, is open for indoor activities most afternoons and evenings most days.

Shopping

There is one shop in Inverarish, which is friendly but not well stocked. Also a post office. Most people go to Portree for supplies.

Nearest Tourist Information Centre: Portree (☎0478 2137).

Introduction to the Small Isles

The parish of the Small Isles forms a compact group accessible from Mallaig. Whatever the ferry times may say, the service can be changed at very short notice to accommodate the needs of the islands, so be warned! From the spectacular grandeur of Rum to the gentler contours of Canna, 'the garden of the Hebrides', the islands offer something for everyone though fitness is essential. All the islands are serviced by a flit boat shuttling between the main ferry and the island so it is only wise to take what you can carry. Shopping is extremely limited, particularly on Rum and Canna, though supplies can be ordered in from Mallaig. Eigg has the most extensive shop.

Rum

(Derivation uncertain. Possibly from Gaelic 'spacious', 'extensive' or 'ridged')

Dominated by the Rum Cuillins, Barkeval, Hallival, Trollaval, Ainshval and Sgurr nan Gillean, one's first impression of the island is of sheer scale. These great hills – three of them Corbetts – rising straight from the sea have an unforgettable impact as you approach. The main anchorage lies in Loch Scresort, the only population centre, dominated at the end by the great bulk of Kinloch Castle. Since 1957 the island has been owned by the Nature Conservancy Council (now called Scottish Natural Heritage) and the population are now entirely in their employ. The NCC's bold idea was to study the possibilities for regeneration in a landscape

stripped and denuded by the activities of man and his livestock. As well as being a key site for the study of red deer, particularly at Kilmory in the north, the island also has numerous sites where reafforestation is being attempted. These already have had a significant impact in terms of numbers and variety of species recorded. Rum was the site for an NCC experiment to reintroduce the white-tailed sea eagle to Scotland, an experiment now happily meeting with some success. Rum is also the home to a herd of ponies, whose ancestors are said to have come ashore from an Armada ship. Feral goats too are present.

While Rum's great size makes for magnificent scenery it also turns the island into one of the wettest places in Scotland. Although rainfall varies dramatically across the island, it is everywhere wet. Kinloch averages ninety-nine inches a year, approximately half as much again as Eigg and Canna, and well over double that of Muck. This means that much of the walking on the island is done even when the weather is dry, through blanket bog. The other feature, encouraged by the woodland around Kinloch, is a midge, blood-crazed and insatiable even by the standards of the west Highlands. From my own experience, the Rum midge regards most forms of repellent as simply another form of tasty snack, an observation confirmed by the workmen on Kinloch Castle who were paid an extra ration of tobacco as a form of midge control! Like most of the Hebrides these two factors make the month of May by far the best time to visit.

The history of the island begins in Mesolithic times with some of the earliest evidence for human habitation in Scotland being found in excavations beside Kinloch Castle. In Neolithic times Bloodstone Hill was used as a source of stone for tools, and evidence of export has been found. Our next evidence for habitation comes in 677 when a priest, appropriately called Beccan the Solitary, is found living on the island. Place name evidence on Rum indicates Viking settlement. Around the summit of Trollaval is a large colony of Manx Shearwaters and the strange calling sound of these birds may have resulted in its eerie name – the Hill of the Trolls. It is an association which occurs elsewhere in the Viking world. Papadil contains the Norse word for priest, 'Papa', and it may have been here that Beccan the Solitary lived, or possibly at the more conventional Kilmory – Gaelic for the 'Cell of St Mary' – in the north of the island. Certainly, the Viking effect on the islands around here is luridly recorded in a verse by Bjorn Cripplehand:

The peasant lost his land and life
Who dared to bide the Norseman's strife
The hungry battle birds were filled
In Skye with blood of foeman killed
And wolves on Tiree's lonely shore
Dyed red their hoary jaws with gore ....

Eventually Rum fell under the control of what became the Lordship of the Isles and the Small Isles became part of the great struggle for predominance on the western seaboard between Norse and Scot. By 1498 the Lordship of the Isles was forfeited to the Scottish crown leaving a power vacuum not to be filled until the rise of Clan Campbell in the 17th century. Numerous revolts took place and law and order broke down. The Isles proved a fertile recruiting ground for the Jacobites and suffered accordingly.

By the 18th century, Rum's population was rising dramatically as MacKinnons poured in from Skye to outnumber the native Macleans. In 1791 the population, aided by the growth of cultivation of the potato and high cattle prices, peaked at just under 450 and remained high until the collapse of the kelp boom (used to provide potash in the Napoleonic wars) just before 1820. But in 1826 a terrible reckoning was to be paid. Financially crippled by the collapse of the kelp industry Rum's landlord had let the island for sheep grazing. For the sum of £5.14s per head almost the entire population was forcibly dispossessed of their land and shipped to Cape Breton. Fifty were left to run the sheep farm. Despairing of his ability to make a profit, the Maclean laird eventually sold on the island as a shooting estate whence it ended up in the hands of the Bulloughs. This fabulously wealthy and larger than life family is responsible for the Rum we see today. In 1899 the old house at Kinloch was demolished to make way for Sir George's grandiose conception of Highland baronial, a shooting lodge was built at Papadil, a laundry at Kilmory. Roads were built, an attempt to dam the river in Kilmory Glen was made and a haunting Doric mausoleum built at Harris for the family (an earlier vault set into the hill was destroyed). The castle is now an extraordinary memorial to late Victorian and Edwardian taste. From the great orchestrion to the giant eagle – a gift from the Emperor of Japan – nothing is too lavish or grand. The ballroom, the piper's platform, the Empire room all bear witness to a vanished age. War and economic change brought an end to the days of glory. The glasshouses fell into ruin, the alligators and turtles were dispersed and the tropical birds and plants gradually disappeared. The population fell steadily until the NCC came on the scene in 1957. In 1967 Lady Monica was laid to rest at the age of ninety-eight beside her husband in the mausoleum at Harris on the island they had both loved so much.

Walking on Rum is immensely rewarding. Across most of the island the views are spectacular. The Cuillins are an extremely long, hard day's walk, and it is probably best to do them over two days. Along their feet the coastal walk to Dibidil and the shooting lodge at Papadil is lovely and slightly less strenuous. The walk over to Harris – with its ruined blackhouses (it was the most extensive place of settlement after Kinloch) and mausoleum is essential. Kilmory is often closed due to the research on deer, but contains the island's only top-quality beach. Another good hike can be had over to Guirdil under Bloodstone Hill with marvellous views over to Canna (there is a bothy at Guirdil). Return by Glen Shellesder. Whatever else you do. though. make sure that you have at least one dinner at Kinloch. Eating in the Bullough dining room from their family porcelain and cutlery before retiring to the library and snooker room while outside dark falls over one of the wildest islands of the Hebrides is one of the most extraordinary and surreal experiences you could have.

How to get there

Ferries
Caledonian MacBrayne operate a ferry leaving from Mallaig (☎0687 2403). It's advisable to book in advance. There are around four sailings a week and the timetable is somewhat complicated as the ferry calls into the other Small Isles on the way.

Day trips to Rum: the MV *Shearwater* runs from Arisaig twice a week, depending on the weather, between May and September. Contact Murdo Grant, Arisaig (☎06875 224).

Accommodation
This is extremely limited and you are advised to book in advance. Contact:

The Reserve Manager
The White House
Isle of Rum
PH43 4RR
(enclose SAE).

Hotels
Kinloch Castle (☎0687 2037)
Open from April to September.

Youth hostel
Kinloch Castle, in the Farmhouse, Stables and 'Foxglove'. Accommodation is basic. Available all year. Telephone number as above.

Campsites
Again, at Kinloch. Book ahead.

Where to eat
Kinloch Castle serves gourmet food. Guests in the hotel stay in the magnificent, if slightly decayed, splendour of a mock-baronial castle, left exactly as it was when the family left it. The quality of the food and the general management of the place is very high.

Things to do and see
Fishing: part of the Kinloch river can be fished for sea-trout and some of the hill lochs for brown trout. Permits can be obtained from the Reserve Office.

Walking: some parts of the island are closed off so check before you set off.

Nearest Tourist Information Centre: at Mallaig (☎0687 2170).

Muck

Smallest and least well known of the Small Isles, Muck is also the most fertile. Its name is derived from the Gaelic for 'pig' and has long caused much amusement, Boswell recording the Laird's squirming embarrassment on being entitled the 'Laird of Muck'. Once again the island was cleared of trees by man though some limited replanting has taken place. Its history is somewhat obscure though no doubt followed a similar pattern to that of its larger neighbours. Population once again peaked at just over 300 by 1821 and once again the profligacy and greed of an absentee landlord – in this case the same Alexander Maclean who had cleared Rum – caused the removal of 150 people. Some scraped a living for a while near Port Mor where the ruins of their huts still remain.

Muck has more recently benefited from the considerably more benevolent ownership of the MacEwen family and a thriving small community of around thirty now exists. Gallanach provides the main beach on the island and there is ample compensation for the smallness of the island in the marvellous views and the wildlife.

How to get there

Ferries
Details are the same as for Rum.

Accommodation

Three self-catering cottages are available. Contact Jenny MacEwan (☎0687 2362).

Camping: contact Jenny MacEwan as above.

Where to eat

There is a little tearoom/craftshop on the island, open three to four days a week.

Nearest Tourist Information Centre: at Mallaig (☎0687 2170).

Canna

Canna (Gaelic: 'porpoise' or possibly 'rabbits') and its linked islet, Sanday, afford the finest harbour in the Small Isles. At present a proper pier is under construction. It has long been a tradition to paint graffiti on the cliffs on the basalt cliffs of the harbour to record safe arrival. Recently the island was gifted to the National Trust for Scotland by John Lorne Campbell. John Lorne Campbell and his wife Margaret Fay Shaw still live on Canna, and it is to their vision

that we owe the preservation of this, one of the most beautiful of all the Hebrides. Although we have little evidence from early sources for Canna, there is plenty of archaeological evidence from the Viking ship burial at Rubha Langan-innis to the Dark Age cross, traditionally on the site of St Columba's chapel near the main farm. A possible early Christian site also exists at Sgor nam Ban-naomha (the point of the Holy women) underneath the cliffs.

Once again the population exhibited the same melancholic pattern as the other islands of a rise to almost 450 during the period of kelp boom, followed by clearances and collapse. By 1871 Canna's population had been reduced to forty-eight as debt forced yet another sale. This time however the island fell into better hands and the population began to stabilise.

Canna is divided by a neck of land into two main sections. The western section consists of a long, high, cliff-girt plateau, roughly egg-shaped. Though the top of the plateau does not make for an interesting walk in itself the views are impressive. It is also possible to walk round the base of the cliffs to some of the main archaeological sites. The Celtic monastery referred to above is certainly well worth a visit, and the Iron Age fort of Dun Channa is at the tip of the island on a rock stack. Near the harbour there is a prominent knoll, known as the Coroghan (probably from the Gaelic for 'fetters'). The fortification on this is probably of 17th-century date. Legend has it that it was used as a place of imprisonment by a Macdonald chieftain for his beautiful wife to frustrate her Macleod lover. Walking on round the coast from here well illustrates the columnar basalt reminiscent of Staffa. Walking too far becomes steadily trickier and is not really worth the effort. Much more interesting is a walk up Compass Hill (so called because of the wildly distorting effects of the rock on compasses) and into the little hillocks and burns which characterise the other part of the island. Once again the views into the sheltered wooded harbour across Sanday to Rum are well worth seeing.

Sanday proves a surprisingly substantial island – its most prominent landmark being its large Catholic church, now abandoned (Canna remained unaffected by the Reformation). Most of the population is now resident on Sanday.

How to get there
Details are the same as for Rum

Accommodation
There is one self-catering cottage which sleeps ten, bookable through the National Trust for Scotland (☎031-226 5922) You could camp but facilities are basic (no toilets).

Where to eat
There are no tearooms or hotels on the island and indeed no shops, save one post-office.

Nearest Tourist Information Centre: at Mallaig (☎0687 2170)

Eigg

Derivation: Gaelic 'Island of the Notch' or Old Norse 'Edge'. Dominated by the great ridge of An Sgurr, one of the most distinctive sights of the Hebrides, Eigg, like Canna, is divided into two main sections, the lochans and hillocks surrounding and behind An Sgurr, and the high basalt plateau shielding the main crofting area of Cleadale.

Despite impressive evidence of iron-age fortification on An Sgurr, Eigg first appears in the historical record as the home of St Donnan. To him and his

monks Columba promised 'red martyrdom' (as opposed to the 'white martyrdom' of exile) and in 617 the Irish annals record his death and that of his community at the hands of pirates. No evidence of his monastery exists today although 'Kildonnan' overlooks the harbour. Viking burial mounds were found here in the 19th century as was a magnificent Viking sword. In 1386 Donald MacDonald was installed as 2nd Lord of the Isles at Kildonnan. His Clanranald brethren were to own the island for the next 440 years. In 1615 Eigg was the site of the last uprising on behalf of the defunct Lordship, a rising as much farce as serious threat. We now come to one of Eigg's most enduring legends, that of Uamh Fhraing – the Cave of St Francis, or Massacre Cave. The story has it that 395 people were burnt alive while hiding here by MacLeods of Harris led by Alastair Crotach in 1577. There are a considerable number of doubts about this story, not least that the population seems to have recovered extremely quickly only to be massacred again a few years later! Yet there do seem to have been bones in the cave until the 1850s. The truth will probably now never be known.

The power of Clan Campbell forced the Clanranald family to pay them for the right to hold their own land in 1627. In 1745 'Young Clanranald' was a figure of some importance in the Jacobite rebellion, leading to the transportation of at least twenty-seven inhabitants. However, Eigg's population grew to a peak of 550 by 1841. Regrettably, their Clanranald owner spent his way through the entire estate, forcing him to sell the island in 1827. The island's new owner proved sympathetic to the population thus delaying and slowing the population decline (there were still 300 people on the island in the 1880s). The fact that the landlord actually lived on the island led to the planting of much woodland and the restocking of the lochs. The death in 1913 of the next owner saw him buried on Castle Island, sheltering the harbour, with a view of all his lands on Skye, Muck and Eigg. The island passed through various hands thereafter including that of the famous Runciman family. One distinguished visitor amongst many at this time was Sir Yehudi Menuhin, 'a handy man for the ceilidh tonight' as one crofter remarked. In 1930 the Runcimans built the present Lodge, the subtropical nature of whose gardens bear witness to the mildness of the climate. In 1975 the island was sold on to its present owner, Keith Schellenberg. At the time of going to press, there is speculation as to the possible sale of the island once more.

Fine walks can be had underneath the Sgurr towards Grulin. The Sgurr itself, of course, is a fine walk as are the hills and lochans behind it, one of which is rumoured to be the residence of a kelpie or waterhorse. The bay around Galmisdale and past the old mill toward the chapel and cross at Kildonnan is particularly attractive in the evening. In the north of the island at Cleadale are some impressive beaches culminating in the famous 'singing sands' of Camas Sgiotaig, which make a noise when walked upon in certain conditions. Near the harbour is the Massacre Cave, not immediately obvious unless you know what you are looking for, and just up the coast the somewhat more authentic Cathedral Cave used for services during the proscription of the Catholic church.

How to get there
Ferries: Details as for Rum.

Accommodation
Full board is available with:
Mrs Carr, Kildonnan Farm Guest House (☎0687 82446);
Mrs Kirk, Lageorna (☎0687 82405).
Caravans also available.

Things to do and see
Fishing: permits available from the Estate office.

Nearest Tourist Information Office: at Mallaig (☎0687 2170)

Coll

Coll and Tiree share the same characteristics, but are as different in nature as it is possible to be. Both low-lying, windswept, almost treeless and desolately beautiful, Coll is the rockier, the wilder and less populated of the two. Just twelve miles long, and three miles across, Coll has a tiny population of 160. Coll's crofting tenants were cleared in the 1850s to make room for dairy farmers from Ayrshire, and though a few crofts still remain, the island is largely farmed. With such a background, traditional life is limited and many of the houses on Coll have been given over as holiday homes. Inhospitable and barren in the north (apart from the northernmost tip, where peat and sand combine to make fertile machair), Coll has sandy beaches to rival Tiree in the south, and an enviable wildlife population including corncrakes, barnacle and whitefronted geese, waders, seals and otters.

Despite their proximity, Coll and Tiree were for centuries under different ownership. While Tiree remained largely a crofting island under the Duke of Argyll, Coll's owners, the MacLeans of Coll, cleared the island in the 1850s to make way for dairy farmers. For eighty years Coll became a leading cheese producer until the market collapsed and the farmers moved to stock instead. Now the main income is from the sale of sheep and cattle, and from tourism.

Coll's capital and the first settlement you reach from the ferry terminal is Arinagour ('shieling of the goats') where the majority of its population cluster. Here the Isle of Coll Hotel, an institution on the island and a favourite with the visiting yachts, cashes cheques (there is no bank apart from the post-office's Giro bank), supplies calor gas, a taxi, hot food and even the luxury of a sauna for weary sailors. It also arranges sea-angling and inland loch fishing. Two churches, two food stores, post-office, a petrol pump, a craft shop and a bistro make Arinagour the centre of Coll life. At Arnabost an old earthhouse with circular chamber and long passage was discovered in 1855 along with several implements and a gold brooch, although nothing can be seen today. Arnabost is also the home of the island's nine-hole golf course. At the north end of the island the almost deserted townships of Bousd and Sorisdale are reminders of Coll's once thriving population. Now only a traditional thatched cottage remains. Sorisdale Bay is a good start for short coastal walks. Turning south from Arnabost you reach Coll's highest point, Ben Hogh, 104 metres high and the best vantage point for views over the island and beyond. Balanced on three tiny rocks near the summit is a huge boulder, an erratic abandoned in the Ice Age and seemingly stable on its precarious perch. Coll is littered with standing stones, the best of which, Na Sgeulachan ('the teller of tales'), can be found at Totronald, reachable from the north on a track through the dunes from Ballyhaugh beneath Ben Hogh, or from the south by a track from the airstrip. At Breachacha stand Coll's two castles. The 'newer' castle was built for Hector MacLean in 1750, sheltered Johnson and Boswell from storms in 1773, was disastrously upgraded by its Victorian owner, and has now been converted into the inevitable holiday homes. Breachacha Castle, a medieval tower house which was the 15th-century stronghold of the MacLeans, has suffered a less ignoble fate and is now fully restored to its former glory. Open to visitors by arrangement, the castle is the home of the MacLean Bristol family and the Project Trust, a scheme to involve young school-leavers in development work around the world. In the south Crossapol and Feall Bays have tremendous shellsand beaches and bountiful wildlife. The RSPB reserve covers most of this area up to and beyond Totronald. The world's most isolated bookshop must be at Crossapol House, hidden amongst the dunes at the southern end of the island. Island Books, with access limited by tide, offers its clients transport if needed – call ☎08793 336.

How to get there

Ferries
Oban to Coll – five sailings a week at peak times, with stops sometimes at Tobermory. Journey time 3 hours 5 minutes. All vehicles taken.
Tobermory to Coll – four sailings a week at peak times. Journey time 1 hour 20 minutes. Some services passenger only.
Tiree to Coll – five sailings a week at peak times. Journey time 1 hour 5 minutes. NB. despite their close proximity there is no regular way of travelling between the two islands except the CalMac ferry. Contact Caledonian MacBrayne for the latest information: The Ferry Terminal, Oban (☎0631 66688).

By air
Although there is a small airstrip, there are no scheduled services to Coll.

Accommodation
The Isle of Coll Hotel, Arinagour (☎08793 334). The only hotel on the island – with the only bar.
Tigh na Mara Guest House, Arinagour, (☎08793 354). Comfortable, licensed guest house by the sea. Contact Mrs Sturgeon.
Acha House (☎ 08793 339) Guest house between Arinagour and Crossapol.
Achamore (☎08793 430). Hires bicycles and golf clubs. Contact Mrs Underwood. For full bed and breakfast contact Tourist Information.

Where to eat
The Isle of Coll Hotel, Arinagour (☎08793 334).
Coll Bistro, Arinagour (☎08793 373).

Bicycle hire
Tigh na Mara Guest House (☎08793 354). Also hires mopeds.
Achamore bed and breakfast (☎08793 430). Also hires golf clubs.

Specialities

Coll ceramics, knitwear and herbal products.

Nearest Tourist Information Centre: Oban (☎0631 63122).

Tiree

Tiree is the most westerly of all the Inner Hebrides – and the flattest. As the ferry glides into Gott Bay the houses seem to rise like ships from the sea, a line of land barely discernible beneath them. Three hills all under 140m dominate the western side of the island while richly fertile crofting land stretches across to the east. Beaches of all types surround the island, rocky inlets with seal colonies, wide bays with Atlantic rollers crashing against silver sands, and intimate sheltered coves with pebble beaches, deserted but for waders and gulls. Only eleven miles long and varying in width from one to six miles, Tiree has some of the richest and most beautiful machair land in the Hebrides, saved from destruction by the island's lack of rabbits. From May to August its surface is a constantly changing blaze of colour and smells as daisies give way to buttercups, clover, wild orchids, ragged robin and 500 species of wild flowers. With its record-breaking sunshine – in May and June Tiree is frequently the sunniest place in the UK – Tiree is a hugely fertile island. Its Gaelic name *Tir-Iodh* means the land of corn, and Tiree was once known as the Granary of the Isles. Now its main exports are cattle and sheep – and fond memories from visitors.

Generations of radio listeners to the shipping forecast automatically connect Tiree with gale warnings, and they'd be right to do so as Tiree is known for its wind. Thousands of people come from around the world to windsurf here, attracted by the knowledge of certain wind. Not always popular with the islanders, the surfers have made a surreal addition to the island over the last ten years, their high-tech equipment and neon colours incongruous against the white-washed walls of a traditional Tiree cottage. In October each year the International Windsurfing Championships are held here and the island abandons itself to neoprene and hip, surfing language. In their frenzy to be out on the waves some surfers have torn up the machair with their four-wheel drive vehicles and caused friction with locals, but the majority are beguiled by Tiree's gentle charm and great beauty and return year after year.

The warmth of its people, who will go out of their way to be of help, and the enchantment of its landscape make Tiree an island on which to relax and recharge. There is little to do and seemingly endless time in which to do it. Strong links with the past, from the brochs and traditional white houses scattered over the island, to the gentle pace and way of life of its Gaelic-speaking inhabitants, make Tiree a timeless place. But the island's special magic is the sense of space and freedom it gives, a heightened awareness of the brilliant colours of nature, and a oneness with sea, sky and land.

The earliest occupation on Tiree dates back to 80 BC. In AD 565 followers of St Columba of Iona founded a monastery at Soroby, which was destroyed when the Vikings invaded the island in 672. For the next 400 years Tiree was occupied by the Norse and many of its current place names date from this period. In 1263 the island came under the Lordship of the Isles, becoming the property of the Campbells, Dukes of Argyll, at the end of the 17th century. Before the potato famine of 1846 Tiree's population was a massive 1,450; during the war the RAF station on Tiree again swelled the numbers, but today the population is less than 800. Crofting is the main source of income, with lobster fishing, and some employment at the weather station.

The main settlement and the island's capital is Scarinish which has a butcher shop, a food store, post-office, and petrol pump at the pier. This was Tiree's main harbour (built 1771) and in former times was jammed with boats bringing in the island's supplies and taking cattle and sheep to the mainland markets. Now only the wreck of the *Mary Stewart* is a reminder of that busier time. Above the village are the impressive remains of one of Tiree's two brochs – Dun Mor Vaul. The second, Dun Mor Caolas, is at the east of the island and has good views to Mull. The Reef or former air force base is the site of the current airport, scrap yards and machine hire – an ugly industrial area with Nissen huts and concrete buildings in the centre of this otherwise untouched island. Crossapol has a good general store (I. & F. MacLeod), and a petrol pump. Just outside is the Island House, the Duke of Argyll's summer residence. A 15th-century castle, with access by causeway and drawbridge, existed on an island previously, but was demolished in 1748 when the present house was built and the channel between the island and mainland filled in. At Hynish, the Signal Tower Museum describes the building of the Skerryvore Lighthouse. Hynish pier and harbour were originally built to transport material for the lighthouse's construction, and were later used in the mid-19th century by emigrants leaving Tiree for a new life in Canada following the potato famine and the division of the crofts. Ben Hynish, the island's highest hill at 141m, sports what the islanders call the 'golf-ball' – the radar station. Ceann a' Mhara (Kennavara), the island's third hill and the headland at the end of the magnificent Traigh Bhi, has three duns, an ancient chapel, a swallow hole, and views to Barra and South Uist. The Sandaig Museum recreates life in a *Tigh Geal* (white house),

and across the road the old Kelp Factory is the only remains of the former kelp industry. Several good examples of thatched cottages are also found at Middleton, Scarinish, Kilmoluaig and Kenovay. Loch Bhasapol has the remains of two crannogs (Celtic loch dwellings usually on artificial islands) and is often used as light relief by sea-battered windsurfers. At Cornaig stands the old island mill, a reminder of the days when Tiree was self-sufficient in grain. Vaul Golf Club has an eighteen-hole links course open daily except Sunday – adults £4, children £2, weekly and monthly rates available. From either Balephetrish or Vaul you can easily walk to Clach a' Choire or the Ringing Stone, Tiree's best-loved ancient monument. This erratic granite boulder, five feet high and covered with cup markings, lies on top of a small hollow and when struck with a hard object produces an eerie metallic sound. Legend says that should the stone be broken Tiree will sink beneath the sea forever.

How to get there

Ferries

Oban to Tiree – five sailings a week at peak times, with stops at Coll and sometimes Tobermory. Journey time 4 hours 15 minutes. All vehicles taken.

Tobermory to Tiree – four sailings a week at peak times, with stop at Coll. Journey time 2 hours 30 minutes. Some services passenger only.

Coll to Tiree – five sailings a week at peak times. Journey time 1 hour 5 minutes. (NB: despite their close proximity there is no regular way of travelling between the two islands except the CalMac ferry. Contact Caledonian MacBrayne for the latest information: The Ferry Terminal, Oban (☎0631 66688).

By air

Glasgow to Tiree – daily flights (except Sunday) to the airport at the Reef at Crossapol. Continues on to Barra. Contact Loganair (☎041-889 3181).

The island's Post Bus meets the plane daily and travels round the whole of the island on Tuesdays.

Car Hire
Tiree does not have the same MOT or licence requirements as the mainland and car hire on the island is cheerfully described as 'rent-a-wreck'. Whatever the standard the cars will get you around Tiree's extensive single-track roads with no problems. Both car-hire companies will deliver cars to the airport or ferry terminal.
Tiree Motor Company at Crossapol. Contact Douglas Hunter (☎08792 469). A MacLennan Motors at the ferry terminal near Scarinish. Contact Angus MacLennan (☎08792 555/559).

Bicycle Hire
Bikes are the best way to travel on the island, as long as the wind is behind you. Contact Vicki and Neil MacLean (☎08792 428), who will also deliver bikes to where you are staying.

Accommodation
Tiree has an extraordinary number of second homes available for rent, but surprisingly few bed and breakfasts and guest houses, which are quickly booked – it is strongly recommended that you arrange your accommodation before you go. The cheapest option is to rent a cottage for your stay. Camping is allowed on the machair, but bear in mind the lack of shelter and the constant winds.

Hotels and Guest Houses
The Lodge Hotel, Gott Bay (☎08792 368). Room for 21 guests, with beautiful views over the bay and the advantage of the downstairs pub and restaurant; fairly pricey.
Scarinish Hotel, The Harbour, Scarinish (☎08792 308). Eleven rooms are available in this somewhat dilapidated hotel.
Balephetrish Guest House, Balephetrish (☎08792 549).
Kirkapol Guest House, Gott Bay (☎08792 729). A converted church with views over Gott Bay. Evening meals.

The Glassary, Sandaig (☎08792 684). The island's only restaurant, 'Taste of Scotland' recommended, with guest house attached.

For cottage rental and bed and breakfast contact Tourist Information at Oban. Not all houses are advertised in the Tourist Information literature, however, so if you are stuck, a good starting point once on the island is to ask at the nearest shop.

Where to eat
All the above do evening meals for residents and some for non-residents. The only coffee house on the island is at Glebe House, Scarinish, open mornings only 10am-1pm.

Nearest Tourist Information Centre: Oban (☎0631 63122).

Mull

'The Isle of Mull is of the Isles the fairest,
Of ocean's gems 'tis the first and rarest,
Green grassy island of sparkling fountains,
By waving woods and high towering mountains.'
Dugald MacPhail

Mull is unashamedly an island for visitors. Since it appeared on the 18th-century tourist map, it has attracted travellers in their thousands, many of whom have stayed and made their homes there, and not surprisingly, as Mull is one of the most beautiful of Scotland's islands. With more than 300 miles of rocky and sandy coastline, the only island mountain over 3,000 feet outside Skye, archaeological remains, remarkable geology and some of the richest island wildlife in Britain, Mull is a magical place. It is also one of the wettest islands in the Hebrides, with the happy result that it has an over-whelming number of indoor visitor attractions, cafes and craft shops. If you are searching for traditional island life then Mull is not the place to find it; many of its inhabitants are incomers (mainly English), the Gaelic language surfaces almost exclusively for the title of the community newspaper – *Am Muileach* – and very few working crofts remain. But if you want to learn more about the history and archaeology of the Hebrides, or participate in energetic outdoor pursuits, or simply soak in some of Scotland's most spectacular scenery, then Mull is an absorbing and rewarding island.

The first human is believed to have reached Mull about 6000 BC, leaving the flint spearheads now seen in the Mull Museum. By the Bronze Age, the *Muileach,* or person from Mull, was erecting standing stones and the impressive Lochbuie stone circle, while two brochs (An Sean Dun and Dun na Gall) and many forts reflect his lack of security in the Iron Age. The island became strate-gically important in the Dark Ages – two cairns standing in Glen More are said to mark the boundary between Dalriada and Pictland (*Carn cul ri Erin*, 'Cairn with its back to Ireland', and *Carn cul ri Albann*, 'Cairn with its back to Scot-land'), while the Way of the Dead, the burial route of the Dark Age Scottish kings, almost certainly ran through Mull. Subsequent Viking invasions gave the Norse dominance until the 13th century.

For the next 230 years Mull was part of the powerful Lordship of the Isles, and its key castles (Aros, Duart, Mingarry) are thought to have formed part of the chain of castles, all within sight of the next, which allowed the Lordship to know from its seat at Finlaggan on Islay what was happening throughout the kingdom. When the Lordship collapsed in 1493, the Maclean clan became

dominant and held sway in Mull until the Campbells took over in 1681.There followed nearly two centuries of pros-perity, as Mull supplied beef cattle for the Napoleonic wars and alkaline ash (from burning kelp or seaweed) for bleaching and soap production. With the end of the wars came the end of prosperity, accentuated by the potato blight of 1846. Emigration and the Clearances began in earnest, and Mull's population of over 10,000 dropped drastically. Today it is under 4,000, and deserted 18th- and 19th-century town-ships are scattered around the island (e.g. Burg, Kildavie, Clac Gugairidh, Treshnish, Cille Mhuire and Tir Fhear-again).

After the ferry trip from Oban with its romantic views of Duart Castle, Craig-nure, the first settlement you reach on Mull, can seem disappointingly func-tional. Like most island ferry terminals Craignure has everything for the tourist but picturesque scenery. Nevertheless, it contains the busiest Tourist Informa-tion Centre on the island and is well situated for day trips. A large camp site, The Ceilidh Place bar and restaurant, The Craig Hotel, a garage and a general store provide all you need. For enter-tainment you can take the Miniature Railway from near the Old Pier to Torosay Castle and Gardens, a twenty-minute journey on a steam or diesel hauled train. The railway shop is a steam-buff's home-from-home with railway books, postcards, train memo-rabilia and guards' whistles.

South (1.5 miles) of Craignure, Torosay Castle and Gardens was designed by two of Scotland's most eminent archi-tects, David Bryce (1803-76), who planned the house, and Sir Robert Lorimer (1864-1929), who laid out the eleven-acre gardens, now complemented with statues by Antonio Bonazza and extended with a Japanese garden, Euca-lypt walk and shrubbery. The Castle is a bizarre mix of Scottish baronial – endless stags' heads and Edwardian furniture – and intimate family history, punctuated by the wonderful humour of its current owner, Christopher James, and his father the late David Guthrie-James, famous as the POW who escaped from Colditz and an adventurer *par excellence*. Witty, handwritten captions to everything you see, photographs of David Guthrie-James' expeditions, his school reports and the original Red Book from his *This is Your Life* appearance make this a fascinating place to spend a wet afternoon. The Castle is family-run – Christopher James may be seen chasing cattle on the 10,000-acre estate, while his mother Jacquetta Guthrie-James is likely to take your money in the ticket office – and extremely welcoming.

Next door to Torosay Castle is the workshop of the Isle of Mull Weavers, a husband-and-wife team devoted to traditional weaving on old dobby looms. Bob Ryan demonstrates his noisy machines and dry humour, while in the small shop Kathie Ryan sells their tweed, ties, travel and floor rugs. Made on the premises, every piece of cloth is unique, with design specifications changed on each weaving.

A bumpy lane from the A849 leads to Duart Castle, the dramatic 13th-century clifftop castle seen from the Oban ferry, and the current seat of Clan Maclean. A small, well set-out exhibition gives a taste of life in the castle over the last 400 years. In 1681 the castle was forfeited to the Crown, returning to the family earlier this century, making much of the exhibition patchy and preoccupied with recent family photographs. In the Main Hall, partially hidden by display cases, is a touching record of the heights of the last Chief's children (now adults), with mum and dad's chest sizes alongside. The last Chief was the No 1 Scout for many years and the castle's top-floor is given over to an exhibition of world scouting. In an outbuilding the cafe serves generous portions of delicious home-baking. Of interest particularly to Maclean family historians (Macleans are asked to sign a special family guest book) Duart Castle is well worth a visit if only for its impressive situation.

North (5 miles) of Craignure on the A849 is Fishnish Point, the ferry point for Lochaline and Morvern. A nine-acre nature walk and nursery are nearby at Balmeanach Park, a camping/caravan site with Cynthia's Tearoom attached (open 8-8 and licensed).

An ideal base from which to explore the island, Salen is the centre of Mull's road network. At the entrance to the northern half of the island, it signals the start of a more relaxed Mull. Coach tours find it difficult to penetrate beyond the village as the road is pot-holed and single-track as far as Tobermory (dubbed the worst A road in Britain by most islanders), and day-trippers from Oban find it easier to head for Iona. Salen is a peaceful village where dogs and cats roam the main street and pretty cottage gardens are the norm. It has most facilities including a grocer, post-office, newsagents, cycle hire, a garage, The Puffer Aground restaurant, two hotels (bar meals available), and the Smiddy gift shop.

On the Dervaig road (6 miles from Salen) in Glen Aros, an inconspicuous Forestry Commission gate leads to what has been described as the commercial centre of Mull in the 18th and 19th centuries – the market place Druim tighe Mhic Gille Chatain. Following the Act of Union in 1707, English buyers could not get enough Scottish beef, much of which was used to fuel the British Army and Navy in their wars abroad, and hundreds of island beasts were walked in droves to the lucrative English markets. Coll and Tiree were big producers, bringing cattle into Croig ('cattle harbour') near Dervaig and walking them to the Mull market at Druim tighe Mhic Gille Chatain. Drove roads also brought cattle from northern Mull, and farmers from Morvern, Ardnamurchan, as well as the Outer Isles and even Ireland, used Mull as a convenient stepping stone to the mainland. From the Glen Aros market site, where traces of huts and booths can still be seen, the cattle headed south across Mull to Grass Point on the mouth of

Loch Dun. Ferried to Kerrera island, off Oban, they were swum across the narrow channel to the mainland, and walked to markets in Crieff and Falkirk. When the landing point moved south from Croig to Kintra (facing Iona on the Ross of Mull), Glen Aros market was bypassed and the site went into decline.

North of Salen (2 miles), on the Tobermory road, lie the ruins of Aros Castle, once one of the most powerful places on the island. It was here that James VI made his audacious move to control the Highland chiefs by inviting them on board the 'Moon' and promptly sailing away with them as hostages. The 13th-century castle was an administrative centre and seat of government until the end of the 18th century. Enough still stands of the 14-15th century keep to appreciate its former grandeur and impressive strategic location on the cliff edge with wide views over the sea-ways.

Tobermory is the island's modern 'capital' and a central place for any exploration of Mull. The hopping point for Coll and Tiree, it also has a ferry connection to the Ardnamurchan peninsula. In 1788 the government developed the small fishing port as part of its wider scheme to pacify the Highlands after the '45 Rising. The original Tobermory was little more than a cluster of houses where the distillery now stands. The present town is focused around the harbour, a tree-lined, gaily painted strip of pubs, restaurants and shops. Few fishing boats now frequent the port, but their absence is made up by a steady stream of yachts and yachtsmen, giving the small town a busy and lively atmosphere.

Part of the town's nautical past is the infamous Tobermory Galleon, anchored in the harbour in 1588 and sunk after a mysterious explosion on board. Believed to be a straggler from the defeated Armada and supposedly carrying a huge amount of treasure, the galleon has attracted treasure-hunters through the ages, from the first attempt in 1608 by the 7th Earl of Argyll to the latest

high-tech dive in 1982, but to date nothing more exciting than a couple of cannon has emerged from the murky depths of its sunken hull.

Another institution is the Tobermory town clock. Mrs Bishop, otherwise known as the Victorian traveller and writer Isabella Bird, erected it in 1905 in memory of her sister Henrietta who died of typhoid in their cottage in 1880. Now its hourly chimes keep a new generation of travellers awake all night in the adjacent Youth Hostel.

On the harbour front is a monument to the Gaelic poet and writer, Dugald MacPhail (1818-87), famous for his song 'An t' Eilean Muilach' (To the Island of Mull). The monument was built from the stones of his birthplace.

The Mull Museum, on the High Street, offers a comprehensive history of Mull and the surrounding islands. A whisky still, a reconstructed schoolroom, bakehouse, and laundry, an archaeological and geological survey and an unbelievable quantity of artefacts of all shapes and sizes are crammed into this tiny, informative museum.

The island's only distillery is at the southern end of the harbour. The Tobermory Distillery gives short tours of the production and bottling processes with a wee dram at the end. The distillery's malt is Ledaig ('little bay') but you won't easily find a bottle of it in any of the local pubs – most of it is sent to the mainland or exported to be used in blends, such as the Tobermory Malt (which, incidentally, is produced in Oban). Formerly a family-run business, the distillery has recently been taken over by a large distillery group and returned to full production, twenty-four hours a day, seven days a week.

A spectacular road runs eight miles from Tobermory to Dervaig, but cyclists beware – it begins with a 1:4 hill out of Tobermory. A rally driver's delight, the road twists and turns alarmingly as it rises high over moorland, with views of the sea, the surrounding hills and the eerie Mishnish Lochs below. Local history says that the road was built by an unscrupulous landowner during the desperate years following the potato blight of 1846. Paying a pittance for their labour he forced the local population to build the switchback road so he could take his crippled daughter sightseeing. Four miles from Tobermory the romantic turrets of Glengorm Castle come into view, with the long low shape of Coll in the distance behind. (The best views of Glengorm Castle are from the Coll-Tiree ferry). The castle is private but its garden shop and pottery are open in the summer. Glengorm means 'the blue glen', but the blue was from the smoke of burning townships at the time of the Clearances. Just before you reach the castle is Glengorm Children's Farm with its collection of rare-breed sheep and goats, rabbits, pigs and horses, all under cover. Beyond Glengorm lies one of the island's two brochs, An Sean Dun, and the remains of a medieval township and galley slip.

At Sgriob-ruadh ('red furrow') farm Jeff and Chris Reade and family operate the island's only dairy and cheese-making operation. A good all-weather visit, the farm demonstrates traditional cheese-making, a tour of the dairy with optional hands-on milking, and sampling of the farm's delicious 'flavells' and 'truckles' in their simple family-run restaurant. A small museum recreating dairy farming and crofting life over the the the last 200 years is also planned for the future. The farm has a long history of dairy farming – up until 1960 its previous owners had for generations supplied milk to Tobermory. The Reade family, experts in cheese-making from Somerset, and now appropriately the only traditional cheddar producers in Scotland using their own milk, rescued the farm from dereliction and in true island-style, recycled whatever materials were available to rebuild it – the stairs were rescued from Tobermory Distillery, the wood came from a Glasgow hospital and the 'Glass Barn' is the former village hall from Salen.

Nestling in the glen beneath Lan Torr at the end of the sea-loch Loch Cuan, the picturesque village of Dervaig is immediately recognisable by its striking nuclear warhead-like church tower. The main village lies to the north-east and consists of two streets of pretty whitewashed cottages, a craft shop (which acts as the ticket centre for Mull Little Theatre) and Dervaig Coffee and Books, selling the best coffee on Mull in some of the most unusual surroundings.

The turn-off for the Mull Little Theatre lies beside the church. With only forty-three seats, Mull Little Theatre is Britain's smallest repertory theatre, and was until recently the smallest in the world. Opened over twenty-five years ago, the theatre has delighted audiences young and old with magical performances in its tiered auditorium, sumptuously decked out with vivid blue velvet seats and curtains. Its tiny company of professional actors gives daily shows in the summer months (twice daily in July and August), and tours the Western Highlands and islands in the autumn. Bookings through Cottage Crafts, Dervaig (☎06884 245) or Tobermory Tourist Office. Information from Mull Little Theatre (☎06884 267).

Off the B8073 is The Old Byre Heritage Centre, housing a remarkable collection of historical models by Nick Hesketh. With painstaking detail he has recreated the history of Mull in miniature, from bloodthirsty Norsemen rampaging through a broch settlement (look out for Conan the Barbarian molesting a Jane Russell lookalike) to an aerial view of life in a traditional black house. The miniature models are fascinating, but the exhibition loses its way amongst additional cases of stuffed animals and an incongruous giant midge. Accompanying the exhibition is an informative video, using the models to good effect in an entertaining history of the island. Downstairs the cafe is 'Taste of Scotland' recommended.

Before crossing the Mornish headland, take a right turn to Croig Harbour, a tranquil stone harbour and formerly the landing point for cattle being taken to the Mull market. Where emigrating families said their farewells to the island as they gathered for the ships taking them to Canada and America, Calgary Bay is one of the most beautiful beaches on Mull and must have made the emigrés' departures even harder to bear. White sands stretch round a wide bay with rocks on either side and views of Coll in the distance. Now a popular picnic and unofficial camp site (campers, the midges are particularly bad here) the beach has public toilets and a parking area. Nearby the Dovecot Restaurant and Art Gallery provide alternative entertainment on a wet day. Beyond Calgary, a track leads to Haunn and the magnificent ruined garden of Treshnish House (a must in May/June for its rhododendrons). When the track peters out, walk over the shoulder of the hill to two of the island's finest ruined townships – Clac Gugairidh and Crackaig. On the tree that still grows in one of them the last inhabitant of the village is said to have hanged himself. Following the burn down over the cliff brings you to an illicit still hidden in a cave. Take a torch!

Beyond Kilninian, with its medieval grave slabs in the church yard, is the spectacular Eass Forss – a combination of Gaelic and Norse meaning 'waterfall waterfall'! From the road the upper falls are impressive enough, but the only way to see them is from the beach. Half a mile further a track leads down to the base of the cliff and it's possible to walk back along the beach to gape up at the huge plunge of water crashing down.

The turn-off for the Ulva Ferry follows a twisty road before arriving at the short stretch of water which separates Ulva from Mull. For years Ulva was closed to general access, but recently the new laird, Jamie Howard, has actively encouraged vistors with 'The Ulva Story' interpretative display, signposted nature walks, the Boathouse Visitors Centre and Oyster Bar, with its freshly-opened oysters, served with wine or Guinness. The Ulva Ferry is summoned in traditional fashion by uncovering a red panel on the mainland jetty, but turns out to be an unromantic modern motorboat. The charge for the short ride includes parking at the jetty, entrance to The Ulva Story and access to the whole of Ulva and Gometra. Make sure you have an early start if you want to visit Gometra too.

On the B8035 to Iona at the turn-off to Gruline Home Farm is an unusual monument in the care of the National Trust of Australia. A huge sign announces that this is a Mausoleum erected for Major General Lachlan Macquarie [sic] (1761-1824), known as the 'father of Australia', but originally from Jarviesfield on Mull. His gothic mausoleum houses his wife and son as well as himself, and is austere and modest, unlike his overwhelming epitaph. Surrounded by a low dry-stone wall and shady Scots pine he must feel a million miles away from the wide open land where he made his name.

The road follows the southern shore of Loch na Keal, with the imposing slopes of Ben More rising from sea-level straight up to 996 metres (3169 feet). Ben More ('big hill') is the only island Munro outside Skye and, once the highest mountain in the North European landmass, is now the highest point for over thirty miles. On a clear day there are unforgettable views of the Western Isles, Skye, the mainland mountains, and south to Islay and Jura. A good path starts from the road by the stream, Abhainn na h-Uamha. Follow this, past waterfalls and pools, up a steep grassy slope to where Beinn Fhada and A' Chioch meet. An energetic scramble up A' Chioch, to the south, brings you to the final rocky ridge and the summit. The quickest way down is along the NW ridge directly back to the day's starting point at Loch na Keal. As well as the usual vital equipment, footwear, compass, food and warm clothing, don't forget to bring a small-scale map of the West Highlands – for island-spotting on clear days – and a good head for heights – the last section of the ascent is exhilarating, but could be nerve-racking for an inexperienced walker.

As it passes the tiny island of Inch Kenneth, the road turns sharply inland and crosses the Burg headland. Named after one of St Columba's followers, Inch Kenneth has the ruins of a medieval church and burial ground, and is now the home of one of the Mitfords. A legend claims that the bodies of the kings of Scotland and Ireland were laid out here temporarily when bad weather prevented their burial on Iona.

The two-mile path to the spectacular MacKinnon's Cave begins near the turn-off to Balmeanach farm. 500 feet long and reckoned to be the deepest on the islands, MacKinnon's Cave is only accessible from half-tide so it's wise to check the tide tables before setting off and to take a torch. The path goes past the farm and to the left of the farm buildings before swinging back to the coast. A short walk through the flotsam of a thousand storms – massive logs, tangled ropes and endless plastic bottles – brings you to a waterfall and a huge protrusion of rock, beyond which lies the entrance to the cave. Some say it was named after an Iona monk who, after various misdemeanours, went to Staffa to pay penance in one of the caves (MacKinnon's Cave), but found its gulls and pounding waves too noisy for effective contemplation and retired to the cave on Mull instead. Others say that MacKinnon the piper once led a band of people into the cave, never to be seen again. Only the piper's dog returned, out of its mind with fear and without a hair on its body.

The Burg headland has some of the wildest country on Mull and is only easily accessible from the east. In the care of the National Trust for Scotland it contains the famous forty-foot-high fossil tree, discovered by the geologist J. MacCulloch in 1819, and believed to be over fifty million years old. The walk to MacCulloch's Tree is an all-day excursion through impressive coastal scenery, interesting for its hexagonal basalt columns, well-preserved dun (Dun Bhuirg), and rich wildlife. Take the Tioran turn-off from the B8035 and continue past Tioran house to the National Trust for Scotland car park. The ten-mile walk is well-marked, but hard going in places and strong footwear is essential.

At the junction of the A849 and B8039 you can either turn right for Iona, or left to return to Craignure through Glen More. An area of wide open country, now being reforested, Glen More divides north and central Mull from the Ross and the Firth of Lorn coast, and has many good walks, while the new road is a cyclist's dream. At the end of the glen a narrow road leads to the beautiful inland Loch Uisg ('loch of water') and the village of Lochbuie, a peaceful place sitting beneath the mass of Ben Buie, with views to Colonsay, Islay and Jura. Its 19th-century church contains a celtic cross. Just outside the village, before the turning to Laggan Sands, lies the only stone circle on Mull. Nearby, the 15th-century MacLean stronghold, Moy Castle, famed for its bottleneck dungeon and a well which reputedly never runs dry, is well-preserved but now too dangerous for public access. Further round the coast at Laggan Sands is a former medieval chapel, restored as a mausoleum for the MacLaines of Lochbuie in 1864.

Grass Point, at the entrance to Loch Don and at the narrowest point of the Firth of Lorn, was the focal point of Mull's 18th- and 19th-century droving trade. It was here that the black cattle produced on Mull, Coll and Tiree were ferried to Kerrera island, and forced to swim to the mainland, before being walked to the huge beef markets at Falkirk and Crieff.

Turning right at the junction on the road to Iona brings you into an area of the island which repays more exploration than the majority of day trippers headed for Iona give it – the Ross of Mull. At Pennyghael, a post office/grocer's and the Kinloch Hotel, with its real fire and collection of long bows and wooden ice axes, provide welcome refreshment and shelter for walkers and cyclists.

Just beyond Pennyghael on the road to Iona, a turn off to the right takes you on a winding road over high moorland, which suddenly plunges 500 ft down through thick forest to a tiny stone pier, where wild salmon, lobsters and crabs are occasionally on sale from the stone boat shed nearby. Carsaig pier is the starting point for a tough but beautiful walk to the Carsaig Arches, two of the most spectacular natural rock formations on Mull. Originally sea caves, they have been eroded into giant tunnels, the largest of which is 140 feet from one end to the other. The eight mile round trip takes in the Nun's Cave, where a group of nuns took refuge after being driven from Iona (look out for the carved early medieval crosses on the walls) and from where the greenish sandstone was quarried for Iona Abbey, magnificent and gigantic cliffs, and views across to Islay, Jura and Colonsay. Another excellent walk takes the opposite direction from Carsaig to Lochbuie, six miles away.

Just off the A849 Ardtun ('cape like a cast') has good short walks, interesting fossilised leaf beds and views of Staffa and the Burg. Tourists pass through Bunessan ('foot of the little waterfall') on the road to Iona, stopping only for the hotel, post-office, grocers, public toilets and cafe. Bad planning decisions in the past have spoiled the character of the village with the ugliest modern buildings on the island. Bunessan's claim to fame lies mainly in the fact that the village is both the source of Iona's new water supply, and the home of the infamous Mull Riviter, produced by the Isle of Mull Wine Co. Free tours and tastings are available; turn off beside the Argyle Arms Hotel.

At the end of the road lies Fionnphort ('white port'), the ferry point for Iona. Inevitably dominated by its more famous neighbour, this quiet village in summer months is overwhelmed by tour coaches disgorging their loads onto the Iona ferry. As you would expect from the quantity of tourists passing through, Fionnphort has some excellent services, mainly centred on the Ferry Shop and Fingal Arts and Crafts. This astonishing 'emporium' has the widest selection of general provisions, hardware, books and things-Mull in the island, as well as a fax machine, photocopier, bureau de change, a flowers by post service, video-hire and tourist information. Its owner, Sandy Brunton, says he believes that an island shop should provide the same service as a mainland shop. He deals with over 250 suppliers and provides daily fresh bread baked in Iona, and local fish and meat once a week. Next door, The Keel Row Bar and Restaurant serves bar meals, while at the end of the village the Cal-Mac terminal building has a small cafe, toilets and a silversmith display. Tickets for Staffa and the Treshnish Isles can be bought on the pier. Bed and breakfast places abound and there is a basic camping ground at Fidden beach, two miles to the south of Fionnphort.

Past Fidden beach, the road leads to the beautiful island of Erraid and a wooded landscape of little coves and beaches. At low tide you can cross to this enchanting island, and recreate the scene in Robert Louis Stevenson's *Kidnapped* when David Balfour was wrecked here.

How to get there

Ferries
Oban to Craignure – up to seven sailings a day at peak times, fewer on Sundays and in the winter months. Journey time: 40 minutes. All vehicles taken.
Oban to Tobermory – one sailing a day (very early start), no sailings Tuesdays. Thursdays or Fridays (or Sundays in winter). Journey time up to 1 hour 45 minutes. Passenger service only on some routes.
Lochaline (Morvern) to Fishnish – up to fourteen sailings a day at peak times, fewer on Sunday. Journey time 15 minutes. Car and passenger service only.

Kilchoan (Ardnamurchan) to Tobermory – seven sailings daily, no Sunday service. Journey time 35 minutes. Car and passenger service only.

Contact Caledonian MacBrayne for the latest information: The Ferry Terminal, Tobermory (☎0688 2017) or The Ferry Terminal, Oban (☎0631 66688).

Some private operators run summer excursions from Oban to places such as Grass Point, Duart Castle and Torosay Castle. Contact Tourist Information for details.

Getting around

A regular bus service operates throughout Mull. Contact Tourist Information or Bowman's Coaches, Scallastle, Craignure (☎06802 313) for the latest timetables.

Island Encounter operates the island's only private hire taxi service; contact Richard Atkinson (☎0680 300437).

Accommodation

Hotels

Assapol Country House Hotel, Bunessan PA67 6DW. (☎06817 258)

The Bellachroy Hotel, Dervaig PA75 6QW. (☎06884 314)

Craig Hotel, Salen, Aros PA72 6JG. (☎0680 300347)

Druimard Country House and Restaurant, Dervaig PA75 6QW. (☎06884 345)

The Glenforsa Hotel, by Salen, Aros PA72 6JW. (☎0680 300377)

The Kinloch Hotel, Pennyghael PA70 6HB. (☎06814 204)

Linndhu House & Restaurant, Tobermory PA75 6QB. (☎0688 2425)

Pennygate Lodge, Craignure PA65 6AY. (☎06802 333)

The Tobermory Hotel, Main Street, Tobermory PA75 6NT. (☎ 0688 2091)

Ulva House Hotel, Tobermory PA75 6PR. (☎ 0688 2044)

The Western Isles Hotel, Tobermory PA75 6PR. (☎0688 2012)

Guest Houses

Antium Farm Guest House, Dervaig PA75 6QW. (☎06884 230)

Ardbeg House, Dervaig PA75 6QW. (☎06884 254)

Ardfenaig House, Bunessan PA67 6DX. (☎06817 210)

Ardrioch Farm Guest House, Ardrioch, Dervaig PA75 6QR. (☎06884 264)

Cuilgown Guest House, Salen, Aros PA72 6JB. (☎0680 300386)

Sunart View Guest House, Eas Brae, Tobermory PA75 6QA. (☎0688 2439)

Self catering

Ach-na-Craoibh, Erray Road, Tobermory PA75 6PS. (☎0688 2301)

Barrachandroman, Kinlochspelve, Lochbuie PA62 6AA. (☎06804 220)

Glengorm Castle, Tobermory PA75 6QE. (☎0688 2321)

Glen Houses (Dervaig), St Mary's, Tobermory PA75 6QE. (☎0688 2111)

Goodfellow Accommodations (Tobermory), 37 Selkirk Road, Curzon Park, Chester CH4 8AH. (☎0244 682128)

Gruline Home Farm, Salen, Aros PA71 6HR. (☎680 300437)

Kentallen Farm, Aros PA72 6JS. (☎0680 300427)

Killiechronan (near Gruline), Highland Holidays, 18 Maxwell Place, Stirling FK8 1JU. (☎0786 462519)

Scoor House, Bunessan PA67 6DW (☎06817 297)

Torosay Castle self-catering apartments, Craignure. (☎06802 421)

Bed and breakfast accommodation is plentiful in all parts of Mull (the Craignure area alone has 22 B&Bs).

Contact Tourist Information for details.

Campsites and Hostels

Free camping is more restricted on Mull than many of the other islands and No Camping signs are beginning to become more common, especially in the area around Ben More. Calgary Bay is a popular place to camp, as are some of the more isolated beaches on the Ross of Mull. As always, it's best to ask at the nearest house before you pitch camp, and make sure you leave no rubbish behind.

Balmeanach Park, Fishnish, 5 miles north of Craignure. Small, friendly, family site, Caravan and Camping Club listed, showers, toilet block and laundry.

Cynthia's Tearoom (licensed) and small shop on site. Bunkhouse planned. Adults £3, Children £1.50. Contact: Alex and Cynthia MacFadyen, Balmeanach Park, Fishnish PA65 6BA. (☎0680 30034).

Fidden Beach (pronounced Fidjen), near Fionnphort. A very basic beach site with excellent views to Iona making up for the lack of facilities. Payment £2 per night, water from Mr and Mrs Campbell at the farmhouse or cottage. Take the Knockvologan Road to the left as you come into Fionnphort, continue past the car park for 1 mile until you reach the beach. Nearest showers at Bendoran Boatyard.

Isle of Mull Campsite, 5 minutes from the Craignure ferry. Good facilities (laundry, showers, wash-up, toilet block etc), but lousy view and expensive. Contact: David Gracie, Shieling Holidays, Craignure PA65 6AY (☎06802 496).

Killiechronan Campsite, on the B8073, at the head of Loch na Keal. Basic site with toilet block and hot water within 3 minutes' walk. No need to book in advance as there is plenty of space. Payment collected on site, £3 tents, £4 everything else. Fantastic views down the length of Loch na Keal.

Newdale Camping & Caravan Site, 1.5 miles from Tobermory on the B8073 to Dervaig. A basic but friendly rural site, with flush toilets and washing basins, hard standing and fresh drinking water. Showers occasionally available in the owner's house. Payment £2.50-£3.50, £1 for shower. Contact Mrs Helen Williams, Newdale, Tobermory PA75 6QF (☎0688 2306).

Tobermory Youth Hostel, overlooking the harbour. A grade 3 basic hostel with 51 beds, open Easter to October. YHA membership required. Handy for ferry connections to Coll and Tiree. Contact The Warden, Tobermory Youth Hostel, Main Street, Tobermory PA75 6NU (☎0688 2481) (7-10pm only).

Where to eat

Unpredictable weather forcing people inside for restoring hot drinks and cakes, added to the high density of visitors, has had the welcome result that eating places are plentiful on Mull. Full evening meals, often making use of fresh island produce, are available to non-residents in most of the hotels listed above, and, if you have a high threshold for chips, Mull's pubs do generous bar meals (NB some pubs stop serving as early as 8pm so don't leave your meal too late). Finding a cup of tea is no problem during the day as almost all Mull's tourist attractions seem to have a cafe attached. Look out for the Taste of Scotland sign (indicating the use of traditional local produce) and expect to pay £15-£30 per head in the hotels and restaurants (advisable to book first) and £5-£10 in the pubs. Here is a selection of eateries:

The Ceilidh Place, Craignure: imaginative pub food, delicious puddings and friendly service. Good value if you want an escape from chips.

Dervaig Coffee and Books, Dervaig: the best coffee on Mull with some of the best books.

Druimard Country House & Restaurant, Dervaig: next door to the Mull Little Theatre for that pre-show treat.

The Keel Row Bar and Restaurant, Fionnphort: varied menu at reasonable prices. Vegetarians catered for.

The Mishnish ('field of deer') Hotel, Main Street, Tobermory: an institution for sailors, travellers and locals. Substantial pub food, well-kept beer, pool, live music and walls tapestried with sailing memorabilia and postcards from grateful yachtsmen.

The Puffer Aground, Salen. Excellent food.

Posh Nosh, Main Street, Tobermory: food stand selling steak rolls, baked potatoes, veg burgers etc. Open lunchtimes and 10.30pm (or as the owner says 'when I fall out of the pub') until late in the summer.

The Ulva Oyster Bar, Isle of Ulva: freshly opened raw or grilled oysters with a glass of wine or Guinness, £6 including ferry fare and walks on Ulva. Leave a gap before the return boat journey...

The Western Isles Hotel, Tobermory: Egon Ronay recommended cuisine and superb views.

Things to do and see

Fishing

Mull has almost 300 miles of coastline, and inland, its mountains hide a variety of lochs and give rise to spate burns and rivers. Freshwater fishing and sea angling are both very popular.

Freshwater fishing: a river board licence is not needed for Mull, but permits or permission are required for all the lochs and rivers. Mull's main fishing lochs and rivers include: Loch Sguabain, Loch Torr, Loch Frisa, the Mishnish Lochs, Aros Loch, Loch Assapol, River Forsa, River Bellart, Rover Aros, River Ba, and River Lussa. You can get permits for Aros and Mishnish Lochs from Brown's Shop, Main Street, Tobermory, while Tackle & Books, Main Street, Tobermory has the best selection on the island of tackle and lures (including their own award-winning range), rod-hire, books and detailed information on local lochs and rivers (☎0688 2336).

Sea angling: from shore and sea. Sea angling trips (including all tackle) available with 'Hooked on Scotland' skipper Brian Swinbanks, book through Tackle & Books. See next section for other sea angling charters.

Boat-Hire/Charter

You can either hire your own boat for the day, or take a trip with an experienced skipper, for sea-angling, seal and bird-watching, trips to the outlying islands or just for the sheer joy of being on the water. All trips depend upon the weather, and the north of the island is better served than the south. From Tobermory: MV *Amidas* takes anglers and sightseers, call Charlie Laverty on (☎0688 2048), or contact Tackle & Books. MFV *Kelowna* is an up-market motor yacht for cruises and angling; call Ian and Jane Slade (☎0688 2440). The 38ft sailing yacht the *Voltaire* can be chartered for short or long trips; call Jeff and Audrey Yard (☎0688 2132/2257). Rowing boat hire available from Tackle & Books. From elsewhere: Inter-Island Cruises take anglers and sightseers in and around the neighbouring islands on board the motor sailer *Jennifer M*, leaving from Croig harbour, near Dervaig. Contact Jeremy Matthew, Ardrioch Farm Guest House, Dervaig PA75 6QR, (☎06884 264). Small boat and windsurfer hire from Bendoran Boatyard, near Bunessan; limited wetsuits (☎06817 435). Regular trips run to Staffa and the Treshnish Isles.

Wildlife

Mull's wildlife, on land and sea, is rich and varied and one of the best ways of seeing it is in the company of an experienced nature-watcher. Most wildlife tours can be made in a day from Oban and operators will pick up from the Craignure ferry terminal. Isle of Mull Wildlife Expeditions, led by ornithologist David Woodhouse, leaves from Tobermory daily. Transport is by landrover and lunch is included in the all-day expedition. Adults £19.50, children (under 12) £15.50. Contact: Ulva House Hotel, Tobermory PA75 6PR (☎0688 2044). Explore Mull Wildlife, led by Andrew Evans, leaves from the Old Byre Heritage Centre. Half or full day trips in a Sherpa minibus cost £10-£14, children under 13 half-price. Lunch is extra. Contact: Shepherd's Cottage, Dervaig (☎06884 209) after 6pm. Island Encounter, led by Richard Atkinson, provides a full day 'safari' in an 8 seater vehicle, leaving from Salen. Lunch is provided, adults £18, children (under 14) £16. 1% of proceeds go to the Scottish Wildlife Trust. Contact: Gruline Home Farm, Salen PA71 6HR (☎0680 300437). Sea Life Surveys do a variety of specialist wildlife trips around the Mull coast and neighbouring islands, including their ever-popular Whale Watching packages, varying from 4 hrs to 7 days (with accommodation), in which you are encouraged to help with data collection and sampling for the ongoing Mull Cetacean Project. Other trips include the Treshnish Isles Special and the Three Isles Cruise (Staffa, Treshnish, Coll). Prices start at adults £25, children £18. For the full range of cruises contact: Sea Life Surveys, Torrbreac, Dervaig PA75 6QL (☎06884 223).

Diving

Tobermory is a well-known diving place with sheltered waters and numerous wrecks to explore. For information on local and off-shore diving contact Seafare, Main Street, Tobermory (☎0688 2277). The Mull Diving Centre at Salen provides accommodation, compressed air and diving sites; contact Richard Greeves, Mull Diving Centre, Salen Pier, Aros (☎06803 00411). In southern Mull, Tormore Diving provides courses and equipment for experienced and first-time divers. Prices from £20 per half day. Contact Jane Griffiths, Fionnphort (☎06817 462).

Cycle Hire

Bikes can be hired all over Mull (just ask locally), and for quality expect to 'get what you pay for'. The main outlet is On Yer Bike, Salen, with mountain, touring and junior models, cycle helmets and advice on where to go. Hourly, daily, weekly hire available. Stockists of British cycle parts and a wide range of spares, On Yer Bike also operates a repairs and spares service (☎0680 300501 or 06802 487) (9-7pm). You can also hire bikes from Pedal Power, Tobermory (☎0688 2007); Tom-a-Mhuillin, Tobermory (☎0688 2164); The Ferry Shop, Fionnphort (☎06817 470); The Gaig Hotel, Craignure.

Pony Trekking

Lochside Ponies, Druimghigha; for pony trekking and riding lessons book by phone (☎06858 206) (after 5pm)

Sports

The only golf course is at the Tobermory Golf Club, a 9 hole hilly course with stupendous views, £9 per day, £30 per week, children half price. Tickets from the Western Isles Hotel (☎0688 2012) or Browns Shop, Tobermory (with club hire) (☎0688 2020). Glengorm Castle has the island's only squash court, tickets from Togs and Clogs, Main Street, Tobermory (☎0688 2579). Details about the Tobermory tennis court also from Togs and Clogs.

Walking

From exhilarating high-level walks on Ben More and its surrounding peaks, to dramatic coastal paths, gentle forest trails, and archaeological and geological walks, Mull is a walker's paradise for all ages and abilities. Three excellent guides to Mull's walks are available locally: Walking in South Mull & Iona, Walking in North Mull and A Walk Around Tobermory, all by Olive Brown and Jean Whittaker, £2.50 each. Contact Jean Whittaker at Tackle & Books for details (☎0688 2336).

Places to visit

Boathouse Visitors Centre and Isle of Ulva Oysters, Isle of Ulva, Aros (☎06885 264). Adults £2, children £1.50, families £6, bikes 50p.

Duart Castle, near Craignure. Open May-September, 10.30 – 6.00, Adults £3.00, Children £2.00, OAPS £1.50.

Isle of Mull Weavers, 1.5 miles south of Craignure. Open all year, 9-5.30. Free entry.

Isle of Mull Wine Company, Bunessan. Free tours and tastings of the famous Mull Riviter, Mon-Sat 10.30-11.30, Mon-Fri. 15.30-16.30, or by arrangement. ☎06817 403 (day) 06817 455 (evenings).

Mull Little Theatre, near Dervaig. Britain's smallest repertory theatre. Bookings at Cottage Crafts, Dervaig (☎06884 245), or Tobermory Tourist Information.

Mull Museum, High Street, Tobermory. Open Mon-Fri 10.30-4.30, Sat 10.30-1.30, closed Sunday. Adults 50p, children 10p.

The Old Byre Heritage Centre, Dervaig PA75 6QR. (☎06884 229). Cafe, gift shop and exhibition. Open daily 10.30-6. (Palm Sunday to end October) Adults £2/Children £1.

Tobermory Distillery, Tobermory. Half-hour tours of production and bottling processes, plus dram. May to October. Admission charge.

Torosay Castle and Gardens open mid-April to end September, 10.30-5.30, Adults £3.50, Children £2.75. Tea room and gift shop. 1.5 miles south of Craignure. (☎6802 421).

Banks

The only permanent bank on the island is the Clydesdale Bank, Main Street, Tobermory (with cashpoint outside), but two mobile banks service the rest of Mull: Bank of Scotland, (☎0631 63639) and Clydesdale Bank, (☎0688 2029). Timetables change seasonally so check at the Tourist Information for the latest.

Showers and laundries

Campers and sailors will be glad to know that many guest houses will let non-residents have a shower during the day for a small fee. Other showers are available from Bendoran Boatyard, near Bunessan, open 24 hours a day. The Boatyard also has laundry facilities (take lots of change as the machines are coin-operated) and a payphone. Tobermory has a laundrette on Main Street.

Tourist Information Centres

Tobermory: Caledonian MacBrayne office, (☎0688 2182).
Craignure: opposite the ferry terminal, (☎06802 377).
Fionnphort: The Ferry Shop (leaflets only).

Events and festivals

It's no exaggeration to say that something is always happening in Mull. June sees The Mull and Iona Provincial Mod 'Mod Ionadach na Dreolluinn' a festival of Gaelic music, singing and recitation and the Mendelssohn on Mull Festival. In July the Mull Highland Games encourages visitors and locals to take part in the open races, while athletes toss the caber and musicians join in the traditional pipe band parade. The West Highland Yacht Week takes place in August, with dozens of yachts gathering in Tobermory harbour to celebrate the end of their race from Oban. October sees the Tour of Mull Rally, a noisy and exciting weekend event when Mull's roads are closed to the public and some of the world's leading rally drivers put their driving skills to the test on the island's incredible switchback roads. All summer, the Aros Hall in Tobermory holds ceilidhs, discos and plays and the Mishnish Hotel puts on tradi-

tional Scottish music. Pubs around Mull hold regular quiz nights and live music evenings – check the free newspapers for details.

Specialities

Tobermory chocolate, Mull shortbread, Mull silver jewelry, Columba Cream (manufactured in Clydebank), tapes of local music, *Gremlins* Jellies and Chocolate Sauce, Mull Weavers Tweed, Mull Pottery, Mull Riviter, *Ledaig* Malt Whisky, Mull Home Videos, Iona Rugs, and postcards.

Iona

The island of Iona has an international reputation many times larger than its tiny size and population. The last home of St Columba, the burial ground of forty-eight Scottish kings (as well as numerous French and Norwegian royalty), and one of the most important places in the history of British Christianity, Iona is a sacred site for Christians around the world. Over 200,000 visitors a year make the pilgrimage to Iona along the ancient road over Mull. They are rarely disappointed. Despite the bustle of its many visitors, Iona has a serene charm which lingers in the memory long after the ferry trip home. Only three miles long and under two miles at its widest point, Iona has all the attractions of a Hebridean island – sandy beaches, rocky inlets, crofts, rich wildlife, clear light and a soothing tranquillity – as well as its own remarkable religious history and beautiful sacred buildings. The combination makes Iona a stirring place. Try to stay on the island overnight, and after the last ferry has returned its coach load of vistors to Mull, the tranquillity of Iona will work its magic upon you. Samuel Johnson summed up Iona's unique effect upon the visitor when he wrote: 'That man is little to be envied, whose patriotism would not gain force upon the plain of Marathon, or whose piety would not grow warmer among the ruins of Iona'.

When St Columba (Colum Cille) travelled from Ireland in AD 563 and built the first wattle and wood monastery on Iona, he was to change the course of Christianity in Britain. One of his monks, St Aidan, went on to establish Lindisfarne in Northumbria and was responsible for the expansion of Irish (rather than Roman) Christianity in England as well as the remarkable flowering of learning and manuscript illustration – the priceless illuminated manuscript the *Book of Kells* is believed to have been partly written by the Columban monks. In the 10th century the monastery moved reluctantly back to Ireland – between 794 and 986 it had been destroyed six times by Viking raids and in three of these attacks the abbot and monks had been slaughtered. Indefatigable, the monks returned and by 1200 a new Benedictine monastery, a convent and nunnery were founded on or near the site of the original abbey. Three hundred years later the monastery was in ruins again and it was not until the end of the 19th century that building restoration work was started. In 1938 Dr George MacLeod founded the Iona Community as a Church of Scotland brotherhood, and the full restoration of Iona as a centre of Christianity began in earnest. In 1979 the island, but not its buildings, came under the care of the National Trust for Scotland.

Today the Iona Community live in the restored abbey buildings and contribute enormously to the local economy of the island. With an indigenous population of around eighty the Community adds another thirty or so people to the total population. Never a constant group, the Community has in the past caused friction with families who have lived on the island for generations, but most local people now agree that life on the island would be a good deal harder without the economic benefits of the Community and the visitors it brings. The island has two farms and eighteen crofts, but the bulk of the population work in tourism, running the two hotels, the extremely well-stocked shops (the only items not sold by Finlay, Ross Ltd are dog leads), boat trips, craft shops and the many B&Bs. An active community council promotes an extensive winter programme including badminton and bridge, and the ever-popular German evening classes – it's said that there are now more German speakers on Iona than there are Gaelic speakers.

Inevitably, the focus of the island is around St Ronan's Bay and the sacred buildings of the abbey. The first building you reach from the ferry is the Nunnery. Founded in c. 1200 it is one of the best-preserved small medieval nunneries in Britain. The adjacent St Ronan's Church, with its collection of carved stones, acts as the Nunnery Museum. Situated in the island's old Manse is the Iona Heritage Centre, an excellent introduction to the crofting, fishing and islander's traditional life over the last 200 years as well as to the geology, flora and wildlife of the island. [Open Mon-Sat 10.30-4.30, Adults £1, discounts for OAPs and children between 10 and 16, children under 10 free.] Iona Abbey itself is beautifully situated with the blue waters of the Iona Sound behind and its rough walls merging into the natural stone of Mull's rugged shores beyond. Simple, low and serene in construction, most of its ornate work is reserved for the Abbey Church, believed to be on the site of successive Early Christian churches. St Columba's Shrine, a small stone room with a simple wooden altar, is traditionally the burial site of St Columba. In the former Infirmary, the Abbey Museum houses an incredible collection of Early Christian gravestones, one of the richest in Britain, as well as many medieval effigies found on the island. The Cloisters and the grassy areas around the Abbey are places to sit quietly and listen for the shuffling of centuries of monks' feet, and imagine their bent figures tending to the vegetable patches, still cultivated today.

Away from the main centre of activity around the abbey buildings, there are many walks and things to see. Visitors are not allowed to bring their cars onto the island so the best way to explore is on foot or by bike. Geologically, Iona belongs to the Lewisian gneiss of the Western Isles and not to the pink granites of the Ross of Mull, and, as such is an island of humps and hollows, amongst which it is surprisingly easy to lose sight of other visitors.

Follow the road south from Martyr's Bay to the sandy beach Tràigh Mor and then west to Iona's machair, overlooking The Bay at the Back of the Ocean. Turn left along the shore to the Spouting Cave, where, under the right conditions, a plume of spray can rise high up over the cliff edge. Follow the track south to Port na Curraigh (St Columba's Bay or Bay of the skin-covered boat), the traditional landing place of Columba in AD 563. A grassy mound at the head of the bay is reputed to represent the size and shape of Columba's coracle (a traditional Irish boat) but extensive excavations have found no evidence to suggest that it was a man-made mound. The shingle cairns on the adjacent raised beach, however, are believed to be the devotional act of medieval pilgrims.

Further around the coast lies Iona's now inoperational Marble Quarry. Iona's white marble with its unique yellowish-green streaks is believed to have been quarried since early times, with the most recent quarrying activity occurring from 1907-14. It's still possible to see the gun-powder store, machinery and cutting-frame, stone quay and reservoir from this period, and a careful search around the quarry can yield some of the famous marble. If none is found, take a look at the magnificent communion table in the Abbey Church, which is entirely constructed from Ionan marble.

Turning right along the coast from The Bay at the Back of the Ocean brings you to Dun Cul Bhuirg, Iona's only Iron Age monument. Remains of a defensive wall still survive on its south and east sides, and excavations indicate a long usage between the 1st century BC and the 3rd century AD. North and inland lies Cobhan Cuiteach (the remote hollow) traditionally believed to be the 'more remote place in the wilderness' to which St Columba is said to have gone to pray. The remains of a small hut are all that can be seen today, but no accurate date can be attributed to the site.

A walk up Dun I, the island's highest point, is well worth the small effort. Take the road north from Martyr's Bay, past the Abbey, to the farm of Auchabhaich. Turn left along the track and continue up the hillside. From the top you can see the whole of Iona. To the west only Skerryvore lighthouse interrupts a direct line to America, to the south the Paps of Jura can be seen on a clear day and to the north and east lie Mull's coast and hills. On the right day you may even be lucky enough to spy the Royal yacht *Britannia*. On her regular visits the Queen is said to enjoy a private paddle in Mull's Market Bay – while she treats herself, the *Britannia* steams up and down to the north of Iona, eventually emptying its crew into Iona's pubs in the evening to 'drink the island dry'.

How to get there

Ferry
Fionnphort to the Pier – frequent sailings from early morning to late afternoon. Journey time 5 minutes. Visitors' cars are not allowed on the island, so leave them at the Fionnphort Ferry Terminal.

Accommodation
Argyll Hotel, PA76 6SJ (☎06817 334). An old-fashioned hotel situated by the harbour.
St Columba Hotel, PA76 6SL (☎06817 304). Modern and close to the Abbey.

Bed and breakfast places are numerous.

Bicycle Hire
Finlay, Ross Ltd, general store, by the Pier – basic bikes of all sizes and conditions from £2 to £5 per day.

Camping sites
There are no official sites and free camping is only allowed at the north end of the island. Ask permission first at the croft or call Mr McFadden (☎06817 341). Hot baths are available on the island for £2, and a laundry service is operated for campers – ask at Finlay, Ross Ltd for information.

Things to do
Guided tours of the island in a traditional horse and carriage. Contact Island Carriages, Ormsaig, Pennyghael, Mull (☎06814 230 after 6).
Boat Hire – Mark Jardine takes chartered trips in an open boat for seal spotting, explorations, landings and basic sea fishing, between May and September (☎06817 537).

Staffa

Only half a mile long, uninhabited but for its huge bird colonies and prolific plant life (over 300 species of plant have so far been recorded on the island), Staffa (Norse: 'pillar island') attracts thousands of visitors each year, keen to see its awe-inspiring basalt columns and giant caverns. During the tertiary period of volcanic activity, a subterranean vent from Skye to Ireland filled with liquid basalt which was then ejected to the surface. The cooling process formed the astonishing hexagonal vertical columns found in particular profusion on Staffa and the Giant's Causeway (eighty miles away in North-

ern Ireland), but also on parts of Mull (The Burg) and Islay. Some of Staffa's columns were worn by the sea into the three great caverns, Fingal's, Burr's and MacKinnon's Caves. Now in the care of the National Trust for Scotland, Staffa is easily accessible from Mull and Iona and can be visited in a half-day.

Staffa was virtually unknown to the wider world before 1772 when the explorer Joseph Banks, passing nearby on another expedition, heard locally of its amazing pillars, and decided to visit. He wrote rapturously about it and indirectly initiated the beginnings of Mull's tourist industry as floods of visitors made their way across the roadless Mull to see the famous island, requisitioning boats and guides for the trip. By 1821 local entrepreneurs were charging up to eighteen shillings to cross between Mull and Staffa – or double this and a bottle of whisky if their passengers were carrying hammers to chip off illegal souvenir chunks of the famous stone columns. Amongst the visitors were Queen Victoria and Prince Albert, the writers Wordsworth, Tennyson and Keats, the artist Turner and, of course, the composer Mendelssohn who was inspired by Fingal's Cave to write his 'Hebridean Overture'.

Fingal's Cave, with its beautiful black columned walls, is the most spectacular of the caverns. Easily accessible at low tide, its ceiling is sixty-six feet above the surface of the sea at mean tide, although on a stormy day the swell fills the whole cave. A walkway takes you deep inside its 227 feet length, and just beyond the final barrier, you can see some original 19th-century graffiti scratched into the walls. It's reported that Joseph Banks himself was the island's first vandal and that his initials 'JB' appear high on the cave's walls. Photographers: the cave gets most sun in the afternoons and almost none in the morning.

Staffa's puffins arrive at the island in mid-April, climb ashore in May and start nesting in earnest in June and July.

Unlike most nature reserves, the birds are not fenced off and visitors are free to wander (with care) amongst the nesting birds. Whales, dolphins and seals are also frequently spotted from the island, and on a clear day it's possible to see the whole of Mull in one view.

The Treshnish Isles

Even if you are unable to visit this string of islands off the western face of Mull, you will be continually aware of their distinctive shapes on the horizon. Uninhabited and treeless, they consist of nine islands running southwest from the tiny island of Carn na Burgh to Bac Beag. Inhospitable to man, there is no permanent settlement on any, allowing the seabirds and seal colonies full uninterrupted use of the land and sea around.

Lunga was the last to be deserted in 1834, when its smallness and the lack of a secure landing made life too difficult to continue for its tiny population, settled at the north end of the island. Now the most visited island of the group, its wildlife is superb and varied. Take a torch – there is the unexpected attraction of an underground passage for the adventurous. To the south lies the distinctive shape of the Dutchman's Cap or Bac Mor. The 'brim' of the Dutchman's Cap and the high terraces on Lunga are all that remain of the massive lava flows from Mull's volcanic past. To the north lie Fladda and the fortress islands of Carn na Burgh Mor and Carn na Burgh Beag. Well nigh impregnable, these islands still have remains of fortifications on them, and were the last places in Britain to hold out for James VII of Scotland (James II of England). It's said that the monks of Iona buried their

library from the ravages of the Vikings on the islands and that one day the lost books of Livy's 'History of Rome' will be uncovered here, although the soil is so thin it's difficult to imagine *where* they could have been buried.

How to get there

Various small ferry services operate from Mull and Iona to Staffa, some of which take in the Treshnish Isles as well. Most trips will land on Staffa, depending on the weather and the swell, but ask the skipper before you leave for the latest report. Booking is advisable from June-August. If you are only visiting Staffa, morning trips might be less busy as the operators for the Treshnish Isles and Staffa trips generally arrive on Staffa in the afternoon. Remember to dress warmly and wear sensible shoes – it is always far colder on the water than on land. The Treshnish Isles are only accessible in the summer months.

Davy Kirkpatrick runs a daily morning service to Staffa only, leaving from Iona and Fionnphort (adults £7.50, children £4) and returning two hours later. For twenty years a fisherman, Davy is the third generation in his family to take visitors to Staffa. On quieter journeys you get the benefit of his wide local knowledge of natural history and his warm sense of humour as he tries to speak to everyone on the trip. For bookings call D. Kirkpatrick, Tigh-na Traigh, Iona (☎ 06817 358).

Gordon Grant Marine runs morning and afternoon excursions to Staffa, departing from Iona and Fionnphort (adults £8, children £4), and all-day trips during the summer to the Treshnish Isles and Staffa, departing from Fionnphort (adults £16, children £8). One-day tours to Mull, Iona and Staffa are also available from Oban. For bookings call Gordon Grant Marine, Achavaich, Iona (☎ 06817 338).

Turus Mara operates day tours from Oban to Mull, Staffa and Iona during the summer, with joining points at Craignure and Ulva Ferry for people already on Mull. Cruises from Ulva Ferry to the Treshnish Isles and Staffa are also available. Prices start from adults £14.50, children £8, depending on the route and the season. For bookings contact Pat & Iain Morrison, Turus Mara, Penmore Mill, Dervaig, Mull (☎06884 242).

Inter-Island Cruises take anglers and sightseers in and around the Treshnish Isles on board the motor sailer *Jennifer M*, leaving from Croig harbour, near Dervaig. Contact Jeremy Matthew, Ardrioch Farm Guest House, Dervaig PA75 6QR (☎06884 264).

Nearest Tourist Information Centre: Tobermory (☎0688 2182).

Lismore

(from Gaelic meaning *Great Garden*)

Lismore (population c.160 people) lies off the west coast near Oban, and is reached from two points on the mainland – Port Appin and Oban. The latter is the car-ferry. It's a pleasant island, with farming being its economy, mainly of sheep; the land is very fertile. The island measures some nine miles by one-and-a-quarter miles, and offers some beautiful views (when the weather's good) of the mainland, up Loch Linnhe, occasionally Ben Nevis and of Mull and Jura.

Historically, Lismore's connections are with the church in medieval times – the bishopric of Argyll had its seat there. The famous 'Book of the Dean of Lismore', a collection of poems in English and Gaelic, is a landmark work in Gaelic scholarship.

The architectural features of the island will be mainly churches, although there are the remains of two castles. The present church, Lismore Parish Church, is built on the site of the cathedral dating from the 14th century to the north of the island. Only the foundations of the cathedral are visible. To the west of the church is Castle Goeffin, date unknown, which can be reached from the main road, and then walking about a mile. The Bishop of Lismore lived in Achanduin Castle for a short while (dating from the 14th century). If you've arrived off the Oban ferry, take the main road and turn left and then right. The castle is reached by a track when the road ends at Achanduin Farm.

Tirfuir, the Pictish broch on the eastern coast of the island, is a couple of miles' walk from the pier at Achnavish. Dating from around 500 BC, it has understandably been ravaged by time, but still has clearly defined walls.

Lismore's saintly connections are with St Moluag, an Irish saint and a contemporary of St Columba (mid-6th century). The story is that, when approaching the island by sea for the first time, he cut off one of his fingers in order to claim the island as his own. The place where he landed is called Port Moluag and is to the north of the island. Artefacts, said to have belonged to the saint, such as a staff and a bell, have survived the centuries, and in the case of the staff can be seen on the island at Bachuil House, while the bell is housed in the National Museum of Antiquities in Edinburgh.

How to get there

Ferries
Car-ferry from Oban to Achracroish daily. Journey time is approximately 50 minutes.

A small passenger ferry leaves from Port Appin around 9 times a day in summer; a reduced service operates in winter. On Sundays the service is reduced also. (This ferry takes bicycles). Journey time is 10 minutes.

Getting around

It's best to have your own transport. If you're stuck in a downpour of rain or need to get back to catch the ferry, there's a taxi service (☎063176 220).

Accommodation

No Hotels, only Bed & Breakfasts.
Mr & Mrs Carter, Achnacroish (☎063 176 241).
Mrs Crossan, Baligarve (☎063 176 262)
Mr & Mrs Lutyens, Brynalen (☎063 176 298).

Where to eat

The Old School Tearoom, Baligarve, is situated some two-and-a-half miles south of the Point ferry.

Nearest Tourist Information Centre: Argyll Square, Oban (☎0631 63122), open all year.

Kerrera

Kerrera (population of around twenty) measures just over four miles long by two miles wide and is visible from Oban. It makes a good day's excursion away from the tacky excesses of the town. In historical terms, it shone at the time of the battle of Largs in 1263 when the Vikings were expelled from the Hebrides. Alexander II died on Kerrera in 1249 at Horseshoe Bay (Dail Righ). (The island was then under Norse rule.) King Hakon moored his fleet there.

The island was settled during the Iron Age, though not much remains from this period. There is a Neolithic burial cairn, now just a heap of stones, to the north of Slaterich Bay, where there is rather a nice beach.

The island seems sleepy now, but in the 18th century the island had a busy port

(serving Mull, until focus switched to Oban), a brewery and a whisky still. There was some industry on the island in the last century, quarrying slate and sandstone, but Kerrera was unable to compete with the other islands further south and fell into decline.

The memorial to the north of the island was built in memory of David Hutcheson, one of the founders of the ferry company, Caledonian MacBrayne. The ruins of Gylen Castle (built 1582) lie at the southern end of the island – it was besieged, burnt by the Covenanters in the Civil War and never restored.

How to get there

Passenger ferry from Oban; actually from Gallanach two miles from Oban. Ferries run throughout the day.

Accommodation

None.

Where to eat

Bring your own provisions.

Nearest Tourist Information Centre: Oban (☎0631 63122).

Seil, Easdale and Luing

These three islands lie south of Oban.

Seil is reached by taking the B844 and crossing over the hump-backed bridge, designed in 1792 by Thomas Telford. It's popularly known as the 'Bridge across the Atlantic'. Seil is a lush island, in summer covered with flowers, and the An Cala Gardens are worth a visit.

Easdale is tiny, reached by ferry from Seil, and has a folk museum with exhibits from Easdale's past as a centre for the slate industry. The 19th-century village itself is well-preserved.

Luing is the largest of the three islands – like Easdale, it too had a slate industry but the island is now given over to farming. It is reached from Seil by car ferry; crossings are frequent. In summer it's possible to use Luing as a jumping-off point for excursions to some of the smaller uninhabited islands off the coast, and some inhabited ones: Mull and Jura. The Garvellachs lie to the west of Luing and have monastic connections.

Nearest Tourist Information Centre: Argyll Square, Oban (☎0631 63122).

Colonsay and Oronsay

There is a golf course at Machrins which presents one or two unusual hazards in the form of rabbit holes and sheep. Colonsay is definitely not the island if your tastes run to discos and amusement arcades. It has possibly some of the most beautiful beaches in the West of Scotland. Kiloran beach is a kilometre wide of white sand and usually the only other inhabitants are about half a dozen cattle. Provided you obey the Countryside Code you can walk anywhere on the island and enjoy peace, tranquillity and views without compare. It is an ideal island for the naturalist. At least 214 species of birds have been sighted and there is a very rich flora.

Colonsay is thirteen and a half kms long by five kms wide at its broadest point. It is separated from Oronsay by a tidal strand just over one km wide at the crossing point. Oronsay is 2.5 kms. from north to south and 4 kms from east to west. The strand can be crossed from two to four hours either side of low water depending on whether the tides are neap or spring.

Geologically, the rocks are very variable from Lewisian gneiss to sandstones. There are many raised beaches and sand dunes are a prominent feature both on Colonsay and Oronsay. The climate is very mild and damp and, because the islands are low, strong winds are a feature. The farms are in the main stock-rearing with cropping only to provide local needs.

Man has been present on the islands from the earliest time. The Mesolithic shell middens on Oronsay have been dated to 4100 BC. The Neolithic period is poorly represented on Colonsay although, because of the chambered cairns on Islay and Jura, it is very probable that there were early farmers on the islands. Bronze age cairns and cists have been found and the remains of cairns can be found at Milbuie, Carnan Eoin and just outside Scalasaig. There are several standing stones and extensive bronze age field systems.

Coming closer to our own times there are eight hill or promontory forts and thirteen duns dating from about 600 BC to the early centuries AD some of which were reoccupied in the Dark Ages. Most of them are now very ruinous although they are all worth a visit if only for the view from the site.

The Norsemen visited the islands but the only traces they left were graves in the sand dunes and place names. The name Colonsay itself is supposed to be derived from the old Norse word for Columba's Isle although the connection between Columba and Colonsay is hypothetical. A stonelined grave at Kiloran Bay yielded a sword, spear, axe head, harness and other finds which are now in the National Museum of Scotland.

The most complete of the early sites is the Augustinian Monastery on Oronsay. The buildings, with the exception of the so-called Priors House, are roofless and have been modified throughout the years. The church and cloister are more or less complete and for many years the reliquary cupboard in the altar of the church contained bones which may or may not have been holy relics. There has been reconstruction of part of the cloister arcade and the Priors House contains a collection of grave slabs many of which are highly decorated. Outside the east end of the church is the Oronsay Cross, one of the finest of the high crosses in Scotland. The priory is dedicated to St Columba and dates from the first half of the fourteenth century. The so-called Kiloran Abbey on Colonsay, which is mentioned in some accounts of the islands, did not exist.

Colonsay is owned by Lord Strathcona whose great-grandfather founded the Canadian Pacific railway. He lives in Kiloran House, the gardens of which were laid out by his father and were in their heyday among the great gardens of Scotland. They were famed for the many species of rhododendron which flourished in the mild, damp climate and for the large number of tender southern hemisphere plants. The garden is being restored and is open to visitors.

How to get there

Ferries
Ferry from Oban on Mondays, Wednesdays and Fridays. Time on passage 2¼ hours. Takes approximately fifty cars and 500 passengers.
Wednesdays in summer only. Ferry from Kennacraig calling at Port Askaig on Islay and Colonsay en route to Oban and returing the same day. This ferry allows passengers to spend six hours on the island and to return the same day.
Both ferries are operated by Caledonian MacBrayne (☎Oban 0631 66688, Kennacraig ☎088 073 253, Colonsay ☎09512 308)

By Air
There are air strips on both Colonsay and Oronsay for chartered flights and the air ambulance.

Getting around
Within the island there is a taxi service and a postbus.

Accommodation

Hotels
Colonsay Hotel, Scalasaig (☎09512 316).
Camping and caravanning are not permitted on Colonsay without special permission.
There are a number of cottages for letting. Contact Colonsay Holiday Cottages, Machrins. Isle of Colonsay (☎09512 316).

Bicycle & Boat Hire
Enquire at the hotel.

Tourist Information
There is no office on the island itself. The nearest is at Argyll Square, Oban (☎0631 63122).

Gigha

There are various derivations proposed for the word Gigha. It may be derived from the Old Norse word Gjedöe which means Goat Island. It has also been suggested that it is derived from the word Gudey which means Good Island, as good a description as any for one of the most beautiful of the islands of the West Coast.

Approximately, 9 kms long by 2 kms wide, rising to a maximum of 70 metres at its highest point it is famed for the gardens at Achamore House which were created by the late Sir James Horlicks.

These gardens are open to the public and successive owners have maintained them since Sir James' death. He left the plants to the National Trust for Scotland with an endowment for their upkeep and the garden is a place of pilgrimage for plantsmen from all over the world. His name is commemorated by one of the rhododendrons in the garden, Rhododendron horlickianum.

Gigha is a long, low, narrow island, much indented by bays many of which are sandy. The central ridge of the island is epidiorite and separates the main centre of population on the east side of the island from the three lochs which could provide a water supply on the west. The only village, Ardminish, is just above the ferry terminal and contains the only shop, the primary school and the hotel. It is a highly fertile island and was once famed for its cheese. Unhappily the powers that be closed the creamery and put the money, which would have modernised it, into a fish farm of which Scotland has already only too many. A very good cheese is still made on a small scale on one of the island farms.

Over 100 sites of archaelogical importance have been recognised on the island and its small southern neighbour, Cara. There are chambered cairns, duns and one fort, Dun Chibhich, north west of Druimyeonbeg. The two ruined chapels are of the typical unicameralate form of the Western Isles. St Catan's Church, which is beside Achamore Garden, is a 13th-century foundation although the present ruined church probably dates from the 18th century. 100 metres to the west of it there is a stone pillar which has an Ogam inscription which has been dated to the 5th to 7th century AD. Tradition has it that Haakon Haakonson in 1263 anchored his fleet of over 100 galleys in Gigulum Sound before sailing to defeat at the battle of Largs and his own eventual death in Kirkwall.

Like Colonsay, Gigha is a bird watcher's and naturalist's paradise and an island for the connoisseur. Long may it remain that way.

How to get there

Ferry from Tayinloan. 9 ferries per day in summer, 5 per day in winter. Time on passage, 20 minutes. First ferry in summer 8am. Last ferry 6pm. In winter first ferry 10 am. Last ferry 5p.m. Takes 12 cars and about 200 passengers. Operated by Caledonian MacBrayne (☎088 073 253).

Accommodation

Gigha Hotel (☎05835 254).
Post Office House (☎05835 251).

Where to eat

Boat House Bistro (closed in winter).

Bicycle Hire
Enquire at the hotel

Tourist Information
No office on island. Nearest is at Argyll Square, Oban (☎0631 63122) or Tarbert (☎0880 820429) in season.

Islay
(pronounced Eye-la)

Islay is famed for two things: whisky and wildlife. It's a curious hybrid of lowland Scotland with its large prosperous farms and farmhouses, and the Hebrides with their expanses of moorland peat, beaches and crofthouses. Islay boasts some of the prettiest island villages in Scotland too – the neat, whitewashed cottages at Portnahaven and Port Charlotte are well-preserved and characterful. It's the most southerly of the Hebrides, measuring twenty-five miles long and twenty miles across, with some 4,000 inhabitants, mainly concentrated in Port Ellen, Bowmore and Port Charlotte.

Historically, Islay was the Seat of the Lordship of the Isles during the 14th and 15th centuries. This was a sort of Parliament or administrative centre based on Finlaggan to the north of the island. There is evidence of occupation from the Iron Age onwards to the Vikings, through to the Highland Clearances.

The beauty of Islay is that it never gets too crowded, even in summer, and you'll be able to find your own tranquil spot, whether you prefer cliffs, machair, fertile cultivated fields, lochs or woodlands. Islanders might add that Islay is for the more discerning island hopper, and that it doesn't yield up its secrets easily. There is Gaelic spoken on Islay, but you won't hear it readily. Efforts are afoot to reverse the decline of the language on the island, and its Gaelic choir takes much pride in competing at the National Mod (the annual festival of Gaelic arts). If you're lucky enough to go in May and June, don't miss Feis Ile (the Islay Festival) which features pipe bands, folk groups, whisky-tasting, dancers and much more.

Your trip might begin at the southern end of the island at Port Ellen, where the Cal-Mac ferry berths. Founded in 1821, the village is named after the founder's wife, Eleanor, and thrives on fishing. On the road heading north you'll pass the Port Ellen Maltings, a rather incongruous and ugly building, but one whose size gives a clue to the economy of the island. Coming north from Port Ellen you have two choices. Take the road left at the distillery and head for Kintra. Just before you reach Kintra you'll find Druim an Stuin (Ridge of the Stone) which marks the grave of Godred Crovan, a rather successful and warlike chieftain who expelled Fingal from the Isle of Man and took possession of the Kingdom of the Isles. He died in 1095. The Mull of Oa, as this part of the island is called, provides good picnic areas. Look out for the monument erected by Americans to commemorate the 266 people who lost their lives in 1918 when the *Tusania* was torpedoed and sank offshore. This area is excellent for wildlife – golden eagles, choughs and grouse abound.

Back on the main road again, head for Bowmore, Islay's administrative centre. This straight road cuts across peat bogs, taking in the airport (built during the war) on the way. The Machrie Hotel, just before you reach the airport, is worth a detour, not only for its superbly-kept eighteen-hole golf course but for the (almost) deserted beach lying behind it, a seven-mile stretch with nothing to disturb your peace apart from the large number of jet trails criss-crossing the sky on their way to and from America. On one particular day, the hotel-owner's dog accompanied the present writer on a two-hour walk on the beach, which was followed by a malt whisky or two in the comfortable lounge by the peat fire. Bliss!

Bowmore is a planned 18th-century village best known for its eponymous whisky and its curious round church, said to thwart the devil by denying him any corners in which to hide. The Bowmore distillery (founded 1779) is beside the school and the swimming pool, partly funded by the company who own the distillery. There's a good tour, lasting approximately 45 minutes, with audio-visual presentation and tasting at the end, taking you through the processes of malting, mashing, fermentation, distillation, maturation in oak barrels and finally, bottling. The number of people employed at the distillery itself is tiny, considering the amount of whisky produced. (See section on whisky in Islay.) The tourist office on the main street is well-stocked, and the service friendly.

From Bowmore, take the road north to Bridgend, a civilised little village with a good general shop and hotel. Islay House, not entirely visible from the road, is not open to the public. Here the road forks in two directions. The first (A847) leads to Port Charlotte and hugs the side of the loch down to the Rhinns of Islay. This road is wonderful for bird-watching, especially for wading birds, and offers a great view of Bowmore 'from the sea'. On the way is Bruichladdich, the newest of the eight distilleries, built in 1881.

Further on, Port Charlotte is arguably the prettiest village on the island, named after the founder's mother. Here you'll find three sites of interest, namely the Museum of Islay Life, the Islay Creamery and the Islay Field Centre. The award-winning Museum is a must for the visitor and is imaginatively laid out. The main part of the collection shows life on the island from its beginnings to the present day. There are room reconstructions and maritime artefacts as well as a library of books dedicated to Islay. The Creamery offers you the opportunity to sample the hard cheese made there. The Islay Field Centre, an information point for wildlife, flora and fauna, is located in the old distillery warehouse. Further on is the Ellister Bird Sanctuary.

Press on to Portnahaven, another planned village built around a small harbour. (R.L. Stevenson's father designed the 1825 lighthouse.) Although Portnahaven doesn't have much in the way of 'facilities' it's a great place to sit and contemplate the past and imagine the way of life in the village in the last century. Its 'twin', Port Wemyss, has the same cosy arrangement of whitewashed cottages. This area, the Rhinns of Islay, is rich in prehistoric and early Christian remains. Taking the B-road north at Portnahaven, you'll pass the Cultoon Store Circle; most of the stones are no longer erect. Two miles further, you reach Kilchiaran Chapel, where there are graveslabs and a fort. St Columba is said to have landed here. Stay on the road and you'll reach Kilchoman Church, known for its Celtic cross, (dating from around AD 1,500) depicting a crucifixion and angels. There are tombs here also. The westerly part of Islay is rather desolate and given over to sheep mainly, but the beaches are superb.

For those interested in fishing, Loch Gorm, the largest freshwater loch on Islay, comes up next. Ornithologists,

pass onto the RSPB reserve at Gruinart along the B8107. The RSPB reserve (covering 4,000 acres) is the wintering site of rare wild geese. In the past, the geese have caused havoc to crops and annoyed farmers, attracting much media attention (and David Bellamy) to the island. The farmers receive compensation for the damage done to their crops and the birds are (in theory, at least) protected.

There's a detour up to Ardnave where the road follows the side of Loch Gruinart and thereafter deteriorates. Ardnave Loch has a crannog or lake-dwelling. You will have to retrace your steps to get back to the main road. Make your way back to Bridgend and take the A846 to Port Askaig. (You will know this road already if you came off the ferry at Port Askaig.) The main settlement on the road, Ballygrant, was once home to a lead and silver mining industry, but doesn't present much more of interest. Further on, you'll come to one of Islay's most important sites: Loch Finlaggan, the Lordship of the Isles. As mentioned earlier, this was the administrative centre of the Lords of the Isles (though it's difficult to imagine this today as the islands and loch which make up the site look forlorn and rather unimportant). Hardly the last word in comfort for such powerful rulers. The ruins are thought to comprise a chapel, a great hall and other buildings. There are also gravestones. In the last ten years or so, a trust has been working hard to restore the area and there's an interpretive visitor centre (opened in 1989). Archaeologists are still in the process of excavation and various artefacts have been found – coins, pottery shards, etc. More detailed information is available from the site. On to Port Askaig where you can catch the ferry to Jura or back to Kennacraig on the mainland. Port Askaig is tiny and, apart from the hotel and ferry terminal, offers little. The views of the Paps of Jura are impressive especially when they are snow-topped.

Those keen on the whisky trail will find two distilleries on this side of the island – *Caol Ila* (pronounced Cool-Eela, roughly) a lesser known single malt. There are tours by appointment only (☎0496 840207). Bunnahabhain distillery (pronounced bunn-na-ha-venn) is reached by a tortuous B-road (well signposted from the A846) and is in a very picturesque location. There are holiday cottages here, with great views and shingle beaches nearby. (They're rather expensive, billed as '5-star luxury self-catering cottages', but perhaps worth it for a sybaritic and tranquil weekend.) Again, tours of the distillery are by appointment only (☎0496 840646). Head back to Bridgend and take the B8016 to Port Ellen, and you'll be passing over a very valuable commodity – peat. Not only is it used to heat houses, but it imparts that very special smoky flavour to the Islay malts, and is probably the smell which best evokes (for me, at least) the Highlands and Islands. The peat in this area was fought over fiercely a few years ago, in a clash between conservationists and distillers, the one wishing to see a natural habitat preserved and the other seeing it as a vital ingredient in their product. A compromise was reached, with the northern half of the area becoming a National Nature Reserve and the south used for the water of life...

Port Ellen to Ardtalla: this little stretch of road heading east encloses three distilleries, Laphroaig, Lagavulin (superb but probably an acquired taste), and the little-known Ardbeg, and one of the finest early Christian crosses in Britain. The coastline here is fretted with little islets, the largest of which is Texa. Just after Lagavulin you'll see the ruins of Dunyvaig Castle, (probably) dating from the early 16th century. Extensively damaged by a siege in 1615, it still makes a pretty impressive sight. Past the Ardbeg distillery (not available to tour) you'll find the Kildalton Chapel and the Cross. Dating from around the 8th century, the cross is well-preserved and is thought to be the work of a local craftsman. The chapel is roofless, but worth poking around, if only to look at the graveslabs from across the ages.

How to get there

Ferries
From Kennacraig on Argyll, there is a car ferry operated by CalMac. The crossing takes approximately 2 hours, and you berth at either Port Ellen on the south of the island (look out for a glimpse of the distilleries as you approach) or Port Askaig to the north. For reservations (and they're crucial in summer) ring CalMac's Head Office (☎0475 33755) or Kennacraig (☎088 073 253). From Jura to Port Askaig on a little regular car ferry. Crossing time is about 5 minutes. Operated by Western Ferries: Port Askaig (☎0496 840681 or Jura (☎982 208). No booking necessary.

By Air
Loganair flies in daily from Glasgow Airport (☎041-889 3181 for reservations). Pricey, but nice views. Time is approximately 20 minutes.

Getting Around

Bicycle Hire
MacAulay and Torrie, Port Ellen (☎0496 302053).
Islay Cycle Hire, Port Charlotte (☎0496 85397).
Bus service operated on behalf of SPTE. Information from B. Mundell Ltd (☎0496 840273/4).

Accommodation

Hotels
Ballygrant Inn (☎0496 840277).
Harbour Inn, Bowmore (0496 810532).
Lochside Hotel (☎0496 810244).
Marine Hotel (☎0496 810324).
Bridgend Hotel (☎0496 810212).
Port Askaig Hotel (☎ 0496 840245).
Machrie Hotel (☎0496 302310).
Self-catering
Enquire at Tourist Information Centre.
B & Bs
There are lots to choose from.
Hostels
Kintra Bunk Barns, Kintra Beach, Port Ellen (☎0496 302051).
SYHA Hostel at Port Charlotte (☎ 0496 853850).

Whisky on Islay

The malts produced on the island of Islay (together with the Isle of Jura malt) are characteristically peaty and strong. For those who have acquired the taste, Islay malts are paradise. There are seven distilleries on the island – most of which you can visit (though you will have to check with the individual distillery beforehand). The whiskies are Bunnahabhain, Caol Ila, Bowmore, Bruichladdich, Laphroaig, Lagavulin and Ardbeg.

The whisky-making process begins with malting. The raw ingredients are barley and soft Islay water. The barley is steeped in the water to germinate, during which time the starch in the barley is converted to fermentable sugars. The grain is then dried in the malt kiln over a peat fire which gives it that distinctive peaty odour. (The whiff of the sea detected in Lagavulin, for example, comes from the water used in the process and the coastal position of the distillery.) The malt is then milled and the ground malt is mashed – mixed with hot water and the starch turns to a liquid called wort which is drawn off to be fermented. The wort is then converted into alcoholic solution by yeast in vessels called washbacks. The wash is distilled twice, put into oak barrels and left to mature for a number of years. During that time, eight, ten, twelve, sixteen or more years, the flavour develops and mellows. At the bottling stage, soft water is added to reduce the strength of the whisky – it is then bottled, sealed, and ready for dispatch all over the world.

Where to eat

All of the hotels provide food, bar lunches, etc. There's also Kilchoman House, Taste of Scotland recommended (☎0496 85382); Croft Kitchen, Port Charlotte (also gifts and crafts) (☎0496 85208); The Old Granary, the Oa, (food available all day) (☎0496 302051).

Things to do and see

As well as the sites mentioned in the text previously:
Islay Lifeboat Station at Port Askaig (☎0496 840245).
Islay Woollen Mill, near Bridgend (☎0496 810563) – Open Mon–Sat 10.00am–5.00pm June to September.
Carraig Fhada, near Port Ellen, a working farm and craft shop.

Golf

The Machrie Golf Course (☎0496 302251).

Diving

Islay Dive Centre (☎0496 302441).

Swimming Pool

Bowmore: Open Tuesday–Sunday. Closed on Mondays.

Shopping and crafts

C. & E. Roy (The Celtic House): a bookshop with a great selection.
Port Ellen Pottery, Tighcargaman (☎0496 302345).

Best beaches

Lossit Bay on the west side of the island. Not good for bathing.
Saligo, again on the west side. Not suitable for bathing.
Tayvulin, nr. Loch Gruinart. Access by foot. Good for bathing.

Birdwatching

RSPB reserve at Gruinart.
Natureguide (Caledonia), Dunfermline, organise wildlife holidays (☎0383 880381).

Tourist Information Centre

Off Bowmore Main Street (☎0496 810254); open all year round.

Jura

(comes from Norse meaning 'deer island')

Jura is now the only major island without a direct link to the mainland. It can be reached from Islay on a small car ferry from Port Askaig, and is almost a one-road island, a single-track road, which begins at the ferry at Feolin. Most of the action takes place at Craighouse, a pleasant village, where there is a hotel, distillery and post office. The rest of the island is mountainous and inhabited mainly by deer, almost 6,500 of them, compared to its 200 human inhabitants. The Paps of Jura, the mountains to the south of the island, rise to over 2,500 feet.

The attractions of Jura are not immediately obvious, but look out for the details: Small Islets Bay facing you as you drive through Craighouse, the herons among the seaweed, the many pheasants and deer, and the brambles spilling over the roadside. Jura is beautifully unpolluted. Occupied since the Bronze Age, there are standing stones (at the southern half of the island), Iron Age forts and duns, as well as more recent ruined villages. The local economy depends on two things – the distillery, dating from the early 19th century, rebuilt in 1876 – and stalking.

The road proper comes to an end after Ardlussa, though a track continues onto Barnhill, a farm in the north. George Orwell came here to seek respite from TB, and wrote the novel *1984* while on Jura. (Not much evidence of Big Brother there.) He almost drowned when his boat overturned at Corryvreckan, the whirlpool to the north of the island; it remains a hazardous place for sailing.

Jura is ideal for walking (you'll find an excellent little publication, *Jura: A Guide for Walkers* by Gordon Wright at the Jura Hotel, which describes various walks and in detail outwith the scope of this guide). The east side you can cover by car or bicycle; try walking on the west side by Loch Tarbet; there are several fine pebbly beaches nearby. For those wishing to tackle the Paps, again refer to the Walkers' guide. The views of Colonsay, Mull and Kintyre, and the Outer Hebrides are excellent.

How to get there

Ferry only
Western Ferries operate a seven-day roll-on/roll-off service from Port Askaig to Feolin. No booking is necessary, and the journey time is approximately 5 minutes. Contact the ferry company at ☎984 681 (Port Askaig) – ☎982 208 (Jura).

Getting around

You will probably need your own transport before arriving on Jura.

Accommodation

Jura Hotel, Craighouse (☎049 682 243).

Bed & Breakfasts
Fish Farm House (☎049 682 304).
Mrs Woodhouse, 7 Woodside (☎049 682 379).

Self-catering
4 cottages are available beside a beach. ☎049 682 323/224 for details.

Where to eat

Jura Hotel: bar lunches and dinners

Things to see

Distillery trip: by appointment only (☎0496 82240).

Pony Trekking (☎0496 82332).

Fishing: salmon fishing in the three main rivers of Jura – the Inver, Corran and Lussa. Fishing is restricted as most of the island will belong to one estate or other. Contact Islay Tourist Information Centre for details.

Nearest Tourist Information Centre: Bowmore (☎0496 810254).

The Outer Hebrides

Introduction

'Probably there's no atmosphere in the
world
that offers so little resistance to people
to look in at Eternity:
there's no need for philosophy
where you can make do with
binoculars.'
  Ruaraidh MacThomais's translation
of his own poem in Gaelic.

The Outer Hebrides, or Western Isles,
lie to the north-west of Scotland in an
archipelago known also as the Long
Isle. There are more than 200 of them
for the truly dedicated island-hopper,
though only thirteen are inhabited by a
total of 31,000 people. The population
of Lewis alone represents two-thirds of
that. The islands take the full force of the
wild and unpredictable Atlantic weather
– the wind being almost constant and
frequently very strong, showers falling
in sheets before the sun returns to
expose the full pallet of pastel blues,
greens, browns and white-golden beaches.

Formed from some of the oldest rock in
the world, the spine of the islands is
made of bleak mountains overlooking
the sea lochs which deeply indent the
eastern coasts. In the central parts, as in
almost all of Lewis, peat bog and freshwater lochs dominate. And on the west
coasts, most islands feature wind-
whipped sand dunes and machair, the
sandy soil on which much of the crofting takes place and which is home to a
carpet of fragrant flowers, especially in
spring.

The islands are the heartland of Gaelic
culture, with the language widely
spoken and enjoying a revival through
parental demand for Gaelic playgroups,
Gaelic-medium schooling and through
recent government funding of a Gaelic
television boom. This has followed a
renewed sense that the islanders are in
control of their own destiny, since the
setting up, in the mid-1970s, of a bilingual local council (Comhairle nan

Eilean) to cover the Outer Hebrides. The
culture is also given vibrancy by the
relative absence of incomers, perhaps
because the islands seem too remote, or
perhaps because the native islanders
have their ways of reminding you that
you always remain an outsider.

The economy is extremely fragile.
Traditionally, it has required islanders
to combine part-time work in fishing,
weaving Harris Tweed and crofting (the
small-scale farming of sheep, a few
cows and potato beds). Many island
men also left for the merchant navy.
Recent decades have added highly
seasonal tourist work, and the shifting,
and usually brief, fortunes of more
substantial industry: fish processing,
oilrig construction near Stornoway, and
servicing the military presence in the
Uists and Benbecula. With big families
and traditional values, women have
been limited in the past to croft work,
but now play the vital role in tourism.
The fragility also results from the
islands' constant loss of their brightest
young people. In a culture which values
education, schools like the Nicolson
Institute in Stornoway are among the
best state schools in Scotland. They
send large numbers to study and jobs on
the mainland, from which they rarely,
if ever, return.

For the visitor, the Western Isles feature
fresh water and sea fishing, bird-watching, water sports, walking, superb
beaches (which are often deserted even
on the warmest day), and reminders of
a prehistoric past and vibrant cultural
present. But more important is the
lesson the islands have to teach
outsiders about peace and quiet and the
value of patience. The time zone is the
same as the rest of Britain, yet hours and
days pass at more leisurely pace. When
God made Hebridean time, he made
plenty of it. So you have to wait for the
weather to change, for a late ferry or for
a dozy sheep to get off the road in front
of you. Here, it takes time to get things
done, and it takes time for things not to
get done at all. (If the latter, it probably
didn't matter much anyway.)

The islands are also a place of reserved friendliness, politeness and gentle humour. Crofters will stop and philosophise at length with a complete stranger on all manner of subjects. And single-track roads force drivers to wait and wave at oncoming traffic – so much so that the first few miles back on the mainland, lacking eye contact with other drivers seems hostile. On CalMac ferries, the crews were recently trained in American customer care techniques to instruct passengers to 'have a nice day'. They ridicule the notion. Here, more than anywhere, it is up to you to decide whether to have a nice day, and nobody is going to force one on you.

Outer Hebrideans are easily ridiculed for what seems to be naïvety, simplicity and a sense of other-worldliness. But beware: there is also a subversive and beguiling quality to the people. Despite the visitor's importance to the island economy, the Outer Hebridean thinks visitors are a wee bit daft – with all those bizarre trappings of tourism, their enthusiasm in bird-watching, looking at standing stones or walking contentedly in the drizzle in search of a rare bog orchid.

Many of the roads are single-track, with passing places both for oncoming traffic and locals who want to get past you – particularly that battered Cortina, full of seventeen-year-olds and bristling with aerials. Many of the roads undulate over rock and peat bog, and can make a back-seat family very unwell. A couple of roads in Harris are particularly stomach-churning. The other key hazard is the constant danger of wayward sheep, particularly on still summer evenings when midge-bites are driving them crazy. And occasionally, on the quieter roads, bored collies confuse cars with sheep and attempt to round up motorists by running beside them snapping at their tyres. Keep petrol well-stocked. There is none on Sunday, and some remote areas have no unleaded fuel.

As the local council is determined to promote the Gaelic language, all road signs have recently been changed to Gaelic, rarely with English translations. This can be perplexing for a visitor, where for instance an attempt to reach South Boisdale requires turning off on the road marked 'Leth Meathanach'. Leverburgh, likewise, has lost its anglicisation, and become 'An t-Ob'. Even where names are identical, it can seem impossible to see any connection between the Gaelic spelling and a word's pronunciation: for Vatersay, read Bhatarsaigh. As Gaelic has an oral tradition, spelling is variable and confounds the learner with apparently random use of silent consonants. True, there is some method to it, but it is well worth getting a map which offers both English and Gaelic. This guide offers the Gaelic translation of place names once in brackets, for ease of reference and as local people still refer to places by their name in English when they are speaking with non-Gaels.

Cycling the Long Isle from north to south or vice versa is a popular route lasting about a week at least, though it often suffers from the unpredictability of the weather and strong winds. Hitchhiking is easy, as there is some assurance that neither hitcher nor hitchee is likely to be a murderous psychopath. Or at least if he is, the Highland Constabulary will collar him at the ferry terminal.

Crofting Code (can be inserted anywhere in the Inner or Outer Hebrides): Take all litter to a convenient disposal point.
Respect and protect all wildlife, plants and trees.
Guard against all risk of fires.
Use gates and stiles properly to cross fences, and close gates.
Keep dogs under control, especially at lambing time.
Do not disturb grazing sheep and cattle.
Respect growing crops.
If crossing croft land, ask permission.
Any crofter will give advice on the best and safest (and driest) routes to take.
Always rely on local knowledge.

Barra

(Barraigh)

When the tide is out, Traigh Mhór (the big beach) stretches a mile and a half across a huge feast of cockles. You can tell something is going to happen when the fire engine sets out to chase the cows away, the driver slapping his door and shouting bovine insults in Gaelic. People begin to point at a speck, little more than a distant seagull, just visible over the Weaver's Castle (a large rock on the horizon). It grows bigger, declining to flap its wings, until an under-carriage becomes clear. This is the daily plane from Glasgow on its final approach to Barra's beach airport. Since first used in 1935, the airline schedule has been dictated by the tides. Such incongruities seem natural in Barra, or Barraigh. The island which anchors the southern end of the Outer Hebrides has all the charming eccentricities of Gaeldom, plus some of the less charming ones: a belief that modernisation requires an L-shaped kit-house and a desire to spend Brussels' ecus on a 'real' airstrip.

For the visitor, Barra offers a small-scale version of all that is most attractive about the Hebrides: the machair, flowers, birdlife, beaches, hills, rocky inlets, a vibrant Gaelic culture and a warm welcome. That makes it a strong candidate for a traveller who hopes to hang out and absorb the island magic, rather than hopping crazily from ferry to ferry in search of it. The sense of community is particularly strong, perhaps because Barra is based on a circular road and Castlebay is a focus where everyone has to go to shop. It may also be because of the island's size and population, roughly 1,400 people, very few of whom are incomers.

The alternative to arriving on the beach is to get the ferry from Oban. This arrives at Castlebay (Bagh a'Chaisteil), which, unsurprisingly, is a bay with a castle in it. The stronghold of the MacNeil clan, it sits on a rock about 150 metres from the pier and, at high tide, appears to be moored there. The MacNeils, with a sea-faring reputation which has been both notorious and renowned, have dominated the harbour since before the 9th century. This makes them relative newcomers, as recent excavations near the causeway to Vatersay have found evidence of settlement 4,500 years ago.

The castle was first built in the 12th century. Its occupants appear to have been either troublesome or very pleased with themselves; one had the splendid title of Roderick the Turbulent, while legend has it that a herald would appear after mealtimes to announce: 'The MacNeil having dined, all the other princes of the world may now eat.' What they didn't seem to realise was that the Barrachs (the people of Barra) had long since finished and were already in the Castlebay Bar.

Such naïvety may have been one reason why the chief went bankrupt in 1838, selling his island to Colonel Gordon of Cluny. History is unkind to the colonel, with good reason. Despite being unsuccessful in trying to persuade the government that Barra could be used as a penal colony, he was responsible for extensive clearances off the land, which first left many perched on useless strips of coast and then forced them to emigrate. Loss of the land also helped establish Barra as a major fishing centre. By the end of the 19th century, the herring boats were so numerous that they stretched right across Castlebay harbour.

A century after losing the clan chieftainship, a competition to prove ancestral credentials was won by an American architect, making him the 45th chief and ensuring that the castle was re-built. His heir, Iain MacNeil, is currently chief and ceases to be a law professor in Chicago each summer to welcome visiting clansfolk when his standard is flying on the castle. This impresses visiting North Americans a whole lot more than the islanders.

The other strand of Barra history is its religion. St Barr (or Finnbarr) is said to have brought Christianity from Columba's monastery on Iona, and there is a 12th-century monastic site connected with him in Eoligarry (Eolaigearraidh), at the north of the island, which is still used as a graveyard and boasts one of the all-time great Hebridean views. Barra remains very loyal to the Roman Catholic church, giving it a feel similar to that of the west of Ireland. It is a lot less dour than the Presbyterian islands to the north, and the Sabbath is observed largely in going to mass and then sleeping off the excesses of Saturday night. Barrachs know how to enjoy themselves with some wild, late dances and with great fondness for the *uisge beatha* (whisky) – a reputation enhanced by their link with Whisky Galore (see Eriskay).

A tour of the island is likely to start in Castlebay, past the school and a football pitch which becomes waterlogged at high tide. On the way to the superb range of west coast beaches, there is a perfume factory and the ruin of a castle in Loch St Clair (good for trout fishing). By the first beach (not safe for bathing) is the Isle of Barra Hotel, a monument to 1970s design and an architect who liked roof tiles. Borve, Craigston and Allasdale (Borbh, Baile na Creige, Allathasdal) feature many of Barra's prehistoric remains, particularly a large dun just above the road at Craigston.

Seal Bay is across the machair from Allasdale road junction, its many rocks home to the grey seals which are greatly unloved by Hebridean fishermen. It is on the hillside above there that the golf course is being built. So far, the road has been gently undulating past magnificent beaches. When it heads inland towards the reservoir and Northbay (Bagh a' Tuath), cyclists begin to find it more demanding. Northbay township is a good reference point for its road junction, church, Post Office (open occasionally) and good anchorage. Near the road, you can see a 1970s statue of St Barr, who appears to be in the middle of a golf swing. Taking the road north to Eoligarry, you will come to the huge expanse of beach which is the airport. You can pick plentiful cockles when the tide is out. (Boil for ten minutes with the shells open.) A large house on the west of the road called Suidheachan was home to Compton Mackenzie, the writer who put Barra on the literary map in the 1930s and 1940s, and made it particularly famous for his book *Whisky Galore*. The building is now a good guest house and a factory turning cockle shell into roughcast wall coating. Behind it are the sand dunes of one of the Hebrides' most beautiful sweeps of sand, Traigh Eais, 1.5 miles long, exposed to Atlantic rollers and safest for bathing at the north end. Eoligarry offers yet more beautiful views over the shallow sandbanks to Eriskay and South Uist. It is more fertile, its sand more chalky and only cows are allowed to be grazed there.

The road down the east side of the island from Northbay is through more populous parts of the island, and past rocky inlets. It rises to the shoulder of Heaval, the highest hill, at 384 metres. From the road, there is a view over Castlebay and down to Barra Head, or for an even better panorama, climb Heaval and, on the way, rest at the 1954 statue of Our Lady Star of the Sea.

How to get there

Ferries

Four times a week from Oban to Castlebay on Cal-Mac's Lord of the Isles. This takes 5¼ hours: two hours up the Sound of Mull, followed by around three hours pitching around the Minch, past Coll and Tiree. It is one of the longest Hebridean ferry crossings, and also one of the most exposed to the full blast of the Atlantic. Pier: Castlebay (☎0871 810306). There is also a regular ferry link with South Uist. The Lord of the Isles takes two hours to Lochboisdale. A passenger/bicycle ferry crosses the shallows between Eoligarry jetty, Eriskay and Ludag jetty, South Uist, two or three times a day. Phone the ferryman: Willie Rusk, in Eriskay (☎0878 720 233).

By air

From Glasgow once a day (except Sunday) by Loganair. The 36-seater plane lands on a beach, so the timetable depends on the tide being out. Flight time is approx. 1 hour. There is also a daily flight (except Sundays) connecting with Stornoway and Benbecula. The airport (☎0871 890 283) is seven miles from Castlebay. For bookings, contact Loganair Reservations (☎041-889 3181).

Things to do and see

Kisimul Castle, open Mon, Wed, Sat afternoons in summer. A boat crosses from opposite the Castlebay post office; be careful of the slippery jetty on the castle side. Members of Clan MacNeil are asked to make themselves known to the chief, if he's visiting from his American home.

Thatched House museum: a mile up a rough track from Craigston (Baile na Craige) road end. Run by local historical society in summer months only. Open 11.30am–4pm. Inclement weather: good swimming pool in the secondary school, one mile to the west of Castlebay shops. Open usually 12 noon–8 pm in summer. Also a public library in school.

Fishing permits are available from Co-chomunn Bharraidh shop next to tourist office. £2 per day, £10 per week. You can hire fishing gear at the tourist office. A golf course is currently being built at Grean, six miles from Castlebay on west coast. Spectacular views, but beware of rabbit holes. Pony trekking from Tangusdale (☎810411). The dances in Castlebay Hall are very late and wild, but well worth the effort. See posters in local shops for details.
Walks: from Castlebay, up to Heaval statue and over the mountain to Borve. Also walk out to Grean Head.

Feis Bharraidh (The Barra Festival) takes place in the first two weeks of July and the island really comes alive with people and activities – piping, dancing, ceilidhs, suppers, and, most importantly, daily classes in all aspects of Gaelic culture. For information before you go, contact the CSS office, Castle-bay (☎0871 810677).

Getting around

Taxis: N MacNeil, Castlebay (☎0871 810302), Hatcher, Castlebay (☎0871 810486), Currie, Castlebay (☎0871 810497), Gillies, Castlebay (☎0871 810689).
Car hire: Gerard Campbell, Castlebay (☎0871 810328). Post Bus, twice a day, slow and timetable depends on meeting flights at the airport. Ask at the post office (☎0871 810286).
Bicycle hire: in a brown hut, just east of shops at Glen junction. Castlebay (☎0871 810284). £7.50 a day. No padlocks available, but who would need one in Barra?
Doctor (in Castlebay 0871 810283). He also runs windsurf club and rental.
Post Office in Castlebay (9 am–5.30 pm, except Saturday 9 am–12 pm) (and at Northbay hall briefly each day ex. Sun). Royal Bank of Scotland in Castlebay, plus six shops (no chemist).

Tourist information office: looking onto main street shops, 100m from pier. Castlebay (☎0871 810336). Open in summer; Mon–Fri 9 am–1 pm, 2 pm–5 pm, Saturday 10 am–5 pm, and briefly after late ferry arrival. Open May–September.

Accommodation

Castlebay Hotel (☎0871 810223) recently refurbished with lively pub. Craigard Hotel (☎0871 810200) also near shops. The Isle of Barra Hotel (☎0871 810383) features 1970s architecture, tartan carpets and coach parties, but is much quieter and away from it all, two miles west of Castlebay overlooking a splendid beach, and bay called Halaman bay.

B & Bs

There are a few dotted round the island. Check with tourist office in Barra. Ask at the tourist office about current self-catering availability. Camping is best at Ledaig, just to the east of Castlebay but there are no facilities. Water and toilets are available at Eoligarry jetty, or water at Allasdale. No caravan site is available.

Vatersay
(Bhatarsaigh)

Vatersay, the H-shaped island just to the south of Barra was a dying community at the end of the 1980s. It was saved, however, by its sex drive.

Until 1990, its link with Barra was a mere motor launch, which proved to be a passion killer for young men in search of marriageable women. Meanwhile, the island required the services of government bulls, employed by Her Majesty's ministers to do the needful for crofters' cows throughout the islands. Such animals could only get to work after swimming across a narrow channel to Vatersay.

But then, the island reached national prominence both for the televised plight of its bachelors, and for the fate of Bernie the bull or B6 as he was known prosaically. He it was who tragically failed to swim the channel from Barra, much to the disappointment of the waiting cows and crofters and much to the pleasure of the press. So Euro-funds provided the money for a splendid causeway, which has completely rejuvenated Vatersay.

The island makes a pleasant meander for visitors, especially on the magnificent beaches. At the time of writing, the local council intend removing Vatersay's rich stock of rusting cars which go there to die, so that should make the dunes more agreeable. Wreckage which still remains is that of the World War II Catalina flying boat, and there is a memorial to the *Annie Jane*, a ship wrecked on Vatersay in 1853, taking 450 lives, at the start of an emigrants' passage from Glasgow to the United States.

The island is also notable for having been invaded in 1907 by crofters (known henceforth as the Vatersay Raiders) from Mingulay and Barra. Eight of them were sent to jail in Edinburgh, but released after public protest. Following the land grab, there were 290 people living on the island: now there are fewer than seventy. An alternative invasion has occurred occasionally during more recent summers, when the royal yacht *Britannia* anchors in the bay and the Queen plays football with her family, staff and islanders on the main beach.

To the south of Vatersay are uninhabited islands: Sandray, Pabbay, Mingulay and Berneray (or Barra Head) which has an unmanned lighthouse. The best to visit is Mingulay, which can be reached after a 30 kilometre journey from Castlebay in exposed seas on a small launch. It has a ruined village, which is said to be haunted, after many of its residents died in a plague. A climb up to the spectacular 213 metre cliffs offers superb birdwatching, especially puffin nests burrowed into the cliff tops.

All services are in Castlebay, roughly five .miles by road from Vatersay's village. A bus leaves from Castlebay and runs between Barra and Vatersay two or three times a day. There is one bed and breakfast on the island in Uidh.

Nearest Tourist Information Centre: Barra (☎0871 810336).

Eriskay

(Eiriosgaigh)

Lying between South Uist and Barra, Eriskay is only 4 km by 2.5 km, populated by 200 people, and therefore one of the Hebrides' most densely populated islands. It doesn't seem that way, though, feeling quiet and not far removed from the back of beyond. A visit will show it to be a well cared-for place with a relatively well-off community, from its fishing of velvet crabs, prawns and lobsters. A day-trip with four hours or so on the island can make for a pleasant walk, but plan carefully, as the tides make ferry crossing times highly variable and bus connections on the other side are poor.

For an island so small, Eriskay is unusually well-known. Its rich tradition in Gaelic song (shared particularly with Barra and South Uist) gave song-collector and translator, Marjory Kennedy-Fraser, the famous Eriskay Love Lilt. It is home to an ancient breed of hardy pony. And it has a special place in Scottish history, as the landing place for Bonnie Prince Charlie, when he arrived in Scotland at the start of the 1745 campaign to re-claim the Scottish throne. As an effete courtier, he is said to have found the smoky atmosphere of the black houses too much and had to take gasps of air outdoors. Legend also has it that he dropped the seeds of a pink convolvulus flower at his arrival at the main beach, Coilleag a' Phrionnsa. Known as the Prince's Flower, that is said to be the only location where it flowers, in July.

But Eriskay's worldwide fame stems above all from the SS Politician, a 12,000-tonne ship which was wrecked near the island on its way to New York and Jamaica in 1941. It was laden with bicycle parts, the equivalent of £3 million in Jamaican currency – and 243,000 bottles of whisky. The Water of Life was almost impossible to obtain during wartime, and to the people of Eriskay, South Uist and Barra, it seemed a terrible pity to let the whisky go to

waste. So they helped themselves to the cargo, reputedly filling every spare space to store it, including the rabbit holes. The tax authorities did not view the wreck with the same generosity of spirit, and eventually sent several islanders to jail for the theft.

The yarn was embellished with some literary licence, and written as *Whisky Galore* by Compton Mackenzie. This went on to be filmed on Barra in 1948 by the Ealing studios and became one of the finest British comedy films ever made – known as *Whisky Galore* to most buffs, or *Tight Little Island* to American in case they missed the point. A bottle of the real stuff can be seen in Am Politician, the recently-built bar, and there are continuing attempts to salvage more, though most has sadly become undrinkable. Also worth a visit is the 1903 St Michael's Church, with seafaring links and Spanish design. Its altar is the bow of a lifeboat from the aircraft carrier *Hermes*.

How to get there

There's a car ferry (5-15 minutes crossing) from Ludag, South Uist, or a passenger ferry from Eoligarry, in Barra. Ferrymen on Eriskay (☎0878 720216 or 261). There are also distant hopes of a causeway to South Uist.

Facilities

A shop, pub, Roman Catholic church, primary school and post office. Sue MacDonald offers bed and breakfast on Eriskay (☎0878 720220).

Nearest Tourist Information Centre: Lochboisdale (☎0878 720286).

South Uist

(Uibhist a Deas)

Many visitors to the Hebrides island-hop onto South Uist across the causeway from Benbecula, to the north, and it doesn't take long for the southerners to let you know the key difference. Roadside shrines to the Virgin Mary show you have suddenly shifted to Roman Catholic turf. And if you miss them, you can't miss the nine-metre granite Madonna on the first major hill, Rueval. Like Barra, there is a more Irish feel to the community; it's more relaxed and not given to the strict Sabbath-keeping of the northerly islands of the Hebrides. Although its services are largely run from the council offices in Stornoway, there is little tension between the dominant Protestants and the southern isles Catholic community - except in the recent campaign led by a South Uist priest to save the local surgical clinic from closure.

It has not always been so easy being Catholic on South Uist. One former laird converted to Protestantism, and used a cane to beat similar belief into his people: some emigrated, others changed back to Rome when he died. Emigration, as with all these islands, played a major part in South Uist's history. Colonel John Gordon of Cluny, who bought the island in 1838, got a government re-location grant to clear the land for sheep. His most infamous action was to call the people to a public meeting, threatening a fine for non-attendance. Once there, police, bailiffs and press gangs seized many from the crowd and put them on the *Admiral*, a ship anchored in Lochboisdale and bound for Canada. Resisters were clubbed and dragged aboard, in what was compared to a slave hunt on the African coast. Around 1,000 people left the island on that ship, many of them to destitution in Toronto and Hamilton. The population, 2,200, is now a third of what it then was.

The island is the second biggest in the Outer Hebrides, 22 miles by eight at its widest point. From the road which runs down its spine, South Uist's distinctive geography can be seen, though it is far better to take detours down the side roads. The dunes to the west hide the golden beach which runs almost all the way down the coast, and the sandy, springy soil of the machair, rich in wild flowers, is the cultivated area where most people live. By the road is the peaty moorland with many lochans, noted for their trout fishing. Loch Druidibeg, beside the road about half way down the island, is the centre of a 4,000 acre (1,677 hectare) nature reserve which is a rare breeding ground for greylag geese. There is a hide near the road at Loch Stillgarry. To the east of the road is a spine of mountains also running the length of the island and overlooking the four large sea lochs which indent the east coast. The highest point, Beinn Mhor, at 2,034 feet, makes for a muddy walk of three to five hours. The east coast is barely populated except in the main harbour of Lochboisdale (Loch Baghasdail), but there are interesting winding roads to see the landscape, the one to Loch Skiport (Sgioport) going through the nature reserve.

The west coast has some wonderful, windy walking opportunities, on the machair or beach. Among the best areas are Askernish (Aisgernis), Kildonan and Howmore (Tobha Mor), but be careful further north in the vicinity of the army rocket firing range. One's Hebridean idyll is not helped by a sign on the beach saying: 'Do not touch anything. It may explode and kill you'. The launchpad itself is an ordinary piece of concrete, onto which artillery is wheeled. It fires bits of military hardware into the Atlantic yonder, and it is the job of trackers on South Uist and St Kilda to the west to find out where the rockets or artillery landed and how many gannets and seals were collaterally damaged in the process. This requires a huge array of aerials and golf ball radars perched atop the hill, Rueval, which is known locally as

Space City. However, they are unable to track bits of explosive shell which wash up again on the beach. For fishing boats and yachties, there are warnings posted to keep out of a firing zone twenty miles by eight. As with the neighbouring islands, the rocket range is a crucial part of the local economy, and means there is a South Uist 'rush hour' in late afternoon when the squaddies come off duty and go tearing home along the island roads.

For history buffs, the most notable ancient remains include the second-century AD wheel-shaped house at Kilpheder (Cille Pheadair), near a striking modern church at Garrynomonie (Gearraidh na Monadh). There are also links with Bonnie Prince Charlie. Although he first landed at nearby Eriskay, his time on South Uist was spent trying to escape government soldiers in 1746. Castle Galvay, on an island in Lochboisdale, was one of the places he hid. There is also a cairn at Milton to mark the birthplace of Flora MacDonald, who helped the Young Pretender escape to Skye disguised as her maid, Betty Burke.

The MacDonalds of Clanranald were the dominant clan on the island, though there are few physical reminders. The most notable is the castle ruin at Ormiclete (Ormacleit), which burned down in 1715, only seven years after being built. But the most significant historical site is at Howmore, which was the centre of church power for the area. There were once five chapels there, dating back to the 7th century, but ruined as a result of the Reformation. Appropriately, a large, yellow Church of Scotland building, with an unusual central communion table, is nearby. So is the Gatliff Trust Hostel, where you can live a grubby thatched-cottage existence with nine others, and inspect the bits of washed-up rocket displayed at the door.

The exit point to Oban is at Lochboisdale, which straggles along the road from equally unprepossessing Daliburgh

(Dalabrog). You may find somewhere to stay there, but make sure you spend tlme exploring the rest of South Uist.

How to get there

Ferries
Ferry from Oban to Lochboisdale six times a week during summer. Four of these are via Castlebay, Barra, adding two hours onto the exposed Minch crossing and always arriving at awkward times in the evening, so book accommodation ahead. There are also plans for a ferry connection twice a week with Mallaig. To reduce time at sea, take the ferry from Skye to North Uist, and the road connects over causeways to South Uist. Or there's a passenger/bicycle ferry link with the north end of Barra (☎0878 720233).

By air
Fly to Benbecula (daily flights, except Sunday), from Glasgow, Stornoway or Barra (Airport ☎0870 602310).

Getting around
Cars for hire from Laing Motors, Lochboisdale (☎0878 700 319/ ☎0878 700 267, or in Benbecula. Bus schedules cover the main centres and the spinal road two or three times on most days but not all, and not even then at the same times. Sometimes, they even connect with ferries and flights. Contact MacDonald Bros (☎0870 620 288/337) or Hebridean Coaches (☎0870 620 237/620 345/620 304).

Accommodation
There's the exclusive Grogarry Lodge, run by South Uist Estates, but for lesser mortals, there's the Borrodale Hotel, Daliburgh (☎0878 700 444) – not the most beautiful part of the island, but a comfortable base. For a far better view, try the unfancy Pollochar Inn (☎0878 720 332), looking out towards Barra, which boasts its own standing stone. The biggest, establishment hotel, with strong fishing and yachting links, is the Lochboisdale Hotel, next to the pier (☎0878 700367).

There are plenty of bed and breakfasts (Curstaidh [Kirsty] MacAskill at Drimisdal Farm does a particularly good herring breakfast, and takes part in the scheme to show visitors the crofting life) while there is plenty machair (field) on which to pitch a tent. In Lochboisdale, the bank usually allows campers to use its lawn, without putting a charge on your monthly statement. There's a water tap behind the tourist office.

Where to eat

There are the hotels above, and the Orasay Inn, Lochcarnan, has a huge menu and good-value shellfish. Remember Benbecula is nearby, which has good facilities.

Things to do and see

Loch Bee is used for good windsurfing by army squaddies.
There is a golf course at Askernish, £3.50 for gents, £2.60 for ladies. In bad weather, the Stoneybridge (Staoinebrig) Community Hall, open 11am–5pm and 1pm–6pm on Sundays, with table-tennis, badminton, darts, snooker, tea, etc. The nearest swimming pool is in Benbecula.

Fishing

The best information is from John Kennedy, fishing manager at Lochboisdale Hotel (☎0870 620332), who has written a booklet about the 70 trout lochs in the area. The opportunities are excellent and cheap, with lets handled by South Uist Angling Club, obtainable on daily/weekly basis, at Lochboisdale Hotel and tourist office, Bornish store and Grogarry Post Office (☎0870 620208) For fishing on Loch Druidibeg Nature Reserve, permits from the warden on Loch Skiport road junction. Sea fishing is not easy in summer, when most boats are working lobsters off the west coast.

Events and festivals

During August, there's a Gaelic *Feis*, or festival, with both traditional skills classes and performances, and Highland Games in July.

Tourist information centre: near Lochboisdale pier, open Apr-Oct 9 am–5 pm and for an hour when the Oban ferry comes in. Have a good crack with tourist officer Joan MacCormick (☎0878 700 286).

Shopping

Much better in Benbecula for most supplies, craft shop at south end of Benbecula causeway.

Benbecula

(Beinn na Faoghla)

First things first – if you don't want others to laugh at you, put the stress on the second syllable – Ben-BEC-ula. Second, remember that Benbecula is largely a means to an end; for the visitor it is part of a holiday covering both of the Uists as well: for its main employer, the end to which it is dedicated is the defence of the realm. The Royal Artillery Regiment has populated the main settlement of Balivanich with a hotch-potch of strong accents from around Britain and a suburban settlement of Ministry of Defence terrace houses. The well-stocked NAAFI supermarket is worth a visit for one of the Hebrides' strongest doses of cultural incongruity, with each side in mutual tolerance and incomprehension. This is a little piece of machair which is forever England.

When the military first brought their missile firing range and 500 troops to Benbecula in 1958, there were strong local suspicions about its effect on the local culture and community. But it brought with it funding for a new causeway to North Uist, an expansion of the airport, regular flights, and local jobs. In 1971, it was substantially expanded to include the base on South Uist. Thirty-five years after arriving, the threat is of a withdrawal by the military, to test their artillery and missiles in Wales instead. Ministry of Defence cuts threaten to tear the heart out the economy of Benbecula and the Uists. A survey in 1993 showed it brought £10 million a year into the islands and the equivalent of 800 jobs, or forty per cent of the total.

The island is similar to much of North and South Uist, but more dominated by both fresh and sea water. Hence its Gaelic name, meaning mountain of the fords – although the mountain is barely a hill, offering a good view from only 149 metres. Bonnie Prince Charlie took refuge from British government ships in the many nooks and crannies of its east coast. A boat is the only way you can get to see much of the east as well. Apart from the fishing in lochs to the east of the main road, visitors to Benbecula spend most of their time on the west, where there is shopping, the airport and most people's homes. This is where Culla beach is, lacking the usual exclusive seclusion one can expect in much of the Outer Hebrides but highly rated. You're unlikely to confuse it with 'Stinky Bay' (Poll na-Cram) to the south, so named because of the seaweed which washes up there. In the early 19th century, the seaweed was greatly valued in the so-called 'kelp boom' and it is still collected by crofters for use as a good fertiliser. Behind Culla is Nunton (Baile nan Cailleach) where you can see the remains of a 14th-century nunnery and chapel. A field beside the road towards Liniclate (Lionacleit) also has the impressive remains of a Clanranald stronghold.

The road from Benbecula to North Uist crosses two causeways and half a mile of the island of Grimsay. This is ignored by most travellers, which is probably why it retains its charm. The road round it was built as part of a relief programme at the time of the 1846 potato famine, and takes you round neat, relatively well-to-do fishing communities and a new harbour at Kallin. Shellfish are stored there until ready to take to markets in France and Spain by truck. For lobsters, they have to stop three or four times on the way to take on fresh supplies of circulating water.

How to get there

Ferries
Ferry connections are via North and South Uist, either to Skye, Harris, Barra or Oban.

By Air
Flights to Glasgow (British Airways (☎0870 602310) are six mornings a week, with flights most days throughout the summer to Stornoway and Barra (Loganair ☎0870 602290).

Getting around
Most buses to and from the Uists stop at Benbecula airport (see numbers in those sections). There is car hire also, from McLennan's Garage (☎0870 602191/2324) and Ask Car Hire (☎0870 602818/602092).

Accommodation
The Dark Island Hotel (☎0870 602414), six miles from the airport, is a favourite haunt and a modern hotel, noted for its excellent food and formidable cook. There is also the Creagorry Hotel, near the South Uist causeway (☎0870 602024) (there's often a good accordion player in the bar at nights) and the smaller Inchyra Guest House (☎0870 602176) (recommended). On the small island of Grimsay to the north, Mrs Macleod runs a flawless bed and breakfast, off the main road and overlooking the new Kallin harbour (☎0870 602029).

Shopping
Balivanich (Baile a Mhanaich) is the shopping centre for the Uists, with the NAAFI supermarket the only such mili-

tary store anywhere which is open to the public. Local tweeds and knitwear are available from nearby MacGillivray's.

Things to do and see

Easy access to anything in North and South Uist, plus sea fishing out of Kallin on Grimsay. Sgoil Lionacleit, the modern community school south of Balivanich, has a good swimming pool with summer watersport courses, a cafe, library and museum displays of local history and culture. It also has a feis/festival in early August and Gaelic Youth Theatre in late July.

Nearest tourist information centre: Lochmaddy (☎0876 500321).

North Uist

(Uibhist a Tuath)

When most folk are curled up in front of a peat fire, or downing the drams at Lochmaddy Hotel Bar, the wardens at Balranald Reserve are outside, in pitch darkness, listening. To the islanders, this kind of eccentric behaviour is only to be expected of mainlanders. But to the wardens, employed by the Royal Society for the Protection of Birds, they are in the vanguard of the battle to save one of Europe's most endangered feathered species – the corncrake, which usually only emits its harsh, grating call between 11 pm and 3 am during the summer breeding season. Sightings of even rarer birds get networked within hours by computer round Britain's 'twitchers' (bird-spotters). Locals talk with amused incredulity of the planeloads who head for the Uists at virtually no notice in a bid (often unsuccessful) to catch the rare sightings for themselves.

For the corncrake, the North Uist nesting ground is one of its last toeholds on survival, because of so much arable crop land (their nesting ground) being converted to sheep farming. Tractor harvesting has also taken its toll, as it usually involves circling round each field towards the middle, and as the birds refuse to rise in daylight, they move to the centre where the blades eventually kill them. Such gory details are explained in a walk around the reserve, guided by the warden. Though he can spot significant specks in the distance – pointing you to dunlin, ringed plover, fulmars, turnstone, redshank and eider duck – he also offers a fascinating introduction to traditional crofting methods, which the RSPB is trying to re-introduce to ensure a sustainable environment for the birds. Forty crofters work the reserve's land, and are paid £30,000 per year in subsidies, mainly to limit the use of chemical fertilisers and pesticides and to rotate the use of their fields for three years, followed by three fallow years. They are also paid to delay harvesting if rare birds like corncrake are nesting, leading to recent, unproven tales of corncrake nests being moved around fields to ensure the maximum RSPB payout. The crofts are made up of separated strips of land which mix the sandy machair with more substantial soil away from the beach. Allowing fallow years makes for a tremendous range of plants, like trefoils, silverweed, orchids, gentians, dwarf pansies, marigolds and poppies in the early years. By the third year, vetches and clovers take over, as they do on most road verges.

Being the first landfall for migratory birds flying to and from Greenland (and, as it happens, airliners from New York), spring and autumn also provide lively times at Balranald, with up to 1,000 Manx shearwaters passing through per hour, along with an abundance of gannets, skuas, petrels, shearwaters. There have been 183 species recorded on the reserve, and fifty can be relied on to nest each year. A boat trip to the now uninhabited Monach Islands eight miles to the west offers more wildlifewatching opportunities, especially its huge seal colony. Check with Estate office, Lochmaddy (☎0876 500329).

There is, of course, more to North Uist. But its most attractive attribute is that there isn't much. This is probably the sleepiest of the large outer isles, with its quiet charm requiring time and patience to appreciate. Many find this is best done from a boat on the trout lochs – the most notable feature of the landscape, with their lilies, nesting geese and haunting reflections. A tenth of the island's surface area is freshwater loch, with the surrounding peat up to twenty feet deep.

It was not always so sleepy. From 1735 until 1822, there was a kelp boom based in North Uist, in which hundreds of people were employed in the gathering and burning of seawood to produce potash and soda. At its peak, 2,000 tons a year was harvested in the Outer Hebrides, but cheaper imports from Spain glutted the market in 1822, and it left North Uist, in particular, over-populated and vulnerable to the potato famines which followed. Part of the reaction to famine was to provide work through the relief projects which built the roads, and the strange Victorian folly on Loch Scolpaig. But, as with other islands, there were brutal clearances of the land. In the north-west township of Sollas in 1849, the landowner, Lord MacDonald of Sleat, brought police from Skye to evict his tenant crofters and burn their homes. This was to leave space for sheep and many people with no option but to go to the United States.

The thirty-five-mile road they left is roughly circular, branching to the north and the Berneray/Harris ferry terminal. The branch to the south leads to the 1960 Grimsay/Benbecula causeway. It allows access to the even older history of North Uist, most notably the chambered cairn of Bharpa Langass, on a hillside seven miles to the south-west of Lochmaddy. Such burial mounds are quite a common feature of Hebridean pre-history, though this one, twenty-five metres in diameter and seven metres high, is unusual in still allowing access for the nimble visitor to one of its inner chambers. It dates back to Neolithic times, 2-3000 BC, probably built by sun-worshippers, and was used also by the Beaker people of the early Bronze age.

Going clockwise further round the road, more up-to-date history is in the ruined chapel buildings at Carinish. Known as Trinity Temple (Teampull na Trionaid), this was once a widely-respected educational centre where clan chiefs' sons were schooled in English and Latin. Founded around 1203 AD by Beathag, daughter of Somerled, the Irish mercenary who fathered the MacDonald clan, it is said the great theologian Duns Scotus studied there. It lies near a causeway to the island of Baleshare (Baile Sear), which has one of the islands' longest beaches, ideal for a long walk.

The circular route takes the traveller past the most populous parts of the island, and many prehistoric standing stones, stone circles, cairns, duns and crannogs, the little islands in the middle of lochs on which people used to live. One group of standing stones to have attracted the attention of local folklorists is known as the Three False Men (Na Fir Bhreige), who, it seems, deserted their wives in Skye and were turned to stone north-west of Lochmaddy by a witch with attitude.

The route brings the traveller back to Lochmaddy (Loch nam Madadh) which is the main village. By any other comparison, it is a random scattering of 300 people, their homes, a few solid granite structures like the sheriff courthouse, a pier and some sheep pens, all perched precariously on the end of a peninsula with nothing much going on unless the ferry is calling. The loch's name is derived either from the 'maddies' or oysters found in it, or the three rocks, known as the dogs (madadh), at the entrance to the loch. As with much of the east coast, Lochmaddy is a watery maze of islets and inlets, measuring up to five by three miles yet with a shore-line reckoned to exceed 200 miles.

How to get there

Ferries
CalMac's *Hebridean Isles* car ferry direct from Uig, Skye, to Lochmaddy (Loch na Madadh) in North Uist, takes 3 hours 45 mins and runs two times on most days, and at least once every day. It covers a triangular route, also including Tarbert on Harris, so it is possible to travel there every day but Sunday. (North Uist observes the Sabbath quite strictly, but not so much as Harris, so there are still ferry sailings.) Lochmaddy pier: ☎0876 500337.

A passenger ferry runs to the south end of Harris from the north tip of North Uist, and there are plans to upgrade this for cars. (☎0876 540230/540250). You can also get a car from here across to Berneray.

By air
North Uist is connected to Benbecula and South Uist by causeway, so it is possible to get there by air or by ferry from Oban to Lochboisdale.

Getting around
There are three postbus routes, each running once a day.

Taxi and hire: Alda's Hire (☎0876 500215). Service buses run between Lochmaddy and Benbecula, with a couple of links south to Lochboisdale.

Bicycle hire
Morrison's, Carinish (☎0876 580240).

Accommodation
Lochmaddy Hotel (☎0876 580331/332), Langass Lodge Hotel (a former shooting lodge; good food), Westford Inn (☎0876 580653) has a lively pub. There's a youth hostel at Lochmaddy (☎0876 500368), also the Uist Outdoor Centre (☎0876 500480) but the hostel at Claddach Baleshare has closed.

Shopping
Try the Weehavitt Store in Lochmaddy, if only for the kitschy name. There's a post office there as well. There are stores at the main road junctions, but it's better if you go to Benbecula.

Things to do
For energetic types, the Uist Outdoor Centre in Lochmaddy runs residential courses and daily options. Purpose-built in 1991 to accommodate 20 people in four-person bunk rooms. Courses include sub-aqua diving, canoeing, water-skiing, hill-walking, rock-climbing, survival skills, wildlife watches and environment studies. Or bring your colleagues for a course in management and industrial development. Contact: ☎0876 500480.

The Royal Society for the Protection of Birds runs the Balranald nature reserve on the western-most part of North Uist. Guided walks are at 1 pm through summer on Monday, Wednesday and Saturday. There is also an otter watch, on Wednesday, meeting at Langass Lodge Hotel (Loch Eport; ☎0876 580285) at 7 pm. (These times may vary so please check.) North Uist Historical Society is planning to renovate the Temperance Hotel, across from the tourist office, as a heritage and arts centre, and other activities for a wet day can be found at the Benbecula secondary school in Lionacleit.

Fishing
The Lochmaddy Hotel is the best place to start, being a very fishing-oriented place which used to have as many as 29 ghillies. You can buy permits and rent tackle there. Ask for Bill Quarm (☎0876 500331/332). Permits can also be had from John Wood, the Estate Office, Lochmaddy (☎0876 500329), or the cheapest option is the North Uist Angling Club (☎0876 500447). Brown trout fishing starts from £4 per day or £15 per rod per week from bank, salmon from £25 per rod per day, with boat hire from £10 per day.

Tourist information centre: Pier Road, Lochmaddy (☎0876 500321).

Berneray

(Eilean Bhearnaraigh)

In a string of islands, all of which offer an advanced state of 'away-from it-all' relaxation, Berneray is the furthest away from it all you can get. This is the place to get in touch with the real you, and out of touch with the pressures of daily mainland life: it offers a special friendliness. This advice comes with the recommendation of Prince Charles, whose reputation for regal battiness has been greatly enhanced by coming to Berneray when the paparazzi weren't looking, staying with local crofter, 'Splash' McKillop, and howking tatties (lifting potatoes).

The tatties are good on this fertile island, 5 by 2 kilometres, which supports a population of 142 in tidy cottages. For such a small island, its worldwide fame is based on being home to one of the world's tallest men, Giant MacAskill, who lived from 1825 to 1863, when he died in Canada working for a freak show. In the 16th century, his forebears could cross to North Uist at low tide, but a freak tide washed away the sandbanks which made it possible to ford not only from North Uist to Berneray, but also to Pabbay and the Monach Islands. Pabbay and Boreray used to be inhabited as well. But, it is said, Pabbay was evacuated as a punishment for illicit whisky distilling. This de-population of small islands may be countered in the next few years, if plans come to fruition to build a causeway from Newtonferry on North Uist to Berneray. So visit it, and its superb beach, before it is invaded by the worldly influences of Lochmaddy.

How to get there

There's a 10-minute car ferry crossing from the north end of North Uist, with seven sailings each day in summer and the last one leaving at 6 pm. A passenger ferry connects Berneray with the south of Harris twice a day, taking an hour. Contact Donald Angus MacAskill (☎0876 540233).

Getting around

The community council runs a minibus, driven by locals on a rota basis.

Places to stay and eat

There's a thatched Gatliff Trust youth hostel with modern fittings. And the Lobster Pot restaurant offers local seafood for dinner on Friday and Saturday evenings, while a coffee shop the rest of the week.

Berneray week: a week of arts and activities in the second half of July.

Nearest Tourist Information Centre: Lochmaddy (☎0876 500321).

Harris

(Na Hearach)

Somewhere in the Hebridean mists of time, the MacLeod clan split into two branches of the family tree, one controlling the north, more fertile end of the Outer Hebrides' biggest island, the other confined to the south end. Thus was born the division between big northerly Lewis (Leodhas) and small southerly Harris (Na Hearadh), helped by the physical barrier of north Harris's particularly inhospitable mountains. Now a road winds its precarious way between the two and the same local council has for years brought the two under one administration. Yet they retain their different communities and dialects of Gaelic, the Lewis people having more Norse influence in their vocabulary. The Harris outlook is also shaped by its short ferry connection across the Minch to Skye – its branch of the MacLeod clan is actually based at Dunvegan on Skye – while Lewis feels a more distant link directly to the mainland at Ullapool. In Stornoway, they talk of Harris as being the home of Western Isles provincialism and yokels – Hicksville, WI. For the visitor, it is more important to note that Harris can boast some of the most spectacular mountain and coastal scenery to be found in the Scottish islands – and some good food as well.

North Harris is dominated by its mountains – huge chunks of desolate grey rock on which little soil, less vegetation and even fewer people cling to existence. You are looking here at Lewisian gneiss, some of the oldest rock in the world, reckoned to have been formed between 1,500 million and 2,900 million years ago. That makes it at least four times older than the Cairngorms or Ben Nevis on the mainland. All the Outer Hebrides are fashioned from such gneiss, but the contours of Harris seems to make it seem particularly enduring and awesome.

Being so close to creation and given the rugged appearance, it is not hard to see a metaphor in North Harris for the austere and forbidding religious faith of the island's people, best known to mainland Scots through the ferocious denunciations of modern life and the Godlessness of the Tory Government penned by young columnist John MacLeod in Glasgow's *Herald* newspaper. He cultivates his prejudices in a cottage near Maarvig (Marvig) on Loch Seaforth – a high-sided fjord that runs eighteen miles into the heart of the island, while Loch Resort on the west coast provides the other watery barrier between Lewis and Harris. Clisham rises by the main road, the highest of the Harris peaks, at 799 metres, and those who venture into such mountains may be rewarded with sightings of deer, hares, wild goats, eagles and buzzards. At the mouth of Loch Seaforth is the tiny village of Rhinigidale (Reinigeadal), famous for long being inaccessible by land except across a demanding mountain footpath. The European Union has recently funded a road – spectacular both for its views and cost – which brings the car and mailvan to the tiny population and youth hostel.

At the heart of the island lies Tarbert, the village/metropolis which barely holds the north and south parts of the island together from the encroachments of Atlantic and Minch sea-lochs. That is where the ferry from Skye berths and where most of Harris's shopping and services are located. If you're waiting for a ferry, wish to pass the time of day or want to find out more about Harris, John Murdo Morrison, proprietor of the Harris Hotel and campaigner against the constant threat of Sunday ferry sailings, is worth looking up. His bar is also notable for a splendid collection of malt whiskies.

South Harris contrasts not only with the north, but also with itself. Taking the road out of Tarbert which branches to the east coast leads to the most populous part of Harris but is a tortuously twisted journey through terrain which resembles the backside of the moon. It is not to be done on a full stomach, and shouldn't be rushed. This is the Bays Road, or the Golden Road, so named because of the cost of building it. It winds through communities shifted there last century from the fertile west coast by landowners who wanted crofters' land to graze sheep. Although all the Hebrides have histories of cruelty and evictions by 19th-century landowners, Harris is particularly striking for showing the poverty of the land on which crofters were expected to live. Today's Bays communities still till the lazybeds (the small patches of earth on which potatoes are grown, fertilised by seaweed). But there was so little space for cultivation that those forced to settle in the east had to take their dead to the west coast to bury them. Such deprivation forced many emigrations to Canada and America, of which there are records available in the local history societies, and it also led to islanders developing a lively fishing industry operating out of the many inlets down the east coast.

At the south tip of the island is Rodel (Roghadal), a tiny village which is home to St Clement's Chapel. To say this ranks as one of the Hebrides' architectural treasures is saying little, but the beautiful church is well worth a visit. It was built probably in the 12th century using sandstone imported from Mull, and was kept in good condition through restorations in 1787 and 1873. Alisdair Crotach MacLeod, 8th MacLeod of Dunvegan on Skye, was responsible for improving it around 1500, building his own tomb which remains the highlight of the superb masonry inside. Below the chapel nestles a snug 16th-century harbour, and an old hotel and bar which have seen very much better times.

Three miles along the south coast of Harris lies the township of An t-Ob, better known as Leverburgh since 1923, when it was named after Lord Leverhulme – one of the most ambitious characters to have settled on Scotland's islands. Born William Hesketh Lever in 1851, the son of a Bolton grocer, he made his considerable fortune in building up the soap company that became Lever Brothers and Unilever. He bought Lewis in 1918 and South Harris in 1919, hoping to turn his business acumen with soap into an innovative fishing enterprise, controlling the business from the sea onto the dinner table. Leverhulme's spectacular ambitions for Lewis were dampened and then thwarted by tensions with local people, which meant he concentrated his resources for a few extraordinary years on South Harris. Obbe, as it then was, was to be turned into one of the west coast's biggest and busiest fishing ports, serving both the Atlantic and Minch and with a population of 10,000. To ease navigation, rocks were to be blasted, and the port was to have three quays for fifty boats, an inner harbour for 200 boats, packing houses and kipper sheds. His lordship even planned, in the early days of commercial flight, to use spotter planes to direct his fleets to the fish shoals, while on the mainland he began to develop a retail chain known as MacFisheries. His fortune was also ploughed into building many of Harris's roads, a water-powered tweed mill at Geocrab and buying the whaling station which can still be seen

at the turn-off of the road to Hushnish (Huisinis). At first, the catch lived up to these high expectations but soon dwindled. Leverhulme had not realised how difficult it would be for large boats to negotiate the shallow waters in the Sound of Harris. When he died, suddenly, in 1925, his executors dropped the project like a stone, selling off £250,000 of harbour works for £5,000. What remains of Leverburgh – so named, he said, because the islanders requested it – is a poignant memory of one of the islands' many grandiose economic failures; harbour works, the foundations of packing sheds and widely spread buildings. It is from there the passenger ferry leaves for Berneray and North Uist.

Before leaving the township, take a look at Roinabheal, the huge chunk of gneiss rising 460 metres above south Harris. The era of the spectacularly ambitious enterprise on the island have not passed, for there is a serious and controversial plan to quarry the entire mountain over the next eighty or so years, largely to provide the foundations for road building in England. This would be loaded onto ships at Lingerabay, a couple of miles north of Rodel. Locals and planners are split over the superquarry plan, as it would provide jobs, but environmentalists fear for wildlife habitats and the discharge by ships of dirty water loaded around the world as ballast.

The west coast of Harris could be on a different planet from the east. Its golden, sandy beaches are among the most beautiful in Scotland: Northton (An Taobh Tuath), Scarista (Sgarasta), Na Buirgh (Borve) Nisabost, Horgabost and Luskentyre (Losgaintir). Since the 1930s, there has been a lot of re-settling the west by crofters. Overlooking the bays are guest houses like the former manse at Scarista, and Borve Lodge, where Lord Leverhulme lived while on Harris. A good walk takes you up Chaipaval for a view of the coast and west to the high sea cliffs of St Kilda. On its southern slope, near the village of Northton is a chapel, roughly the same

Harris Tweed

Throughout the world, an orb and Maltese cross are recognised as the unlikely symbol of the Outer Hebrides' most famous product. Stamped on every three yards of Harris Tweed, it gives the assurance of high quality on one of the most durable of fabrics. The sign was adopted in 1909 by the Harris Tweed Association, and remains jealously guarded as a trademark, representing a woollen tweed that must have been hand-woven in Outer Hebridean homes, and also spun, dyed and finished in the islands. Since 1934, these latter processes have been done almost entirely in mills at Stornoway and Shawbost on Lewis and Geocrab on Harris. The orb and cross come from the family crest of the Countess of Dunmore, who, in the 1830s, recognised the quality of the traditional cloth being woven by crofters on her family's Harris estate. She energetically and successfully promoted it in London society circles, and developed an export earner which remains the attire of the country set, occasionally features on Paris and Milan catwalks, and is one of the main industries of the Outer Hebrides.

Known in Gaelic as clò mór, or the big cloth, Harris Tweed's production process starts with the Blackface and Cheviot sheep which drivers strive to avoid on the islands' roads – though much of the wool comes from the rest of Scotland. It is dyed using natural colours, including the red brown *crotal* made from lichen scraped off rocks. After spinning in the mills, the yarn is delivered to crofts to be woven in the small sheds built onto many Lewis and Harris homes (the click-clack of the foot-powered loom is often audible when walking through a township). A full-time weaver can produce a huge amount of cloth, up to three webs of cloth weekly, each measuring eighty yards by 28.5 inches. Traditionally, crofters only weave part-time, however, mixing the work with agriculture, fishing and formal employment, and the woven cloth would then be dipped in urine and 'waulked' to finish it. For this, traditionally, the women would gather round a long table and beat the cloth methodically while singing the rhythmic waulking songs which are an important part of the Gaelic oral tradition (and available on record). Now, most of the 450 weavers are full-time, and women find their time is too taken up running bed and breakfasts to waulk the Tweed regularly.

Up to one million yards of Harris Tweed are produced each year, but the industry suffers from boom and bust cycles depending on the whim of the fashion market. One of its problems is that its extraordinary toughness means that the more reliable tweedy customers take a long time to come back for more. Hopes for a more stable market are founded on the development, in Stornoway's college, of a double-width loom providing the dimensions most tailors work with, and there are also hopes of diversifying into the tweed's increased use as furniture upholstery.

Many weavers will demonstrate their work – with relative enthusiasm if you are also buying their product. In Liceasto, on the Harris Bays road, Anne Campbell of Clò Mór claims to produce cloth using all the traditional methods, and three shops specialising in the product are in nearby Drinishader. At Shawbost in west Lewis, Kenneth MacLeod's mill offers guided tours (☎0851 710251).

age as St Clement's, Rodel, but largely ruined.

A final part of the Harris road network takes you along part of the north Harris coast and a further winding road to yet another superb beach, this one at Hushnish. Turning off at the chimney remains of the whaling station, this road has the best starting points for the island's walking. Roughly two-thirds of the way along, you pass through a grand gateway and descend briefly alongside a river with a spectacular salmon leap. The road at this point goes past the front door of Amhuinnsuidhe Castle (in Gaelic, Abhainn Suidhe, pronounced Ahvun-sooyah). This turreted baronial pile was built by a former owner of the island, the Earl of Dunsmore, in 1060. It is said that when his new, young wife saw it, she commented that her father had owned larger stables. This may not be unconnected with the fact that the earl sold the castle and this part of the island to Sir Edward Scott in the same year as the castle was completed. More recently, its owner famously tried to get the local council to re-build the road, in a bid to keep riff-raff and day-trippers out of his landscaped garden.

At Hushnish, the road ends looking to the island of Scarp, which has inspired yet more of Harris's strong line in eccentricity. In 1934, a German rocket scientist, Gerhardt Zucher, used this site in a bid to persuade the British government that missiles could be used to send mail and medicines to remote islands. A special stamp was issued, 30,000 pieces of mail were loaded into the canister and the rocket fired from Harris to Scarp. It exploded, singeing the letters and altering the course of postal history for ever. The craziness does not stop there, however, for in recent years, an Asian hotelier bought the island for £80,000, intending to build a five-star hotel and leisure resort on it, complete with swimming pools, saunas, squash and tennis courts and an airstrip. Strangely, the plan has never been carried through.

Though populated until 1971, Scarp is now mainly used for sheep and a handful of holiday cottages. If you want to cross, contact the ferryman Donald Angus Macinnes (☎0859-86238). For a ferry to the island of Taransay (Tarasaigh), off the beach at Luskentyre and last inhabited more than eighty years ago, contact Ewan Macrae (☎0859-85244).

How to get there

There are ten ferries per week from Uig on Skye and three directly from Lochmaddy on North Uist, both sailings taking one hour 45 minutes. As it is the same CalMac ferry on a triangular route, there are seven other sailings from Lochmaddy via Uig. (CalMac Tarbert: ☎0859 502444) You can also sail from Ullapool to Stornoway on Lewis, and travel to Harris by road. It is about 30 miles between Stornoway and Tarbert. Passengers can travel by ferry from Berneray and North Uist, though there are plans to upgrade this route for cars. (Ferryman: ☎0876 540230/540250.) The nearest airport is at Stornoway. Strictly no public transport moves in Harris on Sunday.

Getting around

Some of the roads on Harris are spectacular, but don't expect to cover them at speed. They take time, both to savour the views and to avoid making your passengers very car-sick. Harris Coaches (☎0859 502441) runs three buses a day between Tarbert and Leverburgh, and between two and four daily between Tarbert and Stornoway, depending on the day of the week. It also runs bus tours out of Tarbert. On Tue. and Fri. tours go to South Harris, Stornoway, Kyles Scalpay and the Callanish Stones in Lewis. On Saturday, there is a Callanish and West Lewis tour. These can link in with a £15 day trip from Skye, on Tue. or Fri. taking in South Harris or Callanish.

Accommodation

In Tarbert, there is the Harris Hotel (☎0859 502154), near the ferry, which is one of the island's key institutions – or at least its proprietor is. For half the price and a lot less character, the main township also has the MacLeod Motel (☎0859 502364), presumably so named because it is located next to a car park. There are many bed and breakfasts, but the classiest accommodation includes Scarista House in the beachiest part of the south-west (☎085 985 238) where the away-from-it-all credentials include an absence of TV and radio. There is also Ardvourlie Castle Guest House (☎0859 502307) in the forbidding terrain near the Lewis-Harris border. This is a former hunting lodge, renovated to the Victorian original design with many antiques and a magnificent view down Loch Seaforth. Campers can pitch tent at Drinishadar or overlooking the beach at Luskentyre.

Where to eat

Despite plentiful fresh produce, the Hebrides can be disappointing for the true foodie. But Harris has, for its size, an unusual wealth of quality eateries, almost all run by incomers to the island. The Taste of Scotland guide recommends Allan Cottage Guest House, in the unlikely surroundings of Tarbert's former telephone exchange; Ardvourlie Castle; Scarista House; Siamara Guest House, five miles south of Tarbert on Loch Stockinish; and Two Waters Guest House, Lickisto, between Stockinish and Geocrab on the Bays road.

Things to do and see

Scarista nine-hole golf course, £3 a day green fee, paid in a collection box. Sheep and rabbits help with mowing and bunker creation.

Fishing

Fish the Laxdale river and loch, on the road between Tarbert and Scalpay, £25 per rod per day from the Harris hotel.

Walking is good from the Huisinis (Hushnish) road but be prepared for very rough terrain and unpredictable weather. Amhuinnsuidhe Hotel to Loch Ulladale is recommended, as is Huisinis to Glen Cravandale. There's also the walk to Rhenigdale, the start of which is signposted on the Scalpay road. Mike Briggs runs a professional hill-walking guide service (☎0859 502376).

The Old School House at Northton (☎0859 82256) has Harris history exhibition including census returns, old parish registers, estate rentals, early maps and material from emigrants to Cape Breton, Quebec and Ontario. Open 10am–6pm

Thur, Fri, Sat. Drinishader village hall has some exhibits plus board games and local information, to help while away wet Harris days. Open 10.30am–4.30pm Tue.–Sat.

Genealogy: Bill Lawson runs a commercial service helping people research their Western Isles routes. The 'Co Leis Thu' Research Centre is at the Old Schoolhouse, Northton (An Taobh Tuath) on ☎085 982 258.

Events and festivals

There is a children's Gaelic feis (festival) in July, and a Harris Arts Festival of performances for two weeks in August/September. (Its art exhibition in 1993 caused offence through paintings of nudity, so a local councillor suggested the pictures could be strategically adorned with local produce – tufts of heather and Harris tweed.)

Tourist Information Office: above the pier at Tarbert (☎859 502011).

Gay and lesbian helpline: In Harris? You gotta be kidding.

Scalpay

(Scalpaigh)

Scalpay is in the relative shelter at the mouth of East Loch Tarbert. Like Eriskay to the south, it is held up as an example of how a small island community can not only be sustained, but can thrive. The well-kept houses and islanders' expensive cars show that business acumen with fishing and shipping, combined with a successful co-operative venture, have made this one of the best-off islands in the Hebrides. It is also noted as the very heartland of the Free Church of Scotland, with its associated determination that everyone, including visitors, should observe the Sabbath.

With around 450 people, on an island five by three kilometres in size, Scalpay appears to be relatively densely populated. The village centre is more than a kilometre from the ferry, with a general store and good quality local knitwear for sale. Ask in the shop for a local boatman to take you for a sea-angling or puffin-watching trip around the Shiant islands (Na Eileanan Mora). Or walk the boggy path to the 1788 Eilean Glas lighthouse, the oldest in the Western Isles, at the east end of the island. There are impressive views across to Skye.

How to get there

From Tarbert (Tairbeart) on Harris, eight km along a winding coast road leads to the car ferry at Kyles Scalpay. This runs at least ten times a day, with a crossing of only around ten minutes. It runs late on Friday night, bringing young Scalpachs back from the Tarbert nightlife. But on Sunday, of course, it remains firmly tied up.

Accommodation

There are bed and breakfasts and self-catering: Annie Cunningham, Enfield House, Isle of Scalpay, Isle of Harris (☎0859 84344).

Lewis

(Eilean Leodhais)

A visit to Lewis is bound to concentrate on the rocky coastal areas where people live. But it is an island which might be better understood by contemplation of the desolate Black Moor which dominates the interior. The road from Stornoway to Barvas, or the route through Achmor, is laid across the undulating peat bog which appears to hold little appeal for a tentative tourist industry.

But in summer, you can watch the families which go there to cut peat. This is where the community works together on a bleak and forbidding landscape, digging deep into the earth for the means of survival and each time leaving fresh scars as a memorial to the hard work. The terrain has been this way since 1098, when Norse chief Magnus Barelegs, destroyed the forest that previously covered Lewis, leaving it difficult, if not impossible, for trees to retain a root-hold. The Black Moor is too wind- and rain-swept for too much of the year: it is a soulful place, on an island which takes souls very seriously.

The peat being cut has been in the making over the past 7,000 years, and in some areas it is still being formed. The wet island climate, although once warmer, has been ideal for growing the grass, heather, sedge and moss which form peat, and for arresting the plants' decomposition. In Lewis, the peat is more than two metres deep on average, though it runs as far down as six metres, with eighty-five million tonnes, at a rough estimate, covering much of the island. Cut into bricks and wind-dried on peat stacks outside homes, it has long provided the fuel for heating and cooking in Hebridean homes, releasing the delicate fragrances of its ancient plants into the night air wherever it burns. (See also its effect on Islay whisky.) Each crofter – and there are around 3,500 such units on Lewis – has a right to cut in designated areas of the island. Some hire mechanised cutters which produce rounded log-like bricks. Others laboriously cut by hand, hire the local tractor to haul it home, and take quiet pride in the artistry of their peat stack. However quaint a memento, visitors are not welcome to take a piece of peat. In Skye, such pilfering has put many crofters off bothering to cut and dry any.

The bare-legged Magnus, whose scorched-earth military tactics exposed so much of this fuel source, was one of the Norse invaders who ruled Lewis until it became part of the Kingdom of Scotland in 1266. It retained a high level of autonomy long after that, under the control of three feuding clans: the Morrisons in the north, the MacAulays in the south-west Uig area and the MacLeods coming to dominate by the 15th century from their eastern stronghold. These names, of course, still occur very frequently – so much so that the locally-produced phone directory helps identify people by the Gaelic nicknames, occupations and generations-old family references which separate one Donald MacLeod from the hundreds of others.

When Lewis was ruled by the clan chiefs, the Scottish monarchy was unimpressed by its unruliness. And given the king's frequent fiscal crises, he was conversely deeply impressed by the potential for fishing out of a natural harbour like Stornoway's. In 1598, James VI contracted with a group of Gentleman Adventurers from Fife 'to set up civilisation in the hitherto most barbarous isle of Lewis'. The MacLeods, somewhat weakened by internal feuding, resisted successfully three times before the king finally had his way and Stornoway became a burgh town. The chief of the Mackenzie clan purchased rights from the Fife Adventurers, and after further tussling with the MacLeods, the island had come under the Mackenzies, headed by the Earl of Seaforth, by 1623.

That is how it stayed until 1844, when the Mackenzies sold out to Sir James Matheson, whose company, Jardine Matheson, had earned him a tea and opium fortune in the Far East. He appears to have been, by the dismal standards of the 19th century, an enlightened landlord, developing Stornoway with new houses, gasworks, waterworks and harbour improvements. He built schools, fish-curing sheds and supported people during famine by a major roadbuilding project. He also built the mock-Tudor Lews Castle overlooking Stornoway Harbour and gained a handy monopoly on the first scheduled shipping service linking Stornoway to the mainland. He was,

however, the object of an explosion of hostility by crofters on Bernera, and people were driven out of their traditional grazing territory by the setting up of huge deer-hunting estates in the south-east of the island. In one of the last clashes of the crofters' revolt, in 1887, the people of the Lochs area went into the estate and killed 200 deer to publicise their case. In a stroke of public relations genius, they then offered roast venison to journalists who had come to report on their case. There remains a 57,000-acre deer estate, which continues to make islanders and non-paying visitors feel unwelcome.

In 1918, Matheson's heir sold the island again, to Lord Leverhulme, the soapsud magnate, whose ambitions for Lewis were astonishing. He wanted to develop Stornoway and Carloway fishing harbours with big, new trawlers and to improve transport around the island with a rail system. One snag was that big trawlers required crofters to be more committed to fishing than they wished to be, taking them away from their other part-time work. Another was that men returning from the 1914-18 war refused to see Leverhulme's argument that fishing was a worthy substitute for the land allocations taking place by law around the rest of the Highlands and Islands. There were land raids by those without crofts, which angered his lordship sufficiently to stop his massive investment programme. So he left, giving away Stornoway to stop its occupants, who still own and run it, while the offer of free crofts was taken up by only forty-one people. Leverhulme departed Lewis to concentrate on his similarly grandiose plans for Harris.

His withdrawal of £200,000 per year in investment was a loss to the economy which left a huge gap in employment, and the 1920s and 1930s saw heavy emigration from Lewis not only to Canada and Australia, but also to South America. This followed the loss, in a particularly bitter tragedy, which still resonates today, of 205 men returning from war in the early hours of New

Year's Day, 1919. Their ship, the *Iolaire*, went aground on the Beasts of Holm, rocks at the mouth of Stornoway harbour, and only around seventy of those on board were hauled to safety.

Most visitors to Lewis start their time with a more successful navigation into Stornoway harbour on a CalMac ferry. Stornoway is the only town in the Outer Hebrides, and it has the facilities and sense of superiority to go with it. It is not the most beautiful of places, but is home to more than 5,000 people, the major services, a new hospital, out-of-town supermarkets and a notoriously wild teenage nightlife in its downtown streets and alleys. It is even relatively cosmopolitan, with its own Gaelic-speaking, well-integrated Pakistani community. This is the hub of the Western Isles Council (Comhairle nan Eilean) set up in 1974 to become a focal point for the renewed pride in the islands and their Gaelic culture. Crucially, its employees represent more than a fifth of the Outer Hebridean job market: despite the effects of Thatcherism on the rest of Britain, the Western Isles has only survived through hefty government subsidy. The council has also been the subject of much of the Lewis folk's advanced sense of gently mocking humour. In 1991, it surpassed its reputation for incompetence by losing £23 million in the collapse of the fraud-ridden Bank of Credit and Commerce International, incurring a hefty repayment bill that has been mortgaged over thirty years at the expense of local services.

Above Stornoway's harbour stands Sir James Matheson's Lews Castle, which looks a lot sounder than it is. Behind it is the island's college, with a demonstration croft and a specialism in weaving, while the only use of the castle is for a television studio. Since 1990, government investment in Gaelic television has made this one of the key growth areas in the islands' economy, and courses in TV skills and technology are popular with young people. Around the castle is a huge public garden, cleared of inhabitants by Lady Matheson and cultivated on imported soil with a rich variety of plants and shrubs. It provides a gentle walk and good views over the town. The commuter belt for Stornoway's middle class covers the road north-east to Tolsta (Tolstaigh) and its beaches. East on the Eye peninsula, also known as Point, there is the airport, also a NATO base, and a religious site dating back to the 7th century and sacred burial ground of nineteen MacLeod chiefs.

Getting to know Lewis, and seeing its biggest attractions, requires heading for the west coast. The road to Barvas (Barabhas), north-west out of Stornoway, crosses the bleakest of peat bogs, joining the west coast road which extends up to the Butt of Lewis by shadowing the coast about a mile inland. The land rises and falls gently, with villages apparently designed by haphazardly dropping Monopoly-like houses onto the terrain. Prehistoric sights to visit include the 5.7 metre standing stone at Ballantrushal (Baile an Truisail). Huge, simply-designed churches tower over the communities, the most notable being at Cross, where the Rev. Angus Smith is famed for his uncompromising sermons in Gaelic. He gained national attention while a minister on Skye in 1965, when he lay down on the slipway at Kyleakin with 50 burly Free Kirk men to protest at the start of Sunday ferry sailings. Cross also has the Lionel Stores, one of several village general shops with erratic opening hours and the musty air of a retailing museum. A more deliberate approach to Lewis history, and well worth a visit, is the Ness Historical Society at Habost (Tabost), a former builder's warehouse recently converted for the new Hebridean drive to provide tourists with an interpretation of local culture – and somewhere to go when it's raining. The Ness display is one of the better advanced, including parish records of who owned which crofts, emigration rolls, old newspapers, Free Church sermons from more than a century ago (not far removed from today's), a history of the Gaelic language, local football fanaticism and the tools used in traditional crofting. Forward-looking and in the same building, a tele-croft is planned, providing a community resource to learn and use computer technology, linking through Europe's most advanced telecommunications network to develop (it is hoped) distance learning and data-processing jobs for the islanders.

The prosperous village of Ness has a beautiful beach and small harbour, and nearby, at Europie (Eoropaidh), is the chapel of St Moluag, probably dating from the 12th century. It is still used for services by the Episcopal Church. At the island's north tip, the wind and wave-battered cliffs around the Butt of Lewis (Rubha Robhanais) lighthouse, built in 1862, are home to some of the islands' most accessible birdlife. Geologists have also been known to get excited there, because of the clear example of foliated gneiss. Forty-five kilometres to the north, on the island of Sula Sgeir, thousands of gannets nest on the cliffs, and it is there in August and September that the men of Ness traditionally go to gather the *guga*, or young gannets. These are regarded as a delicacy on Lewis but taste like tough, salty duck to most other people. To the west are the Flannan Isles, famed for a lighthouse where three keepers in 1900 mysteriously disappeared, leaving their meal untouched on the table.

For those spending the minimum time on Lewis, the A858 road south of Barvas and back to Stornoway makes for the best day tripping. It is, of course, more rewarding if given more time. The road passes by a six metre high whalebone arch at Bragar, from which is suspended the harpoon that killed the animal in 1919. First stop for the bus tours, and anyone else who knows what's good for them, is the Black House Museum (tigh dubh) at Arnol, thirty kilometres out of Stornoway. Black houses, until the 1930s, were the homes in which most island people lived: one storey with a thatch and turf roof, thick, unmortared walls and often connecting to the byre,

or animal shed. Their name came from their most distinctive feature – a peat fire burned in the centre of the house, which had no chimney through which to let out the smoke, so the inner walls were covered in soot. This helped keep the thatch and turf dry, but didn't do much for the health of those who lived in them. Black house remains can be seen all over the Hebrides, but Lewis has the most prevalent and extensive ones. The west-coast townships are built around large numbers of their remaining dry-stone walls. At Arnol, near the coast, the black house museum was occupied as a home until 1964, eleven years after electricity had been installed. It was opened to the public four years later, and remains, run by Government agency, with the same fittings and furniture in place: box straw beds, dresses, Harris Tweed bedclothes, the traditional cooking implements, and the peat fire kept burning by a taciturn warden, creating wonderful smoky effects when shafts of light from the small windows cut through the gloom. It is palatial compared with some other such homes, but gives a clear picture of living conditions even for many older Hebrideans who still live in more modern homes. For a more luxurious version of the lifestyle, surrounded by Scandinavian knotted pine fittings, the extensive, though ruined black house village at Garenin (Gearannan) near Carloway has a youth hostel under thatch. It was occupied by a woman who refused to take alternative council housing, because there would have been no byre for her cow. She moved when the cow died. If you visit, mind your head in the doorways.

Shawbost (Siabost), one of the island's main townships, lies to the south, with its own new secondary school, a folk museum created by the pupils and a campsite behind there. Further on are two of Lewis's finer beaches. Dalmore (Dal Mor) is the bigger, but a bit risky for bathers because of the undercurrents. It has a splendid example of the spectacularly beautiful places that Hebrideans, and especially Lewis folk, reserve for their cemeteries. If one gets a view from the grave, this is where to get buried. One of the most awesome Lewis sights, incidentally, is a Free Church funeral, with men – and only men – all wearing black and in solemn procession behind the coffin across the wild machair. Nearby is the smaller and safer bay, Dalbeg (Dal Beag), with a tearoom and picnic site.

The road heads down towards the large inlet of Loch Roag, which provides the shelter for much of the west coast lobster fishing and fish farms. It was here also that Lord Leverhulme wanted to base his fishing fleet. But valuing the loch's shelter and the extraordinary beauty of the landscape and sea in this area is nothing new. Almost two thousand years ago – or to be more accurate, between AD 43 and 400 – islanders chose Carloway (Carlabhaigh) to build a broch, a bottle-shaped stone tower, believed, though this is disputed, to have both a defensive and look-out function. Such buildings were peculiar to Scotland, and today, Carloway's broch is the finest one after Mousa on Shetland. Part of the wall still stands more than seven metres high – slightly less than its original height. The structure is almost fifteen metres in diameter, with its walls more than three metres thick in places, accommodating a stairwell to what was a second storey and thatch roof. The broch is a short walk up a rough path, and you can enter it through a low doorway, but the view on a half-decent day amply rewards such minimal exertion.

By the time the broch-builders got to work, the nearby Callanish stones had been in place for around 3,000 years. Though often compared with Stonehenge in southern England, they are of a different type, without the lintels between stones, which leaves them the most complete and intriguing example of such a standing stone circle in Britain. The stones stand thirty-five metres above Loch Roag, sharing with the broch a commanding view over the surrounding countryside and south to the Harris hills. Forty-seven stones form the shape of a Celtic cross, 120 by forty metres, with the highest ones rising to almost five metres. It remains a mystery – and the site genuinely feels mysterious – as to their exact purpose, but the group of standing stones were almost certainly concerned with burial and cremation, begun when the local cereal growers enjoyed a warmer Lewis climate. At their centre, archaeologists have excavated a crypt, and a chambered cairn added at a later stage. They also believe there may have been around thirty more stones, but these have been taken away or buried. Although the peat in which the stones stand has led to some movement over 5,000 years, there is broad agreement that the only explanation of the stones' pattern is linked to observation of the stars and sun to set an accurate calendar. Take some time to contemplate the stones when you visit. It doesn't require a new-age believer in ley-lines and druidic spirituality to feel this is a special place, not least because of its extraordinary antiquity. Five thousand years of history on this hilltop takes some time just to comprehend. The unworldliness may take something of a knock when a visitor centre is opened nearby, with restaurant, gift shop and, no doubt, tacky Callanish stone trinkets. Indeed, some Lewis people (or at least, some incomers) have objected to the building work. What they may not realise is that the stones themselves would have remained almost completely buried if Sir James Matheson, then the island's proprietor, had not opted to excavate them and remove more than a metre of peat from around them in 1857-58. There are three further stone circles on the hills surrounding the main Callanish site.

Beneath these hilltops and on the shore of Loch Roag are the townships centred around Breasclete (Breascleit). A large, incongruous brick building there used to be the supply base for the Flannan Isles lighthouse, and is now converted into flats. An even larger building was constructed in the early 1970s to boost

Religion

It is hard to travel far in the Hebrides, and even more difficult to understand them, without at least trying to get to grips with their religious cultures and influences. Perhaps it is in the Celtic race, perhaps it comes from the close-knit communities, perhaps from the adversities of life on the island; no one can definitively say the reason why faith plays such an important part in island life. But many visitors bring their backgrounds, misunderstandings and prejudices from the mainland of Britain and beyond, and dismiss the dominant role of religion as the weakness of a simple people who don't know any better, in the grip of overbearing church structures, and repressed by their priests and ministers. It is true these church leaders exercise power in secular island life which can be far from positive, having eroded much of the traditional musical culture from the Protestant isles, for instance. And the community does impose high expectations on the behaviour of church members. But the faith is closely tied to the islands' culture and Gaelic language, and can barely be judged by reference to mainland standards.

One of the most striking aspects of religion in the outer isles is the sharp divide between the Protestants who dominate to north of Benbecula and the Roman Catholics who are just as dominant in the south. (The presence of the British military between the two is, it should be said, purely coincidental.) In the south, the faith and culture appear to be similar to the west of Ireland, but unlike most of Scotland's Catholics, who live in west central Scotland, the Catholicism is not the result of Irish immigration. It probably dates back to pre-Reformation times, when followers of St Columba on Iona travelled throughout the islands spreading Christianity. In the early 17th century, the Roman church was not allowed to organise on the islands, and the people of the southern isles were resistant to conversion. In Barra, for instance, travellers noted that the people had kept a belief in Saint Finbarr, so the Roman Catholic church gradually regained a foothold when priests became re-established.

The Protestants from Benbecula northwards have developed a more distinctive approach, unlike anything else in the world – though visitors from smalltown, Bible-belt America may notice some similarities, perhaps based on a common Scots-Irish ancestry. The outward signs of the church influence are clear, especially on a Sunday, when many on the northern isles observe the Lord's Day with solemn reverence, prayer and Bible reading. The children's swings in Stornoway's playpark are famously padlocked on the Sabbath, and it can be difficult for the visitor to get food or any other service. And even the large, but rather cowed, minority who are not church-goers accept this as part of their culture, though it can reportedly be very frustrating for irreligious teenagers.

Other signs come from the people of the northern isles: generally reserved, quiet, dignified, warm and with a pawky humour. Their social lives are not carried out in public and in pubs, making the townships seem often lifeless to an outsider. But there can be a lively interchange between people's homes, with the occasional dram, great story-telling and ferocious gossip. They also tend to have a disturbingly keen interest in ecclesiastical history, strengthening the impression that island culture and faith are closely linked.

In 1824, a new Church of Scotland minister at the manse overlooking Uig sands began an evangelical revival, which was linked to the recent introduction of classes in reading the Gaelic Bible. This gave weight to Lewis's enthusiastic backing nineteen years later for what became known as the Disruption. This was a split between

Presbyterians over the role of the state in the running of the church: the law then allowed landlords to impose ministers against the will of their parishioners. So the Free Church was formed in 1843, when 430 ministers protested at this interference and walked out of the General Assembly of the Church of Scotland in Edinburgh. It caused a profound split throughout Scotland, but played to the independence of mind enjoyed by Lewis, Harris and Skye people in particular and strengthened their resolve in subsequent battles with landlordism. The Church of Scotland later lost the direct interference of the state and of landlords, and a slow reconciliation began. In 1900 and 1929, amalgamations of the fractured strands of the church brought the bulk of Presbyterian communities under the Church of Scotland – which is inaccurately called an established church as it remains formally separate from the state and the crown.

A minority of the Free Church, who are now known as 'Wee Frees', decided to maintain their independence of the mainstream Church, or Kirk. And although the Free Church exists throughout Scotland, its spiritual heartland is in the island of Lewis and Harris. Meanwhile the Free Church of Scotland had split again in 1893, over a question of interpreting the doctrine of salvation, and the breakaways formed the Free Presbyterian Church.

A bitter rift developed again in 1988, when Lord Mackay of Clashfern, a Free Presbyterian and the Lord Chancellor in Margaret Thatcher's cabinet, attended a Catholic requiem mass for a deceased friend. When his church found out he had been in a Catholic church (it has a profound antipathy to Rome), the elders threatened to expel him. But others disagreed and, with Lord Mackay, they set up their own breakaway church, the Associated Presbyterians Churches.

In the islands of North Uist, Harris, Scalpay, Lewis, Skye and Raasay, the splits remain between the Church of Scotland, the dominant Free Church of Scotland, and the two branches of the ultra-austere Free Presbyterians. Yet they are more like each other than many of their own denominations' parishes on the mainland, sharing a strong evangelical streak and an unyielding approach to liberal interpretations of traditional church doctrine.

Visitors are welcome to join in worship, although this is often conducted in Gaelic. For the Free Church, this is in the simplest of large buildings, barely decorated, with huge central pulpits from which the preacher will deliver intellectual and uncompromising sermons. A precentor stands below the minister to lead the congregation in singing unaccompanied psalms. The result is an astonishing and deeply soulful wailing sound.

Whatever you do, don't trifle with the church. The owner of Stornoway's cinema in the early 1970s wanted to show the somewhat liberal interpretation of the Gospel story in 'Jesus Christ Superstar'. A local clergyman cursed his cinema, but the screening went ahead anyway. Within days, or so the story goes, the movie-house had been struck by lightning and burned down.

the local economy with fishmeal processing. It was one of the more spectacular failures of the Highlands and Islands Development Board (and one they troubled to repeat in Barra with similar results) but the factory is now home to a pharmaceutical and health food company. Across Loch Roag is the island of Bernera, rocky, rugged and bleak, with the well-to-do fishing and shellfishing community of Circebost and accessible by crossing a bridge over the Atlantic. This was built from an' innovative concrete design in 1953, after islanders had threatened to build their own causeway by dynamiting cliffs. At Bernera's north end, Bosta (Bostadh), is another of the west coast's treasure of golden sandy bays.

The moor can take you back across the island to Stornoway or to the southeast townships in the aptly-named Lochs area, passing on the moor by the tiny bothies in which Lewis families used to spend summer tending sheep. But another road branches south from Callanish towards Uig. This road can become quite tortuous, but offers some wonderful scenery as it winds past the exclusive sporting estate centred on Little Loch Roag and Scaliscro Lodge towards the remains of an old nunnery beyond Brenish (Breanais). Towards the furthest reach of the road, the cliffs along this coast and the townships straggling by the roadside, give a real sense of this being the very edge of the world – as, of course, it was long believed to be. Unlike many of the other Hebridean islands, the west coast at this point offers little of the fertile, sandy machair which makes a life of exposure to Atlantic gales worthwhile.

The more hospitable parts of the Uig peninsula are sufficiently different from the rest of the island that even Stornoway people keep caravans here, allowing them to spend the weekend getting away from the frenzy of the east coast metropolis. The main site they use is at Valtos (Bhaltos). The larger dune-backed bay there is relatively sheltered and safe enough for bathing and children, but be careful of the heavy surf at the more spectacular beach nearby at Cliff (Cliobh), which is overlooked by an outdoor centre and the customary cemetery. Better still are the Uig sands, or Traigh Chapadail, a huge, broad and sheltered expanse which often features in Lewis photography. A small guest house and lodge overlook the pristine sands. It was on these sands, near Ardroil, in 1831, that a cow kicked over a large collection of chess pieces that had been buried there, giving its owner the impression that he had just discov-

ered the kingdom of the fairies. There were seventy-eight pieces, believed to belong to at least eight incomplete sets, and had probably been there since coming from Scandinavia in 1150 at a time when Lewis was controlled by the Vikings. The so-called Lewis chessmen, carved from walrus ivory, are reckoned to be the finest ancient set anywhere, and eleven pieces were taken away for display in Edinburgh's Museum of Antiquities and the rest sent to the British Museum in London. Replicas of the humorously depicted, squat figures are easily found in Lewis gift shops.

How to get there

Ferries
By a three-and-a-half-hour ferry crossing on CalMac's MV *Suilven* from Ullapool. Though the Wester Ross town lacks a rail connection, there are good bus connections on the mainland – Citylink from Glasgow and Caledonian Express from Edinburgh. It runs twice a day on most days, though not always at the most agreeable times, and never on a Sunday. The *Suilven* is a bit of an elderly tub, and not well-liked by the islanders who have to use it regularly. But in 1995, it is due to be replaced by a bigger and faster ship, making three trips a day. (CalMac, Stornoway: ☎0851 702361, or Ullapool: ☎0854 612358) Lewis is also accessible – and more cheaply – through the Skye-Harris sailing (see Harris) with day trips by bus available that way from Uig on Skye.

By air
Stornoway has a reasonably sized airport, with regular flights by British Airways from Glasgow, and much smaller Loganair planes connecting daily with Benbecula and Barra. British Airways: ☎0851 703240. Loganair: ☎0851 703067.

Getting about
Afrin Taxis, Stornoway: ☎0851 702092. Car Hire: Arnol Motors, ☎0851 71548, Lewis Car Rentals ☎0851 703760, Lochs Motor Transport ☎0851 705857, Mackinnon Self Drive ☎0851 702984.

Bicycle hire: Alex Dan Cycle Centre, 67 Kenneth St, Stornoway ☎0851 704025.

Buses connect Stornoway with Tarbert in Harris twice a day, and apart from visitors' tours, service buses link the main town with Ness in the north two or three times a day, Callanish and Carloway twice a day, and postbuses meander out to the Uig peninsula and Bernera once a day. (Contact Stornoway Tourist Office for times: ☎0851 703088).

Accommodation

Stornoway is a good base for those with a car, though it lacks the peace, quiet and environment that are the most attractive aspects of a Hebridean holiday. There are loads of bed and breakfasts around town and around the island. The major hotels include the Caberfeidh, two miles from the ferry terminal (☎0851 705572). The Seaforth is also on the edge of town and also caters for a business and bus party clientele, with a nightclub and cinema, on ☎0851 703900. Near the ferry are the Crown Hotel (☎0851 703181), the Caledonian (☎0851 702411) and the Royal (☎0851 702109). Out of Stornoway, lodges and former manses make the most characterful guest houses. These include Baile-na-Cille Guest House, overlooking Uig sands (☎0851 672242) and Scaliscro Lodge, also in Uig (☎0851 672393). There is the Cross Inn, with a bar, at the north end of the island.

Hostels

There is the Stornoway Hostel (☎0851 703628), the Bayble Bunkhouse (☎0851 870863) on the Point peninsula, and a thatched black house at Garenin (Gearrannan). There is caravanning and camping within walking distance of Stornoway centre, at Laxdale (☎0851 703234) north of Stornoway at Coll Sands (☎0851 703561), at Shawbost (indoor cooking facilities and nearby shop, contact Iain Macaulay (☎0851 710504) and at Valtos (Bhaltos) beach on Uig.

Where to eat

Most visitors eat in their hotel or guest house. The best of these, food-wise, is the Park Guest House (☎0851 702485) opposite the Seaforth Hotel in Stornoway. It takes non-residents, but remember to dress smartly. The Caberfeidh and Royal hotels offer quite expensive fare, while the Crown is recommended for good value. Outside Stornoway, there are bars with food or restaurants at several places, including Garynahine, Crowlista, a tearoom in Ness, Cross and Raebhat House in Shawbost.

Where to drink

Bars in Stornoway are designed to make those entering them feel deeply shameful. Drink is frowned upon darkly by the Free Church. One reason is that the Hebridean, for cultural, economic or climatic reasons, is given to quite serious abuse of the whisky bottle, and some of the bars have the seedy feel to go with that. In Stornoway, the Criterion is where the island's main politicking goes on, while the Crown is a reasonably pleasant place. This is famed for being the location of Prince Charles' first public taste of alcohol (cherry brandy), when he was under eighteen and on a school sailing visit. The upstairs bar is renamed the Prince of Wales Suite in his honour. There is a nightclub across the road. Go if you dare.

What to go and see

Arnol Black House Museum, open 9.30am–6.30 pm April to Sept, and shorter hours in winter. On the same west coast road are the Callanish stones and Carloway broch, both free of charge, with a visitor centre being built at Callanish. The Harris Tweed mill at Shawbost has tours at 11am during the week, in the tourist season. Lewis Castle College, behind the castle, has displays of crofting skills, including sheep-dog handling, shearing, spinning and weaving, You can try your own foot at Harris Tweed weaving. Tue and Thur 2.30 to 4.30 pm. There is a fish market at Stornoway quayside also on Tuesday and Thursday evenlngs.

Hebridean Holidays advertise outings including sea angling, shooting, birdwatching, diving and water-skiing

(☎0851 702303). They also hire wind-surfers, canoes, bikes and cars. Sea-angling on the boat *Elena C*: contact M. MacLeod at 5A Knock, Point (☎0851 703000). Or for a genuine feel of the shellfish fisherman's lot, you can go out for half a day lifting lobster and crab creels, tickets on sale at the tourist office. Stornoway's sea angling club is very active, with premises on South Beach Quay and temporary membership available (☎0851 702021). Loch and r1ver fishing requires permits from a variety of source; Stornoway Trust Estate Office (☎0851 702002) for River Creed and two lochs; Scaliscro Lodge for Garynahine, Scaliscro and North Eishken estates (☎0851 672325) or ask at the tourist office. The dedicated sportsperson should read Norman MacLeod's book on *Trout Fishing in Lewis*. Stornoway also has an 18-hole golf course in the castle grounds, with clubs for hire (☎0851 702240). There are guided walks around Stornoway and the castle grounds daily at 10 am, taking up to two and a half hours: tickets from the tourist office.

For wet days, in Stornoway, there is the sports centre, including a swimming pool, at the Nicolson Institute school and opposite the Seaforth Hotel (☎0851 702603). Shawbost's new school has some public facilities, also including a swimming pool. There are about a dozen community associations with centres open to the public for up to eight weeks during summer. They have indoor games, local historical displays, archives and snacks. Some are good, some are just adequate. In central Storno-way's South Beach, there is An Lanntair art gallery attached to one of the few places in the Outer Hebrides where you can get a good cup of coffee (Hebrideans are devout tea drinkers). It also has regu-lar ceilidh entertainments. Museum nan Eilean, the island museum, in Francis Street is also worth a look.

Events and festivals

Highland Games are in mid-July, along with a carnival. Feis Eilean an Fhraoich (the island's Gaelic festival) is in Storno-way primary school in early August, com-bining classes in traditional arts and language for children aged between 7 and 14, with evening entertainment for all.

Tourist information office: 26 Crom-well Street, between the fishing boats and Woolworths (☎0851 703088). Open all year. Plenty of brochures and guides, many at inflated prices.

Shopping

Stornoway is well-supplied for most purposes, with general supermarkets as well as more specialist services you won't find on other islands, ranging across florists, car dealers and a laun-drette. There are 38 Lewis outlets promoted by the island craft associa-tion, mainly producing tweed and knit-ting, with some pottery and stonework. A list is available at the tourist office, and there are craft fairs in Stornoway town hall during summer.

St Kilda

St Kilda is not one island but a group of islands some forty miles west of North Uist. Owned now by the National Trust for Scotland, it is leased to the Nature Conservancy Council, while part of Hirta, the largest island in the group, is sub-leased to the Ministry for Defence. There is an army camp and missile station on Hirta, which is just over three miles long.

The indigenous population were evac-uated on 29 August 1930 (Tom Steel's book, *The Life and Death of St Kilda*, tells their poignant story) leaving behind the remains of their village, testament to a remote and egalitarian community. The people were settled on the mainland, the men finding jobs with the Forestry Commission, which must have seemed odd coming from such a bare, treeless landscape.

The St Kildan's way of life was hard, even by Hebridean seandards. Food was not plentiful and seabirds, especially fulmars, became their staple fare, providing oil for their lamps as well as meat. The birds were stored in cleits – stone and turf construction found all over the island. Catching the birds and collecting eggs was a hazardous affair which involved scaling the terrifying cliffs and stacks on the island. The islanders also kept sheep, a hardy breed called Soay sheep, unique to the island, and some cattle which were kept in Gleann Mor, some miles from the village.

When you approach St Kilda, you get the impression, in Hirta's case at least, that the island is mountainous, but appearances are deceptive: once you climb the mountains you discover there is nothing on the other side but a sheer drop to the sea. St Kilda is often swathed in mist but the views on a clear day are stunning – it seems like the roof of the world. All those romantic cliches spring to mind – towering cliffs, sculpted landscapes besieged by the sea ... They're all very appropriate to St Kilda as this island, more than any other Scottish island, lives in the imagination of many people who will never make the trip.

The main settlement, at Village Bay, has been sensitively restored by the National Trust. In summer, it's possible to join a working party and participate in preserving this vital record of a remote and arduous existence. The houses were built in the 1860s: this is where the people met to discuss the business of the island – the St Kilda Parliament, as it's known. (A famous photograph shows the 'parliament': the men lined up on either side of the 'street'.)

Today, St Kilda has been left to the birds: fulmars, puffins, guillemots, razorbills, kittiwakes and gannets.

How to get there
There are no scheduled ferries to the island but several companies will take you there. It's probably a good idea to contact the National Trust for Scotland before you go there.

For those who fancy a 5-star luxury country-house experience afloat, try the *Hebridean Princess* cruise (☎0756 701338) which departs from Oban and call into various ports, including St Kilda. Prices begin at £750 and go up to £7,000 for a 14-night trip.

Coming back down to earth:
Kylebhan Charters operate from May to August. Private charters available (☎0389 877028). They also sail to Islay and Jura from Oban and to the Small Isles.

Fishing boat cruises on the MV *Monaco* from Oban. Contact Amelia Dalton (☎0254 826591 or ☎0831 121156). The same company also island-hop to most of the Inner Hebrides, the smaller uninhabited islands of the Outer Hebrides and the Isle of Man.

Working parties
Work parties have been travelling to St Kilda for thirty-six years now to restore the buildings on Hirta. In recent years, parties have worked on archaeological excavations. Special skills – building, plumbing and carpentry, for example, are useful but not essential. You will be expected to pay for your time there (around £350–£400 for a fortnight at the time of going to press) – this includes transportation from Oban and all food. More details and a leaflet can be obtained from the National Trust for Scotland, 5 Charlotte Square, Edinburgh, EH2 4DU (☎031-226 5922).

Accommodation
Extremely limited as you'd imagine, unless you're part of a working party. There's a small campsite on the island.

Where to eat
Well, take your pick.

Orkney

Introduction

The southern tip of Orkney is only eight miles from the Scottish mainland, but the high red cliffs of Hoy (easily visible from the Caithness coast) act as a kind of rampart, hiding the green heart of Orkney from the eyes of the south. The surprise is that much greater and more pleasant then, when the ferry hauls around the Kame of Hoy, and comes out of the shadow of the majestic but rather intimidating cliffs and into a world of low, rolling, green-and-gold islands. More fertile and intensively farmed than is usually imagined, the land of Orkney is, on the whole, not particularly 'Highland' at all. In fact, it's not particularly like anywhere, except itself. True, the islands are geologically and botanically pretty similar to nearby bits of Scotland; true too, the accents and attitudes of the Orcadians owe a lot to the centuries their ancestors spent under Norse rule; and certainly true, the trappings of modern British life – from shell suits to satellite TV - are turning up here more and more. What makes Orkney unique is the way all these different elements are blended together: the way people come to terms with the landscape and the climate, the way the islands' history – just as unavoidable as the weather – influences and colours contemporary life.

Acre for acre, Orkney has more archaeological remains than anywhere else in Northern Europe. Several of these monuments – Skara Brae, Maes Howe – are of great individual importance. But most significant for the resident (or visitor) is the fact that virtually everywhere you look you see evidence of six thousand years of continuous inhabitation. This ranges from the standing stones and mud-midden homes of the earliest Neolithic settlers, through the brochs and round houses of the Iron Age Picts, to the cathedral and smaller kirks of the period when Orkney was part of Scandinavia, home to great numbers of Norse settlers and their descendants. And on through the castles and palaces of the Scottish earls who ruled from the 16th century onwards (and earned a much worse popular reputation than the Vikings ever did), on to the harbours and merchants' stores of the last century, the bunkers and gun-emplacements of two world wars, right up to the oil terminal flares and the feed-silos and the supermarkets of the 1990s.

Who could fail to have their ideas about time affected by this? Who could look around and still feel the same about the passing of the days and years and decades? The monuments of six thousand years – and, with a little imagination, the lives of the folk who built them – are laid out in front of you. Individual short-term worries seem less important, less overwhelming somehow, when seen against a background of sixty centuries' struggle. And yet this long-term perspective on human life, and the consequent respect for the endurance of the land beneath the feet of the generations, seem to create precisely the attitudes that place the greatest value on the individual, the greatest respect for human values and needs. It is a rare visitor to Orkney who does not come away with an affection, not just for the great beauty of the islands, but for the warmth, openness and hospitality of the islanders.

George Mackay Brown, who has lived all his life in Stromness, is the author of many novels, poems and stories. They all speak eloquently of island life, of the quality of the minutes and centuries here, and they are all filled with a sharp-eyed but generous view of humanity. They are essential reading before, during and after any visit to Orkney. The novel *Greenvoe* and the story collection *Hawkfall* might be good places to start; his *Portrait of Orkney* is a non-fiction book with many photographs and drawings.

Orkney has produced many writers over recent decades: Edwin Muir is best known for his meditative poetry, Eric Linklater for his comic novels, Hugh Marwick for his work on dialect and place names, Ernest Marwick for folklore and historical studies, Robert Rendall for his poetry (the best of it in Orcadian dialect) and books on shore life. There are many more, stretching right back to the anonymous author(s) of the *Orkenyinga Saga*, 'The History of the Earls of Orkney', which dates to around 1200 (though strictly speaking the saga isn't Orcadian: it was actually written down in Iceland). There are also many excellent individual volumes. Depending on how long you're going to be here for, you might look at (from the briefest to the most in depth): Gordon Wright's *A Guide to the Orkney Islands*, Charles Tait's *The Orkney Guide Book*. Leslie Burgher's *Orkney: an Illustrated Architectural Guide*, Anna Ritchie's *Exploring Scotland's Heritage: Orkney and Shetland*, Gregor Lamb's *Testimony of the Orkenyingar*, William Thomson's *History of Orkney* and Mary Welsh's *Walks in Orkney*. (Tait's Guide includes a long list of other Orkney books, many of them now out of print.) The most informative and readable book covering all aspects of island life from geology to folk tales to modern agriculture and industry is Liv Schei's *The Orkney Story,* which features outstanding photographs by Gunnie Moberg. The best maps are numbers 5, 6 and 7 in the Ordnance Survey's *Landranger* series (1:50 000 scale); depending on which islands you're going to, you may not need all three. The OS's *Pathfinder* series covers the whole area in much greater detail: useful for ambitious walkers. Finally, essential reading while you are here is *The Orcadian,* published every Thursday. This has all the news, a column by GMB, and invaluable timetables for ferries and buses, adverts for concerts and dances etc etc. A more leisurely look at local life is taken in *The Orkney View*, a magazine which comes out every two months.

Finally a word of apology to anyone who lives in Orkney, or knows it well from previous visits, and finds their favourite monument or beach or bird-cliff left out. There simply wasn't enough space to include details of everything worth seeing. That would take ten times this number of pages at least. What I've tried to do is to include all the important sites, and as many of the smaller wonders as possible. Inevitably, my favourite places will not be the same as yours, but I can guarantee everything here *is* worth a visit. First-time visitors: you'll find a lot of great places I haven't mentioned. They should be doubly enjoyable.

How to get there

Ferries
P&O Scottish Ferries operate a service throughout the year between Scrabster (near Thurso) and Stromness. The journey, on the *St Ola* ro-ro (roll-on/roll off, takes an hour and three quarters, and passes the wonderful cliff scenery of Hoy, including the Old Man. During the summer there are several crossings a day. Booking for vehicles is essential, but not usually necessary for foot passengers (☎0856850655). P&O also run a triangular service between Aberdeen, Stromness and Lerwick on the *St Sunniva*, another big ro-ro. This journey lasts between eight and fourteen hours depending on the time of year, and frequently involves sleeping on the boat overnight. Booking recommended (☎0856 850655).

During the summer months, Thomas and Bews operate a passenger-only service between John O' Groats and Burwick in South Ronaldsay. This is cheap and quick (about 40 minutes) and a bus meets the ferry to take passengers on to Kirkwall (though you have to pay separately for that.) No booking required, but for details of times ☎0955 81353.

A relatively new service is the one between Invergordon and Kirkwall run by Orcargo. As the name suggests, this is primarily intended for commercial customers, but it's proved popular with folk wanting to avoid the long drive to Scrabster (☎0856 873838).

If you have a car, then getting to Scrabster or John O' Groats is no problem: you just follow the A9 all the way north.

Public transport is trickier. Scottish Citylink Coaches operate a daily service between Inverness (and connections south) and Thurso/Scrabster. This is cheap and reliable, but you should make sure that you are definitely getting a coach that connects with a ferry. This is espcially important in winter, when ferries are less frequent. Citylink's number is ☎041-332 9191. British Rail operate a daily service between Inverness (and connections) and Thurso/Wick. There are worries that this could be in danger following privatisation, but it's there for the moment. Again, check that your arrival time in Thurso will allow you to catch a ferry. Failing that, there's a youth hostel at John O' Groats. BR will give you up to date information on times, fares etc: ☎041-204 2844.

By Air
British Airways (☎0345 2221111) and Loganair (☎0856 873457) fly six days a week throughout the year to Kirkwall. Between them they come from Edinburgh, Glasgow, Aberdeen, Inverness, Wick and Shetland. Ask about special apex fares; usually you need to book these a couple weeks in advance, but they can bring costs down considerably. Once you arrive at Kirkwall airport (sometimes called Grimsetter), you'll have to get a taxi into town. This costs four or five pounds and takes ten minutes; there's no airport bus service.

Tourist information
The two Orkney Tourist Board offices are listed individually below, but they're so important that I'll repeat them here too. The Kirkwall office is in Broad Street, and its number is ☎0856 872856. The Stromness office is at the pierhead, and its number is ☎0856 850716. For any information you can't find below, phone them.

Camping
There are a few official campsites, and these are listed in the appropriate sections. Generally, though, farmers in areas without organised sites will be happy to let you stay a night or two on a suitable piece of their land. It's a very good idea to check first, though, and not just assume this.

Fishing
Not unusually for an island group, water surrounds Orkney. Sea fishers will therefore find plenty of places to try their luck on mackerel, cod, ling, coalfish etc. Shore fishing is good if you know the right rocks to stand on, and boats can be hired from most harbours; ask the tourist offices for up to date contacts. Inland fishing for both brown and sea trout) is especially good. Access to all the lochs, including the outstanding Harray Loch, is free, though it would be polite and useful to you to join the Orkney Trout Fishing Association. Details of the small fee and other useful information from the tackle shops in Stromness and Kirkwall. Champion flyfisher Stan Headley has written an invaluable guide to all the lochs, recommended flies etc: *A Trout Fishing Guide to Orkney*.

Tours
If you're having difficulty getting around to some of the places of interest, or if you just fancy having an expert guide along, try one of the minibus tours, all of which should be enjoyed, even by folk who usually hate bus tours. Go-Orkney, run by David and Liz Lea, operates a wide range of tours (and associated walks) seven days a week during the summer, less during the winter. They are long-established, and very popular. Bookings via the tourist office or direct on ☎0856 874260. Wildabout concentrate on natural history, but also take in most of the major sites. Details from ☎085675 307. Finally, Rousay Traveller will show you around their own island, and the neighbouring ones by arrangement. Again, good for wildlife and archaeology ☎0856 82234.

How the sections are arranged
There's no 'correct' route to travel around Orkney, and the following island-by-island sections could be

arranged in almost any order. But I've settled on the fact that most visitors still arrive by boat at Stromness, and have started there, gradually moving out to cover the countryside and islands immediately adjacent, then on to Kirkwall and the islands south of there by road, and north by boat.

If you look at a decent map of Orkney, you'll notice that I don't mention about fifty of the islands in the group. Most of these are very small – some little more than skerries – and all now uninhabited, though some, like Eynhallow, Fara, Papa Stronsay and North Faray are sizeable and have been lived on till fairly recently. An interesting afternoon can be spent exploring these – if you can persuade someone to ferry you over there. There are a couple of other islands that are inhabited by just one family, and to which no scheduled ferry runs. I haven't mentioned these either, because, if you know the folk they can invite you themselves, and if you don't know them you probably shouldn't invade their privacy (which is doubtless one of the reasons they wanted to live on an island by themselves in the first place).

Stromness

Stromness must be the most attractive town in the Scottish islands. Its jumble of two and three hundred year-old houses steps right out of the water of the sheltered harbour and climbs away up the steep side of Brinkie's Brae. One long main street runs parallel to the shoreline, and off it zigzag dozens of narrow lanes or wynds with evocative names like Puffer's Close and the Khyber Pass, the gaps between the crammed-together houses create natural frames for glimpses of sea, sky, boats, birds. At times the street is barely three metres across, at other points it opens out into

a quiet square, but always it is paved with big slabs of local flagstone, which blend in with the grey harling or weathered rubble of the buildings. Depending on the time of day and the state of the weather, Stromness can be full of smokey and silvery blues, or warm shadows of pink and brown. At all times, though, except for the coldest, wettest winter nights, Stromness is a busy place, a friendly place, a lively place: a small town that charms just about every visitor that sets foot here.

Although there had been settlements in these parts at least since Viking times, it was in the 18th century that Stromness began to boom as a port, often used by vessels sailing northabout to avoid the dangers of the English Channel. There were also the whalers – as many as 34 at one time in 1816 – taking in stores and crew before leaving for the arctic seas. And for twenty years or so at the end of the 19th century, the port was full of as many as 400 boats and 5000 gutters and packers working on the herring. During two world wars, Stromness again reached peaks of activity, as it became HQ to the massive naval fleets that moved through Scapa Flow. Through the decades, too, the town was carrying on its business as a trading port, a market town, and a focus for the farming lands to the north and east.

It's still all these things today. The fishing fleet is down to a handful of vessels, and the mart is on the point of amalgamating with the one in Kirkwall. But Stromness is still where much of Orkney's freight and most of its people come ashore. And there's a good selection of shops butchers, grocers, the best baker in the islands, craft shops, drapers, hardware stores – to keep drawing folk in from all over the West Mainland – despite the increasing pull of a supermarketised Kirkwall. One shop in particular is a must for any visitor: Stromness Books and Prints in Graham Place (☎0856 850565). All the maps and most of the books mentioned in the guide are available there, as well as an amazingly wide range of others, from

The Social History of the Potato through a good selection of Scottish and Scandinavian fiction to Why *Not Eat Insects?*

Three more cultural essentials: The Pier Arts Centre in Victoria Street (☎0856 850209), the Bu Gallery at the pierhead (☎0856 851169), and the Stromness Museum in Alfred Street (☎0856 850025). The Pier, a converted 18th-century store on its own jetty, features an important collection of works by such artists as Ben Nicolson and Barbara Hepworth, as well as regular visiting exhibitions, often featuring the work of local artists. It's a remarkably lively and forward-looking gallery for such a small town. The large and varied group of painters and sculptors who were born here, or have settled, are featured in the Bu's exhibitions; as well as the art, you can buy antiques and curios here. Downstairs in the Museum is a wide selection of artefacts, pictures and models illustrating the town's historic links with the sea and the lands beyond the sea. Upstairs is a collection of stuffed birds and beasts, and interesting displays of shells, crabs and fossils. (Pioneer geologist Hugh Miller did some of his most important work nearby. Look for your own fossils – they show up as black coal-like shapes in the grey flags – on the shore just to the west of the kirkyard: there's an outcropping of the Sandwick Fish Bed here.)

Once you've seen all of Stromness, head out into the country. A rewarding short walk is up to the top of Brinkie's Brae, the hundred metre hill which shelters the town from the west wind. From the top you get fine views of the harbour and houses below, the hills of Hoy, and most of Scapa Flow with boats coming and going, and the gas flare burning on Flotta. Head out the south end, past the golf course, and round the point. From here you can walk a mile to the kirkyard and the fine beach at Warebeth, then on to the 17th-century bishops' residence at Breckness House and the spectacular cliffs at Black Craig. If you keep on walking, you can spend a whole day heading north to Yesnaby then on to Skara Brae. Great scenery and plenty of seabirds and salty wind all the way.

Heading out of the town in the other direction is the foot ferry to Hoy and Graemsay (see following sections for details). During the summer you can also head out on the schooner *Enterprise* and sail around the Flow for a few hours, watching birds, seals, and the wind in the sails. A light meal is usually served, often of something unusual like Spoot Chowder. (Spoots being razor clams; Orkney is one of the few places in Britain this delicacy is still appreciated.) A great relaxing way to spend an afternoon or evening (☎0856 872856 or ☎0831 101788).

Stromness is the centre for one of the most popular areas for leisure diving in Europe. The blockships and scuttled German Grand Fleet (deliberately sunk in 1919 rather than be allowed into the hands of the enemy, even after the armistice) make the Flow a must for divers interested in exploring wrecks. The water is clear and relatively sheltered, and there is much interesting marine life too. If you're a diver you've probably heard about the Flow already; if you're not a diver, this is mostly pretty advanced stuff – 'it's deep, spooky and dangerous,' one expert said – not ideal for beginners. Information about hiring boats and gear, buying books (including the full guide, *Dive Scapa Flow* by Rod MacDonald) and charts, and finding accommodation, talk to the Diving Cellar: (☎0856 850055 or ☎0856 850395).

Stromness has more to offer than there is space to list here. A few further points of interest, though: swimming pool and fitness suite, squash courts, health centre, putting green (summer only), community centre with children's activities, frequent live music in pubs (good fiddle and accordion in the Royal most Saturday nights), occasional readings, lectures and recitals by poets, painters and musicians, courtesy of the Orkney Arts Society, and some of the best home-brewers in the world.

How to get there

Stromness is the main ferry port to the south (see general introduction). It's an ideal base for exploring the west Mainland by car or bike (both of which can be hired here) and drivers at least will find the rest of the mainland and the southern isles easily within range. Walkers will have to rely on a limited bus service; basically, you can get to Kirkwall (along the main A965) and that's it. (With a bit of forward planning, you can make the connections there for other destinations.) Peace's buses run to the centre of Kirkwall roughly every hour, six days a week, from outside the Town House at the pierhead: ☎0856 872866 for details.

Food and drink

The best place to eat in Stromness is the Hamnavoe restaurant, just off Graham Place; it's only open in the evenings, and only during the summer. Good use of local produce, friendly atmosphere. Booking advised (☎0856 850606). The Coffee Shop, next to the launderette, fifty metres to the right as you come off the pier, has a frequently changing menu, including various vegetarian meals. On the left at the pierhead is the Cafe (formerly Raymie's) which does a lot of pizzas and burgers, has a good view over the harbour, and is open late. It's also licensed. The Peedie Coffee Shop at the start of Dundas Street lives up to its name (peedie is Orcadian for small); a fine place for a cup of tea and a cream bun. All the hotels do bar meals, some of them have slightly more ambitious dining rooms; the Ferry Inn is probably the best. The bars (all in hotels) all have something to recommend themselves: the Braes has the best view, the Royal has the best atmosphere, (and the best fish tank), the Stromness has the best disco. You'll have to try them all.

Accommodation

As well as the town's five hotels, (all of which are adequate, though my first choices would be the Braes (☎0856 850495), there are many B&Bs, and several self-catering flats and cottages. There are also two hostels: an SYHA one on Hellihole Road, and a popular private one, Brown's (☎0856 850661), on Victoria Street (which also hires bikes). There's a council-run camping and caravan site out on the windy Point of Ness; advance booking recommended during the summer: (☎0856) 873535.

Events and festivals

At the end of May each year, the town is the centre for the Orkney Traditional Folk Festival. Formal concerts and pub sessions spill over into parties. A great long weekend for anyone even slightly interested in the music of Orkney, Scotland, and Scandinavia. (☎0856 850516 for details.) Stromness always has some St Magnus Festival events during June; see Kirkwall for more on that. Towards the end of July is the Stromness Shopping Week, which isn't a celebration of consumerism as its name might suggest. It's the town's gala week, with exhibitions of flowers, crafts, and art, also childrens' entertainers, a daft raft race, golf competitions, open air dances at the pierhead and Graham Place, and a parade around the streets of comical and satirical tractor-drawn floats. And much much more!

Golf

There is a fine eighteen-hole course at the Point of Ness. Around midsummer, it's light enough to play till almost midnight. By the clubhouse are a bowling green and tennis court. Non-members are welcome at all of these.

Riding

Horses can be hired from the Traill-Thomsons at Garson: ☎850304. There are many beaches and quiet roads nearby.

Tourist information

In the Terminal Building at the pierhead is a branch of the Orkney Tourist Board (☎0856 850716), an essential port call for information about everything in the islands: excellent leaflet guides to the different islands, help with accommodation, timetables for buses and ferries, up to date details of tours and shows and other events. Also a small exhibition about Orkney life.

Graemsay

'A broad and beautiful sound or strait divided this lonely and mountainous island [Hoy] from Pomona [the Mainland], and in the centre of that sound lies, like a tablet composed of emerald, the beautiful and verdant island of Graemsay.'

Such was Sir Walter Scott's opinion following his visit to Orkney in 1814. Note that, like most visitors to Orkney, he didn't actually set foot on the island; Graemsay remains one of the least visited Orcadian isles: this neglect is quite unjustified.

Graemsay is roughly two miles long and one mile wide. It rises to a height of about sixty metres in its centre, where there is an area of rough heathery moor; most of the island, though, is gently sloping, well cultivated farmland. Viewed from Stromness, or the passing Ola, the strongest impression of Graemsay is still of neat green fields, edged by the long gold blade of Sandside beach on the north side.

The island's size makes it perfect for a day trip, arriving on the early morning boat from Stromness and leaving on the same boat in the late afternoon. Anybody thinking about staying longer should note that there is no accommodation available, and no shop. Anyway, you can probably see all the interesting parts of Graemsay in a single day, if you don't dawdle too much.

You'll land at the pier at the west end of the island. Start walking clockwise round the coast, and you'll soon be passing an outcropping of the Sandwick Fish Bed, the fossil-rich seam of rock that also surfaces to the west of Stromness. Close by you'll see more modern historical remains: the first of many abandoned houses and crofts that are scattered over Graemsay. (The population reached a peak of 250 in the middle of the last century; now it's barely a tenth of that.) Situated right on

the south side of the island is a 19th-century church, now disused; following the road inland from here will take you past the tiny but well-equipped school to the highest point of the island, and magnificent views of the hills of Hoy, and the blockships sunk there to keep out U-boats) in the mouth of the Burra Sound below. The verges are full of flowers; apart from the occasional tractor, the only sound you're likely to hear is birdsong. Oh yes, and the wind; round about here you'll pass the well-named farm of Windywalls!

The west, Atlantic-facing, coast features many interesting rock formations – tiny stacks, cliffs and geos – hours could be spent exploring these nooks and crannies. At the extreme western Point of Oxan is Hoy Low lighthouse, a squat but not unattractive building, with massive surrounds to the accommodation doors, apparently based on the style of Ancient Egyptian temples! Next door to it is a well-preserved Second World War observation tower apparently based on Legoland forts. A short distance to the east of Hoy Low is a tiny cup of a bay, with a sandy beach and small jetty; just offshore from here is the Skerry of Cletts, a favourite seal basking place. A great basking place for humans is the long sweep of clean white sand that edges the Bay of Sandside half a mile further on; rest here a while and gaze across at Stromness, glad to be away from the hectic rush of the place for the day. But don't stop too long, for a little further on is a beach made up of crushed white and pink coral; although you find wee pieces of coral along many Orkney shores, I think this is the only beach entirely made out of the stuff. Just inland from the western end of Sandside Bay is a small wood-panelled community centre; this is probably your best bet if you need to shelter from an outbreak of unpleasant weather. But it won't provide you with anything else apart from basic shelter.

You're almost back to where you started now. But leave time to have a look at the thirty-three-metre-tall Hoy High, 'the

Rolls-Royce of Orkney's lighthouses', as the *Architectural Guide* puts it. Like its stumpy companion, it was built by Alan Stevenson in 1851. A few hundred metres more and you're back at the pier, just in time – if my calculations are right – to be picked up by the boat back to Stromness. At the moment you can only get to and from Graemsay three days a week – so don't miss your return journey, or you could be stranded! – but calls for a much improved service, possibly including ro-ro facilities, seem to be being taken note of by the council. This improvement would certainly be a great boon to Graemsay's residents, but it would also surely encourage more visitors to the island; though not, I hope, too many car-drivers: even one or two visitors driving around would do a lot to spoil the peace of the island, which is one of its most attractive qualities.

How to get there

Stevie Mowat's passenger ferry, the *Jessie Ellen,* visits Graemsay on Mondays, Wednesdays and Fridays, on her way between Stromness and from Hoy. Check details at the pierhead, or by phoning (☎0856 850624. The *Hoy Head* leaves Houton for Graemsay on Wednesday mornings, returning in the afternoon. Check with the Orkney Islands Shipping Company (OISC) on (☎085 681 397 for details.

Flotta

Hundreds of people visit Flotta every day, but it only gets a handful of tourists per year. The visitors are going to work at the Elf oil terminal there, which is one of the four in Britain that receive and process crude oil and gas from the North Sea; Flotta can take up to half a million barrels of crude a day from seven fields – including Claymore and Piper – a couple of hundred miles to the east. The crude is cleaned and separated, then shipped all over the world in the massive tankers which slip in and out of the southern end of Scapa Flow.

Previous to the arrival of the terminal in the mid-seventies, Flotta had been a very quiet island of fishermen and farmers for hundreds of years – except for periods during both world wars, when it became an important link in the Navy's defences around its Scapa anchorage and it seemed likely that it might eventually go the way of its smaller but once populous neighbour, Fara, and be totally abandoned. That now seems unlikely, for the presence of the terminal has brought a lot of modernisation to the island, in the shape of mains water and electricity, improved roads and a good pier; it seems that, even when all the oil has been sucked out of the North Sea (current estimates are that it'll last till 2050 or thereabouts) Flotta will return to the life it's lived for centuries, with rather more security and comfort than would have seemed possible twent-five years ago.

The terminal is vast, and covers virtually the whole of the north of the island, but the southern half is remarkably untouched: still very quiet, still with its flowered verges, its seabirds and seals, still with its farmers working away – seemingly light-years removed from the billion-pound complex a few hundred metres over the hill. There is a plain but peaceful kirk near the southern shore; half a mile to the east of there, near Stanger Head, are two gloups and two small sea-stacks, The Cletts, popular with puffins during the summer.

Popular with rabbits is the north-east leg of the island, Golta; note the number of white, black and ginger animals, descendants of escaped wartime pets. Other reminders of the war are provided by the many impressive (impressively ugly?) concrete gun emplacements and watch towers that are scattered throughout the island.

On the south shore of Pan Hope, a long and broad inlet into the east side of the island, whose name comes from the siting there of salt-pans during the 17th century, lies the post-office at Lairdy. There is no accommodation or tourist information centre on the island, no particular entertainments laid on, but you couldn't hope for a more informed and friendly place to find out whatever you want to know than here. Not much has been written about Flotta, but in 1992 Anne Buxton and Jacqueline McEwan's *The Orkney Chronicles 1900 & 1989* was published; it contains an account of their journey to the island in the footsteps of an earlier traveller, Brenda Murray, as well as Murray's own diary. Both journals contain interesting observations; the modern one is marred by a rather patronising attitude to Orkney and its inhabitants.

Elf are committed to removing all traces of the terminal when they finally leave, and returning the north end of Flotta to its unspoilt state. The fact that the site has won several prizes for the way it fits into its surroundings and for its good record in protecting the marine environment lends weight to their promise. Certainly there is no shortage of folk on Flotta and throughout Orkney keeping an eye on their activities. Indeed, if you live anywhere near Scapa Flow, its impossible not to have your eye caught by the almost-constant orange flare burning off excess gas at the top of its thirty-metre stack. It's worth taking a day-trip to Flotta and seeing the oil-age rubbing shoulders with the sheep-age. It's also interesting to consider that the sheep will certainly be there a long time after the oil has gone.

How to get there

OISC ro-ro ferries leave from Houton on the mainland half a dozen times a day for Flotta and Lyness in Hoy. The journey to Flotta can take as little as twenty

minutes, or as much as an hour and twenty, depending on whether the boat goes to Lyness first. Booking essential for cars (☎085 681 397.

Hoy

Hoy is the biggest island in Orkney, after the mainland; it's also the most popular with visitors, and with good reason. At nearly fifteen miles long, it's one of the few islands where a car might seem essential; I wouldn't go that far, but the fact that the interesting features of the place are divided in two, half at the North end and half ten miles away down in the South with not much in between but heather, hills and views over the Flow – does mean some stiff walking or cycling, if you want to try and see everything. And there is a lot to see...

If you're on foot, you'll probably arrive at Moaness. The road climbs quite steeply for half a mile or so, with the first turning on the left leading to the Hoy Inn (and on to the southern end of the island) and the second one to the youth hostel and the road to Rackwick Bay. But walk straight on, past Sandy Loch and into the deep glen formed by Ward Hill (on your left) and the Cuilags (on your right). These hills are the features that gave Hoy its name – the Old Norse Haey, 'high island' – and Ward Hill (479 metres) is by far the highest of all the Ward Hills in Orkney. From the top you can see all the islands in the group, except the closest, Rysa Little, which is hidden by a lumpy bit of Hoy coast. That's on a clear day. On a foggy day you can't see your feet in front of you, and attempting the precipitous sides of these hills would be extremely dangerous, not to mention extremely wet.

Forge on for an hour or so and, shortly after passing the birches, willows and ferns of Berriedale, the only surviving natural woodland in Orkney, the glen opens out into the magnificient Rackwick bay. This is a mile-wide bite out of the otherwise sheer west side of the island, with great red cliffs rising to over a hundred metres on each side. For a long time Rackwick was known as the loneliest and most beautiful place in Orkney, but now it's so famous for being lonely that it's often crowded out: on a sunny day there may be as many as twenty people here at any one time! It's still beautiful, though.

The full force of the Atlantic and the prevailing wind smashes into Rackwick, and during winter storms the air is filled with an incredible rumbling and crashing, as if thunder were pouring up out of the sea. Actually, it is the waves pounding in and playing marbles with the enormous boulders – some two or three metres across, all rounded like pebbles – that make up the beach. Climb up away from the shore past the hostel, and take the well-trodden path to the Old Man of Hoy. Despite the ubiquity of its image on everything from sweatshirts to oatcake packets, the real thing – a 137 metre stack of fissured and layered sandstone, red as the Forth Rail Bridge, standing clear of the cliffs in the battering Atlantic waves – is still always breathtaking. With a little care and attention to the weather, anyone can make this walk; it's well worth it. Ambitious walkers can carry on northwards over St John's Head – at 346 metres, one of the highest cliffs in Britain – and eventually back to Moaness. In anything but perfect weather, it's much more sensible to head back to Rackwick, and then on through the southern of the two big glens to visit the Dwarfie Stane, a unique five thousand year-old tomb. It's hollowed out of a single enormous block of stone, and lies underneath the louring slopes of the Dwarfie Hammars surrounded by barren boggy moor; interestingly, at the time the tomb was in use, the glen was almost certainly extensively cultivated and settled.

Almost all the present day cultivation is at the southern end of Hoy, and on the peninsula of South Walls, which curls round to enclose the long 'hope' or bay, which gives the village there its name. Longhope has a slightly run-down air about it, its heyday having been at the time of the Napoleonic wars, when it was an important stopping-off place for shipping sailing north to avoid the dangerous English Channel. Francis Groome relates how 'it was no uncommon thing for a fleet of upwards of a hundred vessels to be lying windbound in this harbour; and a fine sight it was to see them spread their canvas to the breeze and move majestically along the shores of the island'. An interesting relic of these days is the massive Martello Tower at Rackness, built in 1815, and now preserved and open to visitors.

Travel back over the narrow 'aith' to the south end of Hoy (known, rather confusingly, as North Walls) and you will see the chimneys of Melsetter House through the trees on your left. Melsetter was designed by W. R. Lethaby in 1898 under the influence of the Arts and Crafts Movement, and is the most attractive large house in Orkney; original Morris fabrics and fittings are still in place. Melsetter is a private home, and viewing is by appointment only; a book by Trevor Garnham has recently been published on it, though, full of descriptions, plans and colour photographs.

Three or so miles north from Melsetter is Lyness; if you arrived by car, this'll be where you'll be heading back to. But it's worth a visit anyway, for a look around the Naval Base and Interpretation Centre. During both world wars, Scapa Flow was one of the Navy's major anchorages (see *This Great Harbour Scapa Flow* by R. S. Hewison for the full story), and the islands around it were swarming with sailors – and the army and airforce personnel who protected them. Lyness was one of the major centres of operations, and the remains of bunkers, gun emplacements, lookout towers, workshops and accommodation blocks are all around. The large building that housed (in fact, still does house, oil-pumping equipment has been restored and provides a history of Lyness's military past; even if you don't fancy playing with machine guns, torpedoes, gasmasks etc., this is still a fascinating piece of social history. Best of all is the unbelievably big oil tank nearby, now emptied of its 12,000 tons of oil, and open for visitors to walk around in and scare themselves with amazing echoes.

I've been concentrating on human activity on Hoy, but in fact the vast bulk of the island is unmarked by any of that at all: 90% of it, everything west of the north-south road that hugs the Scapa Flow coastline, is high heathery moor ending in spectacular Atlantic cliffs. if you like hiking over untrodden hillsides, falling into bogs, being plagued by midges, startled by mountain hares and attacked by the bonxies (Great Skuas), then this is the place for you. The nearest you'll come to another human being all day is when the *St Ola* sails past on its way to Scrabster!

How to get there
Stevie Mowat's foot and bike ferry from Stromness to Moaness in North Hoy, twice a day, six days a week in winter; usually three times a day, seven days a week in summer. Details at Stromness south pier, or from ☎0856 850 624. Also OISC ro-ro from Houton to Lyness, several times a day, including Sundays during the summer. If you're taking your car, booking is strongly advised (☎085 681 397). All these journeys take about 30 minutes.

Hostels
North Hoy Youth Hostel (26 beds): open May till September. Rackwick Youth Hostel (8 beds): open March till September. Both are linked to the SYHA, but bookings should be made direct to the council's education department on ☎0856 873535. Both of these excellent hostels are very popular, and often full up. More spartan is the bothy

at Burnmouth Cottage, Rackwick, a renovated crofthouse, which provides roof, walls, and running water; details from Mr Rendall (☎085 679 262). Campers can find a sheltered pitch within Burnmouth's garden walls.

Where to eat
The Hoy Inn near Moaness Pier does good bar lunches and suppers and has a separate dining room too (☎085 679 313). The Anchor Bar in Lyness also serves lunches and snacks (☎085 679 356). The Lyness Interpretation Centre has a cafe (☎085 679 365). The Stromabank Hotel in Longhope is well-known for its character; unfortunately, at the time of writing the licensing authorities have just decided it has too much character, and have closed it down: let's hope it's open again by the time you get there.

Events and festivals
Every summer Sir Peter Maxwell Davies (who lives on Hoy) and the Scottish Chamber Orchestra (who don't) run a residency for young composers; the pieces they write are performed in the North Hoy Kirk at the end of their fortnight's stay, in a concert that is always popular and stimulating. Special ferries run from Stromness for the occasion, and on a fine August evening the trip is a pleasure in itself.

Nearest Tourist Information Centre: Stromness (☎0856 850716).

West Mainland

The West Mainland makes up the bulk of the biggest Orkney island. Everything to the west of Kirkwall – from the sheltered bays at Waulkmill and Swanbister on Scapa Flow, to the towering Atlantic cliffs at Yesnaby and Marwick Head – gets lumped together under the name. It's a large and varied area, hard to generalise about. It's true that much of it is given over to agriculture, and some of the county's best and biggest farms can be found here (as well as fascinating museums of past farm life at Kirbuster and Corrigal, open seven days a week during the summer), but it also features large areas of rough and hilly moorland (home to rare birds such as Red-throated Divers and Short-eared Owls) and several lochs, including two very big ones: Stenness and Harray.

Stenness is tidal, being connected to the sea by a narrow channel at the Brig o Waithe. A tragic piece of trivia: the first British civilian to die during World War Two was James Isbister, who was hit by shrapnel from a bomb on the night of March 16th, 1940. The bomb was meant for naval vessels in Scapa Flow, but hit farm cottages at the Brig o Waithe, injuring several folk and killing poor James, who'd stepped out of his front door to watch the planes flying over. Harray, just next door, is fresh, 1500 acres in area, and the finest fishing loch in the islands.

But on the narrow strip of land that separates the lochs are two remarkable prehistoric monuments. Slightly to the south, and slightly older (about 4500 years) are the four remaining stones of an original circular setting of twelve: the Stones of Stenness. The height (over five metres) and dramatic jagged shapes of the stones make them extremely impressive. Even more impressive, if only because of its huge size, is the Ring of Brodgar, half a mile further on. Twenty-seven stones still stand (out of an estimated original sixty), in a ditch-surrounded circle over a hundred

metres across. The exact purpose of these monuments is not known, but what's clear by the sheer scale of them is that they must have been of supreme importance to Orkney's neolithic population. Indeed, the landscape here is peppered with burial mounds and single standing stones as well as the two big circles: there's a particularly interesting tomb called Unstan on a spit of land that sticks out into the loch near the Brig o Waithe. A particular type of neolithic pottery, important for determining the culture of the makers of the different cairns and houses, was first discovered here. This area, at the very heart of Orkney, must have been a very special one, whether it was the sun and moon and stars that made it important, or the lochs and the land, or some unknown gods. Along with Callanish and Stonehenge, the Stenness/Brodgar complex ranks as one of the the finest prehistoric monuments in Britain.

Without equal in Britain, probably anywhere else in Europe, is the magnificent chambered tomb of Maes Howe, just a couple of miles away to the east, and clearly intervisible with the circles. Constructed about 2700 BC, its outer appearance is of a grassy mound, seven metres high, thirty-five across. Once you've scrambled in down the long, low entrance passage (which the sun illuminates for a few brief minutes at the winter solstice) you find yourself in a surprisingly spacious chamber, nearly five metres square, with beautifully constructed stone walls, a corbelled roof, and a small cell (presumably where the bones and grave goods were placed) in each wall. Exactly who was buried here and in what fashion will never be known, for Maes Howe was broken into and looted, maybe even reused, long before the archaeologists started excavating it in the 19th century. In fact, almost as important for historians as the tomb itself is the collection of over thirty runes and drawings carved into the walls by 12th century Viking intruders. The best of these will be pointed out to you by the guide, who can be picked up outside

Tormiston Mill on the other side of the road; she should also be able to sell you an excellent illustrated book.

A few miles away towards Kirkwall there is another chambered tomb, on the slope of Cuween Hill above Finstown. It is smaller and less impressive than Maes Howe, but still worth the trek up the hill. Orkney's third biggest village (though quite a lot smaller than Stromness, even) Finstown has a beautiful setting at the head of the Bay of Firth, with its holms and skerries and sheltered waters that are now home to an oyster farm. (You'll see the cages of salmon farms all over the islands.) It takes its name from an Irishman named Phin, who opened a pub here after the Napoleonic wars. Just to the west is Binscarth, a large 19th century house; it's protected by Binscarth Woods, one of the biggest groups of trees in Orkney. The story goes that the man who built the house first erected twelve flagpoles all across the mainland, left them for the winter, then returned and started building on the site of the least-tattered flag! Some way to the east of Finstown is an earth house at Rennibister, and another chambered tomb high up on Wideford Hill: a terrific viewpoint on a clear day.

But we're getting very close to Kirkwall now, and that's reserved for the next section, so let's head back along the A964 away from the capital and towards the parish of Orphir. The road runs parallel to the shore of Scapa Flow all the way; Waulkmill Bay is a particularly attractive place to wander. Good place for birds too: its sandflats are part of a nature reserve. A couple of miles west is the unique medieval round church of Orphir, with the remains of a Viking hall nearby. Further west still is Houton, where the ro-ro ferry leaves for Hoy and Flotta, but more interesting for the sightseer is the 268 metre high Ward Hill just to the north. This is the highest point in the Mainland, and a great place to look out over all of the Flow and the north isles too. There are several paths up it. One more fine spot to visit while we're still in the south is

Happy Valley. This is the name by which the garden surrounding the croft of Bucksburn has become known in recent years, and it captures perfectly the atmosphere of this oasis of trees, flowers and wildlife. Edwin Harrold, now in his late eighties, started expanding his garden some forty-five years ago, and has never stopped. His imagination and hard work have been rewarded by national environmental awards, but you get the feeling that even more rewarding is the genuine pleasure felt by every visitor that comes here to peer into the pools and sluices of the burn, or pass under the wild roses and silver birches. Happy Valley is unsignposted, but is easily found on the right hand side near the top of the dead-end road (signposted Bigswell) that leaves the A965 opposite Brodgar. Mr Harrold still lives here, and his generosity in allowing the public in to see his garden should be matched by our respect for his privacy.

If you continue up the road between the lochs, past the stone circles, you'll soon come to the crossroads at Dounby. Turning left here will take you westwards towards another major neolithic monument, Skara Brae, which is right on the coast at the beautiful Bay of Skaill. The remains of six houses and a workshop, all connected by covered passageways, were preserved remarkably well for about 4500 years under sand dunes till a storm uncovered them last century. Now we can examine the stone-walled rooms, the beds, the hearths, the quernstones – even the stone sideboards! – and get an unparalleled picture of what life was like here about 3000 BC. There is a small museum on the site, and an excellent guide book. Skara Brae is understandably popular – one of the most visited of all Historic Scotland's monuments and can get crowded (a great rarity for Orkney) in summer. My advice is, if there are two or three tour coaches in the carpark, walk along the beach for half an hour till they're gone. That way you can savour the unique, almost ghostly atmosphere of the place without being poked in the back by zoom lenses every thirty seconds.

Just to the south of Skaill Bay are the cliffs at Yesnaby, which are some of the best in Orkney, both for their bird life and for the shapes they've been sculpted into. (And as a good place to spot the rare and beautiful Primula Scotica.) There are two big rock stacks nearby the Castles of Yesnaby and North Gaulton – and several beautiful bays and geos. On a low headland at Borwick there's the ruin of a broch above an attractive cove: a great spot for a picnic. On the other hand, the cliffs to the north of Skaill are excellent too, probably even better for birdwatchers. At Marwick Head (north of the bird reserve at Marwick Bay, with its interesting 19th-century fishermen's huts and boat-nousts) is the impressive if not particularly attractive heughhead monument to Lord Kitchener, who was drowned near here in 1916, when the HMS *Hampshire* struck a mine. All but twelve of the crew drowned with him, in one of the islands' most tragic – and controversial – wrecks.

Further north still (you should be at the extreme north-west of the Mainland by now) is the Brough of Birsay, a tidal island accessible for a few hours each day. Pictish and Viking buildings have been excavated here. It's also a great place to see puffins; July is the best time. Just inland is the village of Birsay, which is dominated by the remains of the 16th century Earl's Palace, now a gaunt ruin, but once 'a sumptuous and stately dwelling'. (That's how the estate agent described it in 1633.)

Follow the A966 onwards, clockwise, heading east now with good farm land and the three lochs of Boardhouse, Hundland and Swannay to your right. There are plenty of quiet roads to be cycled along, and modest hills to be climbed in these parts, but we must speed on to Burgar Hill, above Evie, where three enormous aerogenerators are positioned to catch the prevailing winds. The biggest propeller has wings the size of a jumbo jet. This windfarm does produce commercially-used electricity, but it was mainly intended as an experiment, and has only been partially successful. Pity. From the hilltop you can look across the Pentland Firth towards the alternative: the nuclear power station at Dounreay. Better, maybe, to look inland to the Birsay Moors RSPB reserve; there's a hide close to the aerogenerators where you can watch ducks and divers in the bogs and lochans here.

Two more interesting minor monuments nearby: the primitive water mill – known as the 'Click Mill' because of the noise it makes when operating – half way along the hilly road back towards Dounby, and the 17th-century beehive-shaped doocot at the Hall of Rendall. But the major monument hereabouts, and a good place to end a tour of the West Mainland, is the Broch of Gurness, which is approached by skirting the beautiful Sands of Evie. This is the best preserved and protected broch in Orkney, and in its own way as impressive as Skara Brae or Maes Howe. Brochs were Iron Age defensive structures, built between about 200 BC and AD 200. The remains of small villages often (as here) nestle in about the base of the broch, but it's not entirely clear if the houses were later additions, or if the broch was in fact built to provide refuge for the villagers at times of trouble. Certainly Gurness Broch must have been almost impenetrable, with its protecting ramparts, thick walls, well-guarded doorway, and secure supply of fresh water from a step-down well inside. Nearby is a small interpretation centre with good explanatory material, and the chance to grind some corn yourself with a genuine iron age quernstone! Then walk back to the carpark with the genuine iron age wind nipping your eyes as you peer across to Eynhallow in its quick flowing sound, and Rousay (with its own array of brochs) beyond.

How to get there

The area is crisscrossed with roads, many of them very quiet and ideal for cyclists. Buses are thin on the ground. There's one a week (Mondays) from

Stromness and Kirkwall to Birsay (Shalder Coaches: 0856 850809) and one a day from Stromness and Kirkwall to Dounby (Peaces: ☎0856 872866). Most useful is the Rosie Coaches seven-day service (six in winter) from Kirkwall bus station to Evie, a good centre for exploring the north of the Mainland. This route ends at Tingwall, where the ferries depart for Rousay, Wyre and Egilsay. Up to five journeys a day: (☎085 675 227/232 for details).

Accommodation

As well as the hotels below, there are many B&Bs and cottages for rent. And youth hostels at Birsay (book via the council: ☎0856 873535) and Evie (☎085 675 270/254). Also at Evie (and part of the Eviedale 'complex', along with the hostel and cafe) is a popular campsite.

Events and festivals

There is a Finstown gala-day every summer, but the area's really big event is the West Mainland Agricultural Show, better known as the Dounby Show, and held there every August. A great day out, with livestock judging, games, side-shows, and a very popular beer tent.

Where to eat

There are quite a few country hotels, all of which serve good bar food, some of them striving to do more than that. The best supper I've had recently was at the Plout Kirn (part of the Smithfield Hotel in Dounby (☎085677 215). But the others are fine too: Barony Hotel, Birsay (☎085 672 327), Scorrabrae Inn, Orphir (☎085 681 262), Merkister Hotel, Harray, once the home of novelist Eric Linklater, (☎085 677 366), Standing Stones Hotel, Stenness (☎0856 850449). You'll find the Eviedale Centre does good meals and snacks in a very pleasant atmosphere with books to read, an open fire etc. (☎085 675 270/254). And there are various other places to eat: *Wylie's Tearooms* at Harray serve enormous helpings of cakes and scones and biscuits for afternoon tea; there's a good wee cafe in Birsay village, and a good big one at Evie called Woodwick Stores and Restaurant; Northdyke Restaurant has a great view over the Bay of Skaill and Woodwick House in its wonderful wooded garden on the shore at Evie achieves a very high standard, including a lot of vegetarian stuff (☎085 675 330) – booking essential; finally, there's a craft shop and restaurant at Tormiston Mill, half way along the main road from Stromness to Finstown. Let us turn to drink. There's an interesting old pub called the Mistra at Evie, above the shop there. There are two pubs in the village of Finstown: Baikies (which has a restaurant section too) and the Pomona Inn, a lively spot. And at Quoyloo near the Bay of Skaill is The Orkney Brewery: (visitors welcome: ☎085 684 802), home to four fine beers: Raven Ale, Dark Island, Dragonhead Stout and Skull-splitter strong ale. All are widely available in bottles, the first two sometimes on draught too. Highly recommended. Hic.

Leisure

The Eviedale Centre (numbers above) hires canoes and other water-sport equipment. They can also arrange trips to Eynhallow, the uninhabited island half way between Evie and Rousay, which has the remains of a medieval monastic settlement on it, plus lots of birds and seals.

Nearest Tourist Information Centre: Stromness (☎0856 850716).

Rousay

Rousay is a heathery hill rising out of the water, with a narrow strip of fertile land around its base. Blotchnie Field, at 227 metres, is the highest point in the north isles; there are magnificent views from the top over the islands, skerries and rocks that are scattered black and green against the blue of the sea all around. While you're up the hill, keep an eye open for birds, especially moorland varieties such as Hen Harriers, Short Eared Owls, Merlins and Golden Plovers (and Great Northern Divers on the lochs); this is the RSPB's Trumland Reserve.

The thing that draws most folk to Rousay, though, is its archaeology, which is outstanding, even by Orkney standards. Indeed, Rousay is sometimes referred to as 'The Egypt of the North' – and it's not because of the seaweed-eating camels that roam the shore. On the Loch of Wasbister near the north of the island is an artificial island or 'crannog' dating from the Iron Age, and at Taft o' Faraclett at the north-eastern extremity there is an interesting broch-mound and a standing stone nearby which reputedly visits the Loch of Scockness for a drink each Hogmanay. But the south-west coast of Rousay features one of the finest collections of ancient monuments in the country.

Less than a mile from the pier, moving clockwise round the road that rings the Island, is Taversoe Tuick chambered cairn, an unusual two-storeyed burial tomb which you can climb down into and spook yourself. Half a mile further on is another well-preserved chambered tomb, Blackhammer. More ruinous cairns and barrows, and an impressive 2.2 metre standing stone, the Langsteen, are scattered all over the hillside here. Don't miss the tomb at Knowe of Yarso, a little further up the slope: a tomb with a view. A mile or so along the road is the start of the Westness Walk, which has signposts and a footpath close to the shore, and its own explanatory leaflet. The walk takes you from the elegant Westness House (an 18th-century laird's residence), past the almost invisible Viking cemetery at Moaness, and onto a complex of tumbling walls and buildings above the seal-filled Bay of Swandro. This site features a simple 12th-century chapel, and the remains of a square tower called

The Wirk, which was probably part of a Norse hall; this part of the coast was very badly affected by the storms and high tides of January 1993, and some of these interesting ruins are on the point of collapsing into the sea. See them before it's too late! Five minutes further on is what looks like an aircraft hangar. In fact it is the shed built in the 1930s to protect the newly excavated and still very impressive Midhowe Chambered Tomb, with its twenty-four separate burial compartments. There are believed to be the ruins of at least eight brochs on Rousay, but the best preserved one is just a few metres further along the coast. Midhowe Broch is rivalled only by its counterpart across Eynhallow Sound at Gurness, and is an essential visit. Notice the massive defensive rampart and ditch on the landward side, and the natural barrier of the sea. See how similar the internal hearth and furnishings of the broch are to those used at Skara Brae two or three thousand years earlier and to features seen in small croft houses occupied right up to the present century.

A couple miles beyond the end of the Westness Walk, is the remains of the crofting township of Quendale 'cleared' by George William Traill in 1845. What remained when the people left is around sixteen small houses, (now ruinous), patterns of feelie (turf) dykes, and the clearly visible outlines of the old runrig land divisions. Nearby is Tafts House, dating back to the 15th century, said to be the first two-storey house in Orkney and at one time obviously the centre of this community. It's a sad and eerie spot.

Traill's successor as laird was General Frederick William Traill Burroughs, who gained the reputation of being the cruellest, most autocratic and grasping of all Orkney's lairds. And there was a fair bit of competition in the 19th century! At one point, his dispute with some of the crofters he was trying to evict reached such a pitch that a navy gunboat was called in to quell the 'revolt'. Edwin Muir wrote about him in his poem 'The Little General', and William Thomson's book, *The Little General and the Rousay Crofters*, is essential reading for anyone spending more than a day or two on Rousay. Burroughs' main monument is Trumland House, finished in 1873; it dominates its corner of the island, but is not particularly attractive: in both ways similar to its original inhabitant.

The road around the island is great for car drivers, but is too long to walk in a day, and too hilly for cyclists. (Bikes can be hired, by the way, from Helga Tait's Craft Shop at the pierhead.) Better to spend a day or two here, I'd say. That'll give you time to have a good look at the extraordinary cliff scenery at the north end's Sacquoy Head as well. And if you're lucky, you might happen to be around while one of the famous Rousay dances takes place (several times during the summer); don't miss the chance to attend, but do take spare feet: the dancing's wild.

How to get there

MV *Eynhallow*, a small OISC ro-ro, goes back and forth between Rousay (and Wyre and Egilsay) and the Tingwall Terminal at Evie on the Mainland, from around seven in the morning till about six at night, seven days a week from May to September, six the rest of the year. The journey time is about half an hour. Cars are advised to book, especially during the summer, when the boat is often full up (☎085 675 360).

Accommodation

As well as the Taversoe Hotel, and a few B&Bs and self-catering cottages, a well-equipped six-bed hostel has just been opened on Trumland farm, half a mile west of the pier. Bookings (☎085 682 252). In the grounds of the hostel is a campsite with space for two caravans and six tents.

Where to eat

There's a pub with a small restaurant just as you come off the pier; they're meant to be good, but I've never been in.

The Taversoe Hotel a mile or so west of the village serves ambitious and inventive food, including a lot of great vegetarian stuff; the bar has an enormous choice of malt whiskies. It's a bit expensive, but you'll be very well looked after (☎085 682 325).

Festivals

In July there's the Rousay and Wyre Regatta, and a month later there's a Horticultural and Handicraft Show.

Nearest Tourist Information Centre: Kirkwall (☎0856 872856)

Wyre

Growing up in Wyre is beautifully described in the *Autobiography* of Edwin Muir, recently reprinted in paperback. The poet was born in Deerness, but spent his formative years at the largest farm on this island, The Bu, before moving – unhappily – to near Kirkwall, and then disastrously – to Glasgow. Not only is this book essential reading for anyone interested in Muir himself, it also provides an incomparable account of Orkney rural life a hundred years ago. By the by it touches on ballad-singing, folk legends, how to slaughter a pig and much more.

Wyre came to represent a lost Eden for Muir, but a visitor today will find it less idyllic. The size of the island (two miles long by one wide) and the consequent small amount of good land has made it hard for a decent-sized community to be sustained. There are no shops at all, and no accommodation for tourists; children have to commute to primary school in Rousay. But the old school has been done up as a community hall, most of the island is still being farmed, there is a modern ro-ro pier; these things indicate a more positive future for Wyre than similar-sized islands such as Faray and Stroma, both abandoned in recent decades.

The visitor can spend an interesting day on Wyre. Its main landmark is Cubbie Roo's Castle, halfway down the island's main road on a grassy knowe. The *Orkenyinga Saga* gives the original form of its name: 'At that time there was a very able man named Kolbein Hruga farming on Wyre in Orkney. He had a fine stone fort built there, a really solid stronghold.' The time referred to is about 1150, making Cubbie Roo's the oldest stone-built castle in Scotland; the base of the square keep and its surrounding ditch-and-bank defences are well preserved.

One field to the south lie the ruins of St Mary's Chapel, a romanesque building of the 12th century; it is a roofless shell now, but the skill of the stoneworkers is still obvious, in the fine arched doorways Hruga's son Bjarni was the third bishop of Orkney (as well as a poet), at a time when St Magnus Cathedral was being built; maybe that explains the presence of such an impressive church on such a small island.

A hundred metres to the north-east lie the extensive steadings of The Bu, with its south-sloping gardens; the house is without a permanent occupant at the moment, which seems a pity given its small but significant part in Scottish literature. It would seem to present an ideal opportunity for a museum or literary centre such as MacDiarmid's cottage in Biggar or the Soutar House in Perth; as well as being a living memorial to one of Orkney's greatest writers, this would bring money directly into the community that formed him. Read George Marshall's *In a Distant Isle*, a study of Muir's years on Wyre and their effect on his writing; it contains a lot of interesting information about social change on a small island in the second half of the last century. Does that sound boring? It's not meant to: it's a fascinating book.

How to get there

The Tingwall/Rousay ferry calls here four or five trips a day, six days a week, seven during the summer. Advisable to book in advance; some of the crossings depend on there being definite bookings; phone Evie (☎085 675 360).

Nearest Tourist Information Centre: Kirkwall (☎0856 872856).

Egilsay

In the year 1117, Hakon Paulson and Magnus Erlandson were joint Earls of Orkney. Magnus had early on shown aberrant behaviour for a Norseman – refusing to fight during a Viking raid on Anglesey, for instance, singing hymns instead as the battle raged around him – but the differences between the two men did not seem insuperable. A summit meeting was arranged for a day just after Easter, on the neutral island of Egilsay. But, encouraged by jealous followers, Hakon broke the agreed rules and brought a large number of warships and warriors with him. Magnus knew when he was beaten, and offered to leave Orkney forever. Hakon wasn't satisfied with that, nor with Magnus's next suggestion, that he'd allow himself to be imprisoned forever. Finally, Magnus asked Hakon to mutilate and torture him, and *then* imprison him. After a moment's hesitation, Hakon ordered his cook to kill Magnus. Without a moment's hesitation, his cousin's treacherous behaviour obviously coming as no surprise, Magnus told the cook, 'Stand thou before me, and hew on my head a great wound, for it is not seemly to behead chiefs like thieves. Take good heart, poor wretch, for I have prayed to God for thee, that he be merciful unto thee.' Only obeying orders, the cook did what he was told.

Magnus was buried at Birsay, and very soon stories of miraculous cures and strange lights around the church started to circulate. Hakon repented his evil deed and made pilgrimages to Rome and Jerusalem, and in 1137 work began in Kirkwall on the great cathedral named after his victim. A more modest church of about the same date stands near the spot of Magnus's murder, and is also known by his name. It is roofless, but otherwise virtually intact, its most impressive feature being a fifteen-metre-high round tower, which seems to have been as much a defensive keep as a religious monument. It dominates Egilsay, and is clearly visible from all the surrounding islands; it is the most impressive ecclesiastical building in the outer isles.

Since the death of Magnus, things have been quiet in Egilsay. It is another smallish island, whose population worked hard as fishermen and farmers for centuries, till the particular pressures of the twentieth century conspired to make such a life almost impossible. But not quite impossible. In the early seventies, it was one of the first of the Orkney islands to be settled by escapees from the rat-race in the south. Ruth Wheeler describes her family's attempt at self-sufficiency in her revealing book *Living on an Island*: 'A person may imagine that they can come here, stay for a while, and leave unchanged. This isn't so. When you step from the boat onto the shores of this or any other island you are at the beginning of an affair. The affair may involve love and a lasting union or hatred and despair.'

Now Egilsay is almost entirely populated by incomers. Whether their arrival was a curse, in that it brought new ways and expectations to the place, thus driving out old traditions and ways of life, or whether it was a blessing, in that they are keeping alive an island that was on the point of abandonment, is an argument that could rage from now till next year. It's also an argument that applies, not just to Egilsay, but to several places in Orkney, and through-out Scotland; probably to thousands of small and isolated communities through-out the world. It's discussed in a very interesting book by Diana Forsyth: *Urban-Rural Migration, Change and Conflict in an Orkney Island Community*.

As well as historians and peace-seekers, who will enjoy a walk down the attractive east coast, Egilsay is worth a visit for bird watchers, as it has a relatively large area of water and boggy ground. On the lochs breed waders such as snipe and redshank, as well as various breeds of duck. If you're lucky, you might hear the call of the corncrake – like a straik on a rusty scythe – a bird once common throughout Orkney, but now very rare.

How to get there

The Tingwall/Rousay/Wyre ferry: four or five trips a day, six days a week, seven during the summer. Again, advisable to book in advance; some of the crossings depend on there being definite bookings (☎085 675 360).

Accommodation

There's one B&B on the island (☎085 682 308).

Nearest Tourist Information Centre: Kirkwall (☎0856 872856).

Kirkwall

Kirkwall is the capital of Orkney: where the council meets, where most of the trade and commerce takes place, home to nearly half the islands' population (about 8000 folk, four times as many as live in Stromness) and still growing! More and more, it's also the place where the big shops, factories and amenities (such as the planned new library and sports centre) are to be found. People who live in Kirkwall often say it's the only modern, lively place in Orkney: the place to be if you want to participate fully in the consumer society of the 1990s. A lot of visitors might think that's a good reason *not* to live in Kirkwall, but that's not so easy a position to maintain on a dark and stormy winter's evening when you have to travel five miles from your remote idyllic croft to get a pint of milk, or your kids have to bus for an hour in the darkness to get to school, and the same back in the afternoon. Stop your moaning! Kirkwall's a great place, and shouldn't be missed by anyone visiting Orkney, no matter how briefly.

The town is dominated by the St Magnus Cathedral, and has been for more than eight centuries. It was started in 1137 by Earl Rognvald Kolsson, and dedicated to his uncle Magnus, martyred on Egilsay twenty years earlier; it took nearly four centuries to complete. It was worth the wait, though, for despite its relatively small size, the elegance of its proportions and the marvellously warm red and yellow sandstone used in its construction make it one of the most impressive cathedrals in Scotland. There is much fine external carved decoration, and inside there's a fascinating display of early tombstones. There are services every Sunday; on other days St Magnus is open to visitors, who should have a read of the excellent guide book on sale inside. The extent to which the cathedral is the centre point of the islands can be judged by the fact that its spire is visible from as far away as Westray!

Across the road on the south side of St Magnus are the ruins of the Bishop's Palace (parts of it built as early as the twelfth century) and the Earl's Palace, built in 1607 by the notorious Earl Patrick Stewart. (Read the full terrible story in the recent book, *Black Patie*.) At the time of his execution in 1615, he was described as having left 'no sort of extraordinary oppression and treasonable violence unpractised', but no one is entirely bad, and Stewart certainly knew a good architect when he saw one: his palace is one of the finest Renaissance buildings in the country.

Throughout Kirkwall there are many fine and attractive old buildings (see Spence's Square, Gunn's Close, and the old Main Street, for instance) and in one of them, the 16th century Tankerness House on Broad Street, is the town's museum. It's open seven days a week during the summer, six in winter, and contains fascinating permanent displays on Orkney life from prehistory to the present, as well as temporary exhibitions focusing on some particular aspect of island life, such as Orcadians' part in Arctic exploration, or the history of the kelp industry. Anyone interested in finding out more about Orkney's history (or anything else) should visit the excellent library in Laing Street; ask to see the Orkney Room, which contains an unparalleled collection of books and maps, old and new, on every part of island life through the centuries. Founded in 1683, this is the oldest public library in Scotland.

Near where Laing Street joins the main shopping area of Albert Street, is the Big Tree, the most famous but certainly not the *only* tree in Orkney. Once situated in a private garden, the walls of which were demolished to widen the thoroughfare, the tree was too popular to be chopped down. It flourished for another century until, in 1987, it had to be severely trimmed back for safety reasons. For several years little more than a stump, it is now starting to shoot out new branches: there's hope for us all. On either side of the Tree are many shops, including chemists, jewellers, craft shops, newsagents (with good selection of Orkney books), bakers, butchers, junk shops, record and video stores, a chip shop, and a couple of all-purpose emporiums. The bakers and grocers, Cummings & Spence, is a good place to buy different Orkney cheeses, as is the fishmongers just round the corner in

Bridge Street. In fact, anything you want can be bought in Kirkwall from a tuppenny chew to a tractor: more than ever it's the commercial centre of Orkney.

The cultural side of life isn't neglected either. Through the summer (and especially during the Festival) there are usually one or two art exhibitions on at any time. The Phoenix cinema, a vast wartime barn on Junction Road, shows commercial releases on Thursday and Saturday nights. (If you're going in the winter months, take a blanket and a hot water bottle.) Just along the road from the Phoenix is Scapa Books, second-hand store, which often has interesting Orkney books for sale. (There's a branch in Stromness too.) Local amateur and visiting professional drama goes on in the Arts Theatre in Mill Street, and live music (both local and imported) crops up all over the place. Worthy of special mentions are the Accordion and Fiddle Club, that meets in the Ayre Hotel on a Wednesday night, and the Strathspey and Reel Society, that plays in the Community Centre on Tuesday evenings.

Does whisky-drinking count as a cultural activity? Yes, you go on the guided tour of the Highland Park Distillery at Holm Road, a mile or so from the centre of town. (☎0856 874619 for details of times etc.) For as well as seeing the malting, distilling and barrelling work, you get an audio-visual presentation on the history of Orkney. And a free dram. That's not to be sniffed at (well you can sniff it, but you should swallow it immediately after) for Highland Park twelve-year-old is generally considered to be one of the finest whiskies in the world. I've done extensive tests, though, and can recommend the products of the nearby Old Scapa distillery equally highly.

There are several interesting walks in the vicinity of Kirkwall. You might try going out beyond Highland Park to the beach and busy jetty at Scapa Bay. Or you could go west to Wideford Hill with its chambered cairn, (mentioned in the West Mainland section) or maybe out the north side of the town towards the Head Of Work. Here you will find an interesting burial cairn, about fifty metres long with a curving 'horn' at each end defining a semi-enclosed area similar to the one at the Tomb of the Eagles (see South Ronaldsay). Round to the east of the Head is the beautiful sandy beach of the Bay of Meil. Orkney conchologist Robert Rendall said that this area (along with Birsay) was the best place in the islands to find rare sea shells. His observations drawn from a lifetime walking the coastline and *thinking* are collected in *Orkney Shore*, a fascinating book, sadly out of print at the moment, as is *Kirkwall in the Orkneys*, the definitive history of the islands' capital.

How to get there

There are frequent buses to and from Stromness, (Peaces: ☎0856 872866), and others meet the short sea crossing into Burwick (see general introduction). You can also sail direct to Kirkwall from Invergordon, and of course the harbour is the main point of departure and arrival for the north isles. (See introduction and relevant island sections.) The town is centrally situated, ideal as a base for touring anywhere in Orkney; cyclists should note that the roads around Kirkwall tend to be busier than those elsewhere, though.

Accommodation

There are half a dozen hotels in Kirkwall, all of which are adequate. The Kirkwall Hotel is the grandest and overlooks the harbour (☎0856 872232). As well as a big selection of B&Bs, and flats and cottages to rent, there is an SYHA hostel on Old Scapa Road (☎0856 872243) and a large caravan and camping site at Pickaquoy Road (bookings via the council on ☎0856 873535).

Where to eat

There are two Chinese restaurants – the Empire and the Golden Dragon – and one Indian – the Mumtaz in Albert Street. All of these can be good on occasion, poor at other times. The Mumtaz has just been refurbished and is probably the best of the three: bookings on ☎0856 873537. The Foveran is a hotel a couple miles outside the town towards Orphir; it serves good food in a pleasant setting, but is rather expensive (☎0856 872389. All of the pubs do bar meals, some just at lunchtime. Most of the hotels do slightly more ambitious food in their restaurants. None stands out as being particularly better than the others. There are three cafes in Albert Street, the Atholl, Trenabies and the Pomona; they serve snacks and meals and lots of cakes and bakes. All popular and crowded, too, and not open late. There's the utilitarian council-run St Magnus Café opposite the cathedral, and a sit-in section in Bews chip shop on Junction Road. Finally, varied vegetarian food is available at Rejane's healthfood café and shop in the Anchor Buildings in Bridge Street. There are at least seven bars (I lost count after that...) all of which are fine. The Bothy Bar in the Albert Hotel has a good open fire for cold nights around midwinter. Or midsummer.

Golf

There is a good eighteen-hole course on the west side of the town, at Grainbank, with a luxurious new clubhouse. Clubs are for hire, and visitors welcome (☎0856 872457).

Leisure facilities

Kirkwall Grammar School (the secondary for most of the outer isles as well as the immediate surroundings) has a swimming pool and other sports facilities (☎0856 872364). There is a bowling green in the Watergate near the Earl's Palace. The Pavilion, a grocers/confectioners in Main Street, has a couple of snooker tables.

Events and festivals

The Ba is an event (a game? a spectacle?) unique to Kirkwall. It takes place on Christmas Day and New Year's Day every year, starting off outside the cathedral when a small leather ball is thrown up into the air. The hardy men of the town are divided into two teams, the Uppies and the Doonies, and each team attempts to seize the 'ba' and move with it into the other team's territory. Not easy when you're in the middle of a scrum of two hundred or more folk, half of them struggling violently to stop you moving! The battle can go on for hours, including long periods of apparent deadlock; then a new tactic will be tried and a group of players will rush off along a side road like bulls down the streets of Pamplona... Usually you don't get more than an odd glimpse of the ball from the start of the game to the end! Much more refined, and almost as interesting, is the St Magnus Festival, which happens each June; it has events in Stromness and elsewhere, but Kirkwall and the cathedral in particular is its spiritual home. There is a great deal of classical music each year, some of it specially commissioned (one of the founders of the festival was the composer, Peter Maxwell Davies); there's also a distinguished visiting poet, who does several readings, as well as art exhibitions and various other cultural activities. A great time to visit Orkney for anyone interested in the arts. Ask the tourist board for up-to-date information. Every August there's a regatta, (starting from the harbour), and in the same month takes place the County Show (in Bignold Park). Half the population of the islands comes to the Show, though whether they're most drawn by the livestock competitions, the sideshows or the beer tent is hard to say.

Tourist Information Centre

An office full of leaflets, guidebooks, up-to-date posters and information about events locally and throughout the islands is situated just to the left of the cathedral. The friendly staff can help with accommodation too, and are generally a mine of information on what's on where and when. Their number is ☎0856 872856.

East Mainland

The area of country to the south and east of Kirkwall is much smaller than the big lump of the West Mainland, and it's comparatively short on spectacular visitor attractions. But there are at least two stretches of outstanding coastline, and several other places well worth a visit. And as with other relatively untouristy parts of Orkney, the peace and quiet of much of the East Mainland is something worth seeking out in its own right.

The A961 travels down from Kirkwall through unexciting farming country all the way to the village of St Mary's at the south of the parish of Holm (pronounced 'ham'). The village itself is small and attractive, very quiet now since the construction of the barriers (see next section) took away its importance as a port to the south isles. There's not much to see though, so head on a mile or so out the far side of the village to Graemsehall, a large 19th-century house, now home to Norwood Antiques: open May to September, certain days only (check with tourist office for times). There s plenty to see here. In fact Graemsehall contains one of the most astonishing collections of antique clocks, watches, frog mugs, furniture, guns, porcelain, statues, Staffordshire figures, silverware, ivory carvings, music-machines, books and pictures that you'll ever see. And it was all collected by one man, Norrie Wood, a stonemason from Firth, now in his eighties. His obsessional collecting is remarkable not just for its intensity, but also for its diversity: you'll find the work of great craftsmen and artists next to curios and knick-knacks. It's all fascinating, made even more so by Mrs Cilla Wood, who shows you round with genuine enthusiasm. There's a small admission charge.

There are pleasant sandy bays and the vestigial remains of Norse settlements out towards Rose Ness to the south-east of Graemsehall, but more to see if you continue eastwards to the peninsula of Deerness, the extreme eastern point of mainland Orkney. There are some excellent beaches here: Sandside Bay with the old Skaill kirk, Dingieshowe where the whale scenes in *Venus Peter* were filmed, and Newark Bay, where a mermaid was seen by many people over several years in the 1890s. The Gloup, towards the top-right hand corner of Deerness is an impressive chasm where the roof of a sea-cave has collapsed. A mile or so's walk from there takes you to the Brough of Deerness, a dramatic clifftop site for the scant remains of an early monastic settlement. This point was used for target practice during the war, so it's hard to tell which holes in the ground are priest's cells and which are craters... Seals can be observed swimming about in the clear waters below the cliffs. Another mile round Mull Head (or else back to the road and follow the signposts) takes you to the Covenanters' Memorial, a monument to a shipload of religious prisoners who drowned nearby in unsavoury circumstances in 1697. The farmer on whose land the Memorial stands recently offered it for sale. There were no takers. Still, with the housing shortage being what it is, I'd go and see it quick if I were you.

Between Deerness and Kirkwall is another peninsula, the relatively unvisited one of Tankerness. It too has a great sandy beach, at Mill Sand: a good place to see Shelduck and also waders such as Turnstone and Redshank. And its east coast is a fine walk of low but fascinatingly eroded cliffs, with many caves, several stacks and natural arches, and a lot of seabirds, including numbers of cormorants – 'skarfs' as they're called in Orkney. Fans of Second World War architecture will want to see the gun emplacement and lookout tower at Rerwick Head; indeed, if they keep their eyes open they'll find a lot of concrete all over the east mainland. At the opposite, southern, end of the Tankerness cliffs, is a cannon of uncertain age – 17th century? – mounted at the end of a taing of land called Gumpick. Nearby was found a Pictish carved stone, now housed in Tankerness Museum in Kirkwall (originally the townhouse of the lairds of this area.)

One wing of the lairds' country residence, the Hall of Tankerness, can be rented as a self-catering accommodation. Perhaps even more exclusive is the lighthouse-keepers' house on the small, wedge-shaped (and now uninhabited) island of Copinsay, off the south-east of Deerness. You can rent this and live in perfect solitude – except for the thousands of pairs of guillemots and kittiwakes that nest there. See the tourist board's accommodation brochure for details.

How to get there

There are two main roads through this area, and several quiet minor ones. The bus service is minimal: just a very few buses per week between Kirkwall, Deerness and Tankerness. The times are odd too. W. J. Stove is the operator (☎085674 215). More useful is the Causeway Coach service through to St Margaret's Hope. This operates several times a day, and can let you off anywhere along the A961 (☎085 683 444). Likewise the Shalder service to Burwick (☎0856 850809).

Accommodation

The Commodore Motel provides rooms, and also self-catering chalets (☎085 678 319). There are also various B&Bs and cottages for rent.

Where to eat

In Tankerness, just off the main road, is the Quoyburray Inn, a comfortable pub that does bar food. Its Kiln Bar has an enormous fireplace in the shape of an old malt kiln. Just outside the village of St Mary's in Holm is the Commodore – the only motel in Orkney! It does good bar food too.

Nearest Tourist Information Centre: Kirkwall (☎0856 872856).

South Ronaldsay and Burray

At one o'clock in the morning on October 14th 1939, a German U-boat torpedoed the battleship HMS *Royal Oak* as it lay anchored in the supposedly safe haven of Scapa Flow, then slipped out the way it had come in: through the narrow channel separating the Mainland and Lamb's Holm. 833 crew died, and Winston Churchill immediately ordered the construction of the four massive barriers that still bear his name, linking the two major islands and two small holms that stretch down towards John O'Groats. But the Italian prisoners of war who were to provide most of the labour refused to work on an enemy defensive project, so the barriers were officially declared causeways for civilian use, and work began. Several years and over a million tons of rock and concrete later, it was possible to drive across what had previously been treacherous, swiftly flowing sounds.

The nature of the southern isles had changed forever: no longer islands at all, really, they are now easily accessible to anyone with a car or a bike or a bus-ticket. And the first thing to visit, on the north side of Lamb Holm, immediately after you cross the first barrier, is, fittingly, the beautiful Italian Chapel, constructed out of two Nissen Huts and various bits of scrap metal and concrete by the POWs who lived and worked here. It is a monument to the survival of the spiritual and artistic impulse even under the severest of conditions; its frescoes and mock wrought-iron work are moving both for their skilful execution and for the witness they bear to the story behind their construction. The chapel is open all day every day; a booklet with full text and illustrations is available inside for a donation.

Pass quickly over Glimps Holm (unless you've got peat-cutting business there) and you'll find yourself on Burray, a well-farmed island, three miles by two in extent. Much of the east side of Burray is taken up by the wide and duney Bu Sands; at the western tip is the small islet of Hunda, connected to the main island by a narrow causeway which is holm to sheep, seals and many birds. Talking of birds, Echna Loch, which the road skirts right in the middle of Burray is very popular with swans. Take the road to the right immediately after the loch, and you'll find yourself at the Orkney Fossil & Vintage Centre (open most days: ☎085 673 255 for details). It may not be Jurassic Park, but this small privately-run museum is stuffed with interesting fossils, many of them found within a few miles, and is fascinating for kids or adults. There is vintage farm machinery too, and a good cafe with a varying menu: Thursday is chip supper night! Burray Village features one of the last working boat yards in Orkney (in the same family for five generations), and overlooks the fourth barrier, on the east side of which a beautiful curve of sand has built up over recent years. The rusting hulks of several blockships (superseded by the barrier) stick up out of the sand like a scene from a Terry Gilliam movie.

The largest of these connected islands is South Ronaldsay; it also contains the largest and most attractive settlement, Saint Margaret's Hope, which is home to the Orkney Wireless Museum and the Old Smiddy Museum (both open most of the time during the summer) as well as several shops, and places to eat and drink. The centre of the village hosts the parade which leads up to the famous (and now unique) Boys' Ploughing Match. This takes place on the third Saturday in August, and is always well advertised. In the early afternoon, the young girls of the area line up in amazing costumes, supposed to be imitative of the show-dressing of working horses; indeed, this part of the proceedings is sometimes known as the Festival of the Horse. Some of these costumes have been handed down unchanged over generations, others are improved from year to year with the addition of fun-fur

fetlocks, silver horseshoes, and what look like Christmas tree decorations... Following this, the boys and their miniature ploughs are taken to a nearby beach where, with the encouragement of their fathers and grandfathers, they compete to create the neatest pattern of furrows in the wet sand. You won't see anything like this anywhere else in the world: see it here.

South Ronaldsay is maybe not the most exciting of islands, scenically, but there are more than a few small sandy coves (like Kirkhouse on the east side), medium-sized cliffs (like the Kame of Stews, a couple of miles south of Kirkhouse, where there's also a standing stone) and attractive groups of old houses (such as Herston, half way along Widewall bay on the west side.) One place not to be missed by any visitor to Orkney, let alone South Ronaldsay, is the Tomb of the Eagles, otherwise known as Isbister Chambered Cairn, which lies at the south end of the island at Liddle Farm. The farmer, Ronald Simison, was in fact responsible for much of the excavation of the tomb, and made many interesting and important discoveries, which have greatly increased knowledge of stone age life in Orkney. (See John Hedges' excellent book *Tomb of the Eagles* for details.) Best of all, Mr Simison and his family are on hand most hours of the day to give guided tours, answer questions, and pass round some of the artefacts and entombed skulls he discovered. ☎085 683 339 for further information; there's a small charge.

At this point you're very close to Burwick and the ferry terminal, but I'd advise not heading south. Not yet. Never! If you must leave, take the time to look in at St Mary's Kirk near Burwick, where there is a remarkable and mysterious monument: a large lump of stone with the impression of two feet carved into it. One legend has it that St Magnus miraculously crossed the Pentland Firth on the stone, but it doesn't look like a very efficient surfboard to me.

How to get there

The ferry from John O' Groats arrives at Burwick in the south of South Ronaldsay; see general introduction for details, including connecting buses. Assuming you're already on the Orkney mainland, it's a straightforward drive or cycle south from Kirkwall on the A961; it's about five miles to the first barrier, eighteen to Burwick. Alternatively, Causeway Coaches run several buses each way six days a week (☎085 683444).

Accommodation

The Creel offers B&B accommodation, as does the Murray Arms Hotel, just round the corner, which also serves bar meals. There's a small privately run ivy-clad hostel in Herston Bay (☎085 683 208) and one called Wheems Bothy (☎085 683 537). In Burray Village is The Sands Motel, with a range of accommodation, full licence and bar meals: (☎085 673 298).

Where to eat

Pride of place must go to The Creel, Front Road, St Margaret's Hope, one of the leading restaurants in Scotland; the prizewinning chef makes good use of local produce in a variety of imaginative dishes. Open throughout the summer, but only on a limited basis during the winter; reservations are usually necessary (☎085 683 311). The Coach House Tearoom is open during the day in nearby Back Road, and in the middle of Burray the Fossil Centre (see above) also serves good basic food and snacks.

Events and festivals

The third Saturday in August sees the Boys' Ploughing Match, described above; details advertised in *The Orcadian* and on posters.

Nearest Tourist Information Centre: Kirkwall (☎0856 872856).

Shapinsay

The approach to Shapinsay is dominated by the baronial turrets and crowsteps of Balfour Castle, the home of the island's lairds for nearly two centuries till 1961. It has been said that the Balfours represented 'paternalism at its best'; the families evicted in 1847 in the name of agricultural improvement might have felt that, even at its best, paternalism has its drawbacks. What can't be disputed is that, following David Balfour's imposition of a grid of large square fields with long straight roads in between, and the subsequent construction of a model village, water mill, and even a gasometer (all still there around the shores of Elwick Bay), Shapinsay became a prosperous and proud agricultural community.

It's still that today. If Shapinsay isn't the most exciting destination for visitors to Orkney, it's certainly one of the prettiest: the fields are neat, the cattle sleek, and Balfour village is filled with charming buildings and flowery gardens. While in the village, don't miss The Smithy, which has a small but interesting Heritage Centre featuring old farming implements, household gear, and hundreds of photographs covering the past hundred years. Upstairs there is the cafe, and there is also a small craft and produce shop attached, which is open seven days a week during the summer.

Shapinsay is ideal for cyclists, as there are only a few gentle hills. At less than four miles by six, it's small enough for walkers to see a good deal of in a single day, but big enough to make taking a car over almost worthwhile. Whichever way you're travelling, let's get going. On a low hill towards the south-east corner of the island, is Mor Stein, an impressive lichen-covered standing stone about three metres high. Half a mile due east from there, across the island's last small area of rough moorland, lies an unimpressive mound with the impressive name of Castle Bloody. As an old joke has it, you can look as hard as you like, but you'll find no bloody castle. In fact, it's almost certainly the remains of a chambered cairn, just one of several archaeological sites on the island that remain tantalisingly unexcavated. This is a good bit of coast to walk for an hour or so, by the way; you should see seals, otters if you're exceptionally lucky, and certainly the rock formation known as the Foot of Shapinsay.

The north-east leg of the island has two sites with interesting stories attached. Near Linton Bay is the ruin of a chapel, which probably dates to the 12th century; in the early 1900s, an imprudent farmer removed a lintel from the ruin to use in his new byre. Within days he was punished for his impiety, when two of his cows were found mysteriously hanged in the new byre... He didn't hang around before returning the lintel. Further north and facing west, is the small house known as Quholme, where, in 1731, was born one William Irving. He emigrated to America in his thirties, and fathered a son by the name of Washington, who went on to be one of the first celebrated American authors. And what is his most famous piece of writing? *Rip van Winkle*, an adaptation and Americanisation of an old Orkney legend: a weary traveller rests by a mysterious greeny mound, and disappears for years or decades. Then suddenly he appears again, unaged, having been living with the trows or the fairies, and has to come to terms with a world where his job has been taken, his true love has married another and he is barely remembered...

Veantro Bay is the large bite out of the north edge of Shapinsay. A fine beach stretches out along half its length, and half way along that beach lies Odin's Stone, a two and a half metre long block, that is of a distinctive, darker rock than everything around it. Its name suggests that it had some ritual or magical significance in Norse times, but exactly what purpose it served is long forgotten. Shapinsay has several more stretches of interesting if unspectacular shore, including sandy beaches (mostly on the west side); birdwatchers will find that Vasa Loch and Lairo Water are especially good for various breeds of waders.

Finally, back to Balfour Castle. A special guided tour of the house and gardens, a homebake tea in the Servants' Hall, and a return ticket on the ferry, is available as a special package tour on Wednesdays and Sundays from May onwards; tickets must be booked at Kirkwall Tourist Office for this deservedly popular excursion.

How to get there
A half-hour ferry journey between Kirkwall harbour and the pier at Balfour Village The OISC ro-ro, MV *Shapinsay*, makes about six journeys each way per day. Booking advised for cars (☎0856 872044).

Where to eat
The Gatehouse, Balfour Village, at the foot of the drive leading up to the castle, has to be one of the most unusual pub-buildings in Scotland (☎085 671 216). There's a cafe in The Smithy in the village; it sells good home-made snacks and light meals, seven days a week during the summer. (☎085 671 258).

Leisure
Appropriately for this intensely cultivated island, at least two farms run guided tours and other activities, ideal for kids: East Lairo Goat Farm (☎085 671 341) and Lucknow (☎085 671 271). Paul and Louise Hollinrake provide accommodation, equipment and guiding for anyone interested in 'wildlife, birdwatching and adventure holidays' (☎085 671 373). Mrs Wallace of Girnigoe also gives guided tours to folk staying at her B&B (☎085 671 256).

Nearest Tourist Information Centre: Kirkwall (☎0856 872856).

Eday

After Rousay, archaeologists will probably find Eday the most interesting of the outer isles. In the north end of the island there is a remarkable grouping of monuments between Mill Loch and the summit of Vinquoy Hill: three chambered tombs (including the well-preserved Vinquoy, the northmost), and the Stone of Setter, the most impressive single standing stone in Orkney. It is 4.5 metres high, and weathered into the shape of a gigantic hand reaching up out of the heather. Further south, near where the road branches off to Fersness (where much of the stone used in St Magnus Cathedral was quarried), can be seen a Bronze Age burial mound, and another chambered tomb; this is another of the pattern with a horn or spur wall arching out from each end, similar to the Tomb of the Eagles. The official explanation is that ritual events took place there, but I think it was a kind of patio where they could have barbecues on sunny neolithic afternoons. At the extreme south end of the island at Stackel Brae is a large eroding mound; it is believed to be a small Norse castle, similar to the famous one on Wyre.

Seven and a half miles away, at the extreme north end, lies Noup Hill, and the Red Head's magnificent sandstone cliffs, seventy metres high. The usual seabirds – guillemots, razorbills, puffins – are here in numbers; back towards the south end, around the 100 metre Flaughton Hill (a Site of Special Scientific Interest) can be found one of only two breeding sites in Orkney for the whimbrel, as well as various birds of prey such as hen harriers, merlins, and short-eared owls, which thrive on the rough heathery moorland.

In fact, as if there weren't enough interesting archaeological remains already visible, the blanket peat (only two or three thousand years old) which makes up a lot of this moorland, is believed to be covering many more relics – field systems and buildings – of prehistoric farmers. Until the 1940s, a lot of peat was exported, both to the other outer isles, and as far away as Edinburgh, where it was used by whisky distillers; peat is still dug for domestic use – who knows what might turn up under the tuskar one day?

One of the best beaches in Orkney is the linked Sands of Mussetter and Doomy, on the western side of the low isthmus that joins the two lumpy ends of Eday, and gives the island its name (Eithey = 'Isthmus Isle' in Old Norse). One of the best small laird's houses in Orkney is Carrick House overlooking the Calf of Eday at the north end, the oldest parts of which date to 1633. (It is a private house, but there are guided tours on Tuesdays and Thursdays, June to September: (08572) 260.) In 1725 the Carrick House hit the headlines – well, word got around as the site of the capture of Pirate John Gow, who had been attempting to lead a buccaneering life for several months since the captain of the ship he was second mate on was murdered off the Barbary Coast. It has to be said that Gow wasn't a very successful pirate; despite this, or maybe because of it, Orkney is very proud of him. Outsiders, too, have found him a dramatic figure: Daniel Defoe wrote an account of his life, and Sir Walter Scott used him as the model for the central character in his Northern Isles novel, *The Pirate*. It would take pages to relate all Gow's blunders; his final two were to run his ship aground on the Calf, and then to allow himself to be tricked into capture by a not-very-subtle ploy of James Fea of Clestrain and Carrick House.

Mention of the Calf reminds me that it holds its own attractions, well worth a few hours' visit: there are two chambered tombs dug into the hillside, and another, long stalled burial cairn, now completely excavated and open. Most interesting, perhaps, are the ruins of a saltworks, which began operating in the 1630s and provided most of Orkney's salt for a century. There are two buildings, both with their original enormous fireplaces (to aid the evaporation of the seawater) more or less intact. Ask at the co-op about hiring a boat to take you across to the Calf. Access may be restricted during the breeding seasons of the important colonies of great black-backed gulls, cormorants and terns that live there.

How to get there

The OISC north isles ro-ro ferries call here seven days a week during the summer, six during winter. In the summer only it is usually possible to make the return trip in a single day, allowing yourself a few hours on the island (though note that the pier is at the southern tip of the island, several miles from most of the interesting sites). The journey lasts between an hour and a quarter and two and a half hours depending on whether the boat goes direct or via another island. Booking essential for cars (☎0856 872044). Till May 1993, Loganair ran a twice a day air service to London Airport in the middle of the island; due to competition from the recently improved ro-ro service, that has been reduced to just two planes one day a week. Check with Loganair for the latest (☎0856 872494).

Accommodation

There is a SYHA-administered youth hostel (open April to September) just north of the Loch of Doomy; camping is allowed alongside it. Contact Alan Stewart for details (☎08572 267). There are several B&Bs and self-catering cottages.

Where to eat

Eday Community Enterprises runs a well-stocked grocery shop, which also sells alcohol and petrol; connected to that is a café which serves snacks and light meals, in the summer months at least. Also a local heritage display. (☎08572283).

Things to do and see

The community centre is attached to the school, near the south end of the island; visitors are welcome to use it during bad weather (☎08572 263).

Nearest Tourist Information Centre: Kirkwall (☎0856 872856).

Stronsay

From the air, Stronsay looks as beautiful as a tropical coral island. It has three curving legs of bright green fields, and in between the legs are shallow bays, blue as lagoons, rimmed with flawless white sand. Seals can be seen basking on the islets and skerries that are scattered around the island, occasionally slouging off into the clear water. Viewed from ground level, the look of the place is often less stunning: Stronsay is a very flat island, and it's also intensively farmed, only a small area of slightly raised moorland on the south-west leg (Rothiesholm) giving much relief from either. On a grey day, the outlook can be pretty monotonous: grey land, grey sea, grey sky... But let's give the weather the benefit of the doubt: there are many places worth visiting on Stronsay, and if the sun's shining it can be beautiful, even seen from five feet off the ground.

All three big bays have good beaches; the southmost one, at the head of the Bay of Holland, is particularly fine: a mile long, completely clean and white, and reportedly a good spot for finding rare seashells. Just to the west is an area of wet dune slack, where interestingly-named plants such as the Adder's Tongue Fern and the Green-flowered Frog Orchid can be found. If you find them, they're probably interesting to look at, too.

The shallow-curving Odin Bay on the south-east coast is an interesting walk along low cliffs. You'll see the Vat o Kirbister, a seacave that has collapsed, leaving a gloup with the biggest natural arch in Orkney. There is a natural swimming pool in the rocks near Bluther's Geo (soon to be superseded by an indoor, chlorinated, *heated* one) and on top of a stack there, the first of no less than three monastic cells, used by clerics in retreat or contemplation or bird-watching in the early years of Orkney's Christianity. Finally, there is a small Iron Age promontory fort, with a earth and stone rampart blocking off the narrow pathway to the clifftop.

From the approaching boat, Whitehall is an extremely attractive village, with its two piers and its curve of well-proportioned two-storied houses stretching out around the bay. The harbour is sheltered by the small island of Papa Stronsay (which features in the sagas as the site of Earl Rognvald Brusason's murder); the last time I arrived by ferry, there were swans swimming around the bow of the boat as it pulled in. Once you see the village closer up, it's disappointing how many of the houses are empty and starting to deteriorate, but still, Whitehall has a fascinating history, the evidence of which is all around. Stronsay had been exporting live lobsters to London since the end of the 18th century, but by the middle of the 19th it had become the most important herring port in Orkney. At its peak, up to 400 fishing vessels worked out of the island; on Sundays it was possible to walk from deck to deck all the way from Whitehall harbour to Papa Stronsay. No doubt more than a few folk did just that, for there were long corrugated-iron dormitories built there for many of the thousand or more women who came here to work at the gutting and packing. By the start of this century, Whitehall could boast – not only the longest bar in the north of Scotland (in the original Stronsay Hotel) – but also a chip shop, an ice-cream parlour, and a cinema! But, as all economic explosions do, the herring boom ended. By the mid-thirties a combination of overfishing and modern shipping meant that Stronsay's

glory days were over. There are still old folk around who remember the hard work and the bustling social life of the later herring decades; much of their history and many of their stories have been collected in a series of books by local author W. M. Gibson, e.g. *Herring Fishing, Old Orkney Sea Yarns*.

Another writer raised in Stronsay – at Mount Pleasant, on the low sandy arm that leads to Rothiesholm – is Douglas Sutherland, whose books *Against the Wind* and *Born Yesterday* contain colourful evocations of an island childhood. While we're down this end of the island again, have a look inside the Moncur Memorial Church (built in 1955, though it feels much older), a simple, graceful building that features a stained-glass window by Marjorie Kemp.

How to get there

The OISC north isles ro-ro ferries call here seven days a week during the summer, six during winter. In the summer it is sometimes possible to make the return trip in a single day, allowing yourself a few hours on the island. The journey lasts between an hour and a half and two and a quarter hours depending on whether the boat goes direct or via another island Booking is essential for cars: (☎0856 872044). Loganair fly to the airstrip, a couple miles north-west of Whitehall village, twice a day.

Where to eat

Stronsay Hotel in Whitehall is fully licensed (☎08576 213). There are various B&Bs and self-catering cottages, including a full range of accommodation at Stronsay Bird Reserve, on the shores of Mill Bay (☎08576 363). John and Sue Holloway also welcome campers on the reserve, and will be happy to provide information about birds and other wildlife. Woodlea Restaurant, in the village, is open seven days during the summer and has a table licence: (☎08576 337). Food and drink can be bought from several shops in Whitehall, and there is another small store, just south of the school, in the middle of the island.

Nearest Tourist Information Centre: Kirkwall (☎0856 872856).

Sanday

Rarely has an island been so well named. Coming in by plane, you might be forgiven for thinking that Sanday is entirely made of sand. But not quite; there is a small area of moor at the euphoniously named Gump of Spurness, and a lot of good farming land, mostly given over to raising cattle. The beaches really are remarkable, though: they surround most of the island (except the rocky south-west), and are uniformly clean, dazzlingly white, and quite deserted except for seals, birds and the occasional pulled-up fishing boat. Large sand-flats at Cata Sand, Otterswick and elsewhere are home or temporary lodging to a large number of waders such as bar-tailed godwit, knot, dunlin, grey plover, and turnstones. Large numbers of breeding ducks and waders – including whooper swan, pochard and goldeneye – can be seen at appropriate times of the year at Bea Loch, Roos Loch and North Loch; the Northwaa area around this last loch is a Site of Special Scientific Interest, notable for its wetland plants such as Frog Orchid, Adders Fern and Early March Orchid.

After its beaches, Sanday is most remarkable for its archaeological monuments. Indeed, the island probably has more important sites than any other; unfortunately for the visitor, few of these have been excavated recently, fewer still made accessible to the non-

expert. One of Orkney's finest chambered tombs can be seen at Quoyness (key from Lady PO); others are visible (though less impressive) at Tres Ness (suffering badly from erosion), Rethie Taing and at Maesry on the tidal island of Start Point. This last named was used for a number of years as a tattie store by the keepers in the nearby lighthouse, which is a remarkable structure in itself, not least because it is painted in enormous vertical black and white stripes; it looks as if it's about to blast off for the moon. A couple of years ago, 'the finest Viking grave in the UK' was revealed by erosion at Scar; archaeologists then raced against the wind and the waves to excavate the site before it was washed away completely. A remarkable collection of grave goods, including a sword, beads, and the remains of the small wooden boat used as a coffin, were recorded and taken away to museums in Kirkwall and Edinburgh, before the forces that revealed the site for the first time in nearly a thousand years washed it away forever, almost overnight. Similar damage is being done to the Pictish and Viking settlements at Pool on the south-west leg of Sanday, and indeed, throughout Orkney; changing weather patterns in the Atlantic – with an all-time record low pressure being measured in January 1993 – are washing away our coastline, and important parts of our heritage, faster than ever before. Come and see it while it's still there! (I'm not exaggerating: County Archaeologist Raymond Lamb has said that the ever encroaching sea is likely to bring about 'catastrophic losses to European – even world – archaeology.)

More recent history can be seen (in chronological order): at the ruined Cross Kirk, near Kettletoft, a 16th-century building built on the remains of a Viking settlement; at the Model Farm at Stove, an early (1860s) attempt at industrialising agriculture, which features extensive and sadly ruinous steadings, including a steam-engine shed and a red-brick chimney; at Lettan at the eastern extreme of the island, where there is the shell of one of the earliest (1940) and largest of Britain's air-defence radar stations. One spot definitely worth visiting is the abandoned fishing village of Ortie, on the north side of Otterswick. At one time sixty people lived here; now it is an eerie, ghostly place, its unusual long, straight, very narrow street – or 'kloss' – populated only by rabbits.

Which leads me on to the Breckan Rabbits Craft Centre in the north of the island, where specially trained rabbits produce raffia-work baskets and... no, sorry, my mistake... where angora wool is produced and prepared for export. Another local industry is knitting; the Isle of Sanday Knitters Ltd is a cooperative pooling the resources of more than 125 women in Sanday, Eday, Stronsay and North Ronaldsay, creating jumpers and other garments in both traditional and modern designs. Visits are welcome at both Breckan and at the Wool Yall in Lady.

Sanday has a population of over 500, a junior secondary school, and a lively social scene (e.g. the Agricultural and Industrial Show in early August, the St Colm Model Yacht Club Regatta on Roos Loch every Boxing Day), if that's what you're looking for. It's big enough, though, that you could spend a week walking around and never see another person, if that is what you want. It's a big island, as long as Hoy (though much spindlier), and taking a car or bike is definitely worthwhile, though not essential; alternatively, you can hire both from the garages at Kettletoft and Quivals, and there is also a post bus. Pedestrians arriving by ferry should note that the new pier is at Loth, at the extreme south-west tip of the island, a long way away from most of the places mentioned above. My advice is: befriend someone with a car during the crossing from Kirkwall...

How to get there

OISC ro-ro ferries make at least one return journey per day from Kirkwall to Sanday, seven days a week during the summer, six during the winter. The journey lasts between an hour and a half and two hours, depending on whether the boat goes direct or via other islands. Booking for cars strongly recommended (☎0856 872044). Loganair provides two return flights (about ten minutes each way) per day, six days a week: book on (☎0856 872494).

Accommodation

As well as the hotels below, Sanday is well supplied with B&Bs, self-catering cottages and caravans for hire.

Where to eat

Both the Kettletoft Hotel (☎08575 217) and the Belsair Hotel (☎08575 206) are open to non-residents for drink and bar meals; the Belsair also provides packed lunches and has a good reputation for its à la carte cooking. Most of the island's B&Bs will also provide packed lunches or evening meals on request. There are two licensed grocers (at Kettletoft and Roadside) and several farms sell milk, eggs etc. A special mention goes to Mrs Sinclair at How farm (☎08575 361) – who makes great Orkney cheese.

Golf

There is a basic nine-hole links at the Plain of Fidge; clubs can be hired from the nearby farm of Newark.

Westray

First a word of warning: the new ro-ro pier at Rapness is at the extreme south end of Westray, about six miles away from the village and most of the amenities. This long walk can come as a shock to non-car-drivers lulled into a false sense of comfort by the well-equipped-ferry journey. All is not lost, though: during the summer at least, Sam Harcus operates a feeder minibus service to connect with the foot ferry to Papay, and he will carry other visitors too, if he has space. Better check with him, though, if a lift is essential (☎08577 432).

This problem underlines something important about Westray: it's a big island! At nearly ten miles from Rapness in the south-east to the cliffs of Noup Head in the north-west, and four across the way at its widest point, Westray covers a lot of land. It's not the kind of place you can see all of in a day trip; nor do the island's attractions consist of a handful of spectacular monuments that can be chalked off one after the other. No, ideally you should spend a week or so here, gradually getting to know the place and its people, exploring its many interesting corners at a leisurely pace.

Bird watchers will want to head straight for the RSPB reserve at Noup Head, which has the second largest population of breeding seabirds (after St Kilda) in Britain. Guillemots, fulmars, kittiwakes and razorbills fill the air all along the rugged red sandstone cliffs which stretch for more than four miles south of the lighthouse. The area just inland from these cliffs is windswept and soaked in salt spray: a good place to find various maritime heath plants such as thrift, sea pink, meadow rue, alpine mistort, mountain everlasting and the rare and tiny primula scotica. At the opposite end of the island, near the bay of Rack Wick, is a stumpy sea stack called the Castle of Burrian; puffins nest here in large numbers, and can be observed close up for hours. July's the best time to go, just after the chicks have hatched.

The single most impressive building in Westray – indeed, probably in all of Orkney, outside Kirkwall – is Noltland Castle, overlooking Pierowall (keys from the farm opposite). Dating to around 1560, it was built for Gilbert Balfour, arch-plotter and conspiricist, implicated in the murder of Cardinal Beaton and various shady goings-on in the court of Mary Queen of Scots. The massive walls linking two square

towers are pierced by a huge number of gunloops: in anyone else's castle they would seem evidence of extreme paranoia, but in Balfour's case they were probably quite justified! (He was finally put to death in 1576 for his part in an attempt to assassinate the king of Sweden.) The interior of the castle is very impressive, with a large great hall and a sweeping main staircase: 'one of the finest in Scotland' according to architecture experts. Fine views over most of Westray (and as far as Fair Isle on a clear day) can be had from the top of the towers, which are semi-ruinous (this on top of the fact that the castle was only half-finished when Balfour fled).

Westray is full of interesting archaeological remains, but unfortunately very little has been prepared for public viewing. On the Links at Noltland, for instance, an extensive area of prehistoric settlement was excavated, then covered up again. And on the southern shores of the Bay of Tuquoy, a large Viking village has been partly surveyed: very big stone walls and middens of bones and seashells are being eaten away – and revealed to the shorewalker – by erosion. Westray is thought to be one of the first islands settled by the Norsemen; it would have provided a good harbour at Pierowall and excellent farming land throughout. These conditions still prevail – Orkney's largest fleet of white fish boats operates from here, and the island is a big exporter of beef cattle – making it the most prosperous of the northern isles. As a direct result of its prosperity, natives have not been forced to leave to make a living, (the population has been stable at around 700 for years now), and so there are few incomers. Visitors will certainly be given a friendly welcome though.

There's a ruined medieval church, St Mary's, at Pierowall, which contains two intricately carved 17th-century tombstones. On the west side, right on the shore at the Bay of Tuquoy, are the evocative remains of a 12th-century chapel, Cross Kirk. The attached graveyards of both of these kirks contain many interesting old stones, some of them grand, some of them touching in the simplicity and crudeness of their inscription. Look out for several mentions of the surname Angel. These are descendants of a single boy – real name unknown – who was washed up half-dead after a shipwreck 250 years ago. The only information about him (he spoke some strange language, and there were no other survivors) was a piece of wood from his ship with the Russian placename Archangel painted on it. The boy remained on the island, became known as Archie Angel, and his descendants (though none, unfortunately, still bearing the name Angel) live here to this day. There's another fascinating and lengthy shipwreck story, to do with the Spanish Armada and the stranded sailors who started new lives on the common land to the north of the village, building homes for themselves, the shells of which are still standing, and still known as the Dons' houses... But I'll leave you to find that one out for yourself.

It should be clear by now that, like all the Orkney islands but more so because of its size, Westray is a place that will reward the unhurried, inquisitive visitor, who is prepared to soak in the sights and sounds of the place, rather than anyone who rushes around trying to take in everything in an afternoon. If time is at a premium, though, or if you are without transport to get to the more remote parts of the island, Sam Harcus (number given earlier) is usually available to give very informed and very personal guided tours. He knows all about the Spaniards.

How to get there

Big OISC ro-ros make return crossings from Kirkwall to Rapness usually twice a day, seven days a week, during summer months; they are less frequent but still regular during the winter. The journey takes about an hour and twenty-five minutes. Booking advised for cars (☎0856 872 044). Loganair fly to the airfield in the north of the island twice a day, six days a week, throughout the year (☎0856 872 494).

Accommodation

Both the hotels below are very popular during the summer, as are the B&Bs and the self-catering cottages, and advance booking is strongly recommended.

Where to eat

The Pierowall Hotel is reputed to serve the best fish and chips in the north of Scotland; they are good, and the bar is very pleasant too, with an open fire and pictures of fishing boats on the walls: (☎08577 208). A wider range of more ambitious food is served at Cleaton House Hotel, half-way down the east coast; it has recently become very popular with visitors from Kirkwall (and beyond) for both lunches and evening meals. Local seafood is a speciality: (☎08577 508). There are several B&Bs, and most of them are happy to provide evening meals on request; apart from that, there are two well stocked shops (not licensed) in Pierowall, and another at Surrigarth down the east side. The chip shop in the village closed down recently, but there is talk of a new carry-out restaurant opening soon.

Things to do and see

There is a games hall and swimming pool at the Community Complex in Pierowall, open to the public at certain times: Mrs Kent (☎08577 436) has the details. On the Links near Noltland Castle at the north end is a nine-hole golf course. Clubs can be rented locally, details at the clubhouse (which is, I reckon, the smallest in the country: room for a single golf-club inside).

Events and festivals

One of the major events of the year in the north isles is the Westray Sailing Club Regatta, usually held at the end of July. The sun on Papa Sound, and on dozens of sails skiting over it, is a sight worth seeing (☎08577 281) for details.

Nearest Tourist Information Centre: Kirkwall (☎0856 872856).

Papa Westray

'A most beautiful little isle, rich in
excellent corn and luxuriant natural
grass. The uncultivated part like a
carpet spread with all the flowers in
season.' So wrote the Reverend George
Low in 1771. Two centuries later, there's
not much corn being grown, but there
are still plenty of flowers: 230 different
species at the last count! These include
yellow flags in Tredwell Loch, sea pink
by the shore, and the insectivorous
sundew on the boggy North Hill.
Birdlife is also abundant, both migrants
and residents such as razorbills, guillemots and great skuas; the North Hill is
a bird sanctuary, important to the
expert for its 6,000 pairs of Arctic terns,
and to the novice for its warden, who is
generous with advice and information
about where and when to see what. He
can be found in a cottage by the gate that
leads into the reserve.

Birds were not always so well protected
on Papay. In 1813 the last surviving
Great Auk – a very large, flightless
version of the puffin – was shot at Fowl
Craig on the north-east cliffs. What's
always puzzled me is, if the Auk
couldn't fly, how did it get up the cliff
in the first place? From big birds to
small planes. The Loganair flight (more
of a hop, really) from the Papay airfield
(and I mean field) to the one across the
firth in Westray, is officially timetabled
as lasting two minutes, making it The
Shortest Scheduled Flight In The
World. The day I did it there must have
been a following wind: it was more like
45 seconds between take-off and landing!

Another record-holder is the two-celled
stone-built house at Knap of Howar, on
the west side; it is the oldest standing
dwelling in northwest Europe. Similar
in appearance to Skara Brae, with its
stone shelves, hearth and querns, it was
in use from about 3800 BC. Around the
same time, chambered tombs were
being built on the Holm of Papay, an
islet on the east side; three have been

identified there, indicating the presence of a relatively large and well organised community. The organisation is
most obvious in the large and unusually
structured South tomb; its outer shell is
estimated to have been over thirty
metres long, and various decorations –
some likened to patterns of eyebrows –
have been chipped into the stonework
inside. A small boat can usually be
hired to take you over to the Holm: ask
at the Co-op. And bring a torch.

The Co-op is a great boon to the visitor;
along with the renowned friendliness of
the folk here, it helps make Papay one
of the most popular of the small islands.
In a row of converted farm cottages, a
shop was started in 1980; soon after, the
hostel and the hotel opened next door.
The Co-op also runs self-catering accommodation, and generally makes visitors
very welcome. (Phone number below.)

Have you been paying attention? If so,
you'll've noticed that I've been referring
to the island as Papay. This is closer to
the original Old Norse name, Papey,
which means 'island of the monks'. All
the maps say Papa Westray, but the
older name is generally preferred
locally. There seems little doubt that
the island was an important centre for
early Christianity. St Boniface's kirk,
north of the airfield, is being examined
by archaeologists as I write; it is
believed to date to the 12th century, and
has a Norse hog-backed gravestone
close by. Even more interesting, though
almost completely ruinous, is St Tredwell's chapel, which lies on a point of
land sticking out into the loch of the
same name. The legend is that Tridu-
ana, a Celtic abbess, was visiting the
Pictish court when Nechtan, their king,
admired her beautiful eyes. She
plucked them out and had them
presented impaled on thorn-twigs, to
impress upon him the folly of his
worldly ways and the strength of her
faith. How she came to be associated
with Papay is unknown, but the island
became a centre of pilgrimage for her
followers, and the waters of the loch
were believed to have magical proper-

ties: people came here from all over the north, right up till the 18th century, seeking a cure for their eye-troubles. Now there's an optician in Kirkwall, but there are many other reasons why a few days here will stick in your memory for more than a few years.

An excellent booklet – *Papay: a Guide to Places of Interest* – has been written by Jocelyn Rendall, and is essential for anyone visiting the island.

How to get there

Loganair flies from Kirkwall to Papa Westray twice a day, six days a week; there is a special low return fare in operation, which puts the flight within reach of those on a tight budget (☎08568 72494). The OISC runs a complex six-day timetable of ferries – some direct, some involving changing boats and crossing Westray by bus or taxi. Get them to explain it (☎0856 872044).

Accommodation

Papay Community Co-operative coordinate all visitor accommodation, including several farmhouse B&Bs, and their own sixteen-bed hostel and four-room hotel, both part of Beltane House in the middle of the island (☎08574 267). They'll also usually collect you from the pier or the plane if you ask in advance.

Nearest Tourist Information Centre: Kirkwall (☎0856 872856).

North Ronaldsay

On a clear day you can see Fair Isle from North Ronaldsay. On a very clear day you can see the cliffs of Foula in Shetland. One night in 1902 the sky to the north-east was filled with flickering red

and yellow lights; much later, word reached the island that the Norwegian town of Bergen had suffered a terrible fire...

But North Ronaldsay is not only the northmost island of the group; it is also the most remote – in several ways. There is only one ferry a week to the island, and even that is subject to delay or cancellation due to bad weather. It's not a ro-ro, either, so no casual day-trippers can scoot around the island in an hour or two then head home: you have to really want to visit North Ronaldsay. It has the reputation amongst other Orcadians of being the most old-fashioned island of the group: ways of talking and working and living survive there decades or centuries after disappearing from more worldly parts. On the down side, this isolation meant that the island wasn't connected to the electricity grid until 1983; it means that there is little work for young people, except the hard and precarious life of crofter-fisherman; it means that supplies of essentials including food are often interrupted, always expensive. On the positive side, the people of North Ronaldsay – the vast majority of them born and bred there – have a knowledge of and respect for their island's history and culture that is an example to small communities everywhere. Visitors can hope to experience the unique atmosphere of the island, and the unique character of its inhabitants.

A good day's walking can take you right around the coastline, but why rush? There is plenty worth taking your time over. If you land at the pier, one of the first things you'll see is the standing stone; it's about five metres high, with a small hole punched through the middle of it about half way up. It's been suggested that the hole was used – similar to the now demolished Odin Stone at Stenness – during ancient marriage rituals. It is recorded that, up to a couple of hundred years ago, the people of the island used to dance around the stone on New Year's morning singing strange songs. The songs are lost, unfortunately: you'll just have to look at the stone, listen to the birds, the seals the waves, the wind – and use your imagination.

On your right you'll pass Holland House, which was built in the 18th century for the Traill family, who bought the island in 1727. Their descendants still own the house, though much of the land has – since the land act of 1976 – been sold to the people who farm it. Feudalism was another thing that lingered on in North Ronaldsay.

A right turn at this point will take you down past the new school and community centre which is open to visitors: enquire at either of the two shops about a key) towards Bridesness Point, a particularly quiet and flower-swathed corner of the island. The road passes a large structure like a railway embankment at one point: this is the remains of the Muckle Gersty, one of two prehistoric dykes that divide the island into three roughly equal parts. (The other is called Matches Dyke, and can best be seen at the roadside between North Manse farm and Ancum Loch.) The legendary explanation was that three brothers divided the island between themselves like this in olden times; there isn't a satisfactory scientific explanation of who built the dykes, or why. But more and more of these fascinating structures are being identified throughout Orkney – on parts of Sanday they are maze-like! – and more and more evidence and theories are being brought forward to justify the immense amounts of work involved.

A further antiquity at the south end of the island is Burrian Broch, about half of which is now washed away into the sea. Go and examine the other half quickly, before it disappears too! The farmer here is sensitive about people crossing his land; best to approach along the shore. That way, too, you can carry on to the fine sandy beach and seals of Nouster Bay.

But don't hang around the southern end

of the island all day! Walk or cycle (bikes can be rented from the Treb shop by the airfield) up the road that runs along the spine of the island (though it's a low-lying spine, nowhere higher than about twenty metres), bear right once you pass the swans and irises of Ancum Loch, and soon you'll be at Dennis Ness, the eastmost point in Orkney. Here you'll see one of the four oldest lighthouses in Scotland; it was built in 1789, and looks like a giant chess-piece. Its successor (built 1852) stands nearby; at forty-two metres, it is the tallest land-based lighthouse in Britain. It's also one of the last to be manned, though it'll be going automatic within the next few years. Get there quick and see the breathtaking view from the top. Enquiries to the Headkeeper (☎08573 225.)

I haven't mentioned the sheep yet! But you're bound to have noticed them, for they outnumber humans on North Ronaldsay thirty times over (there are 2000 sheep: work out the rest yourself) and they're usually to be seen scavenging the foreshore, often right down at the water's edge, eating the seaweed there. It looks like they're munching on giant strips of red and green pasta. Do they like the stuff? They don't have much choice: the island's most remarkable architectural architectural feature is a two-metre-high wall entirely encircling it, designed to keep the sheep off the valuable crops and pasture inside! You've never seen sheep like these before; they are the survivors of an ancient breed once common throughout Orkney, and can now be found nowhere else but here. They look as much like goats as sheep. Their meat tastes of seaweed. They are rounded up ('punded') by all able-bodied islanders at set times of the year for shearing and slaughtering; if you're lucky you may be able to help with this. At least ask at the shops for some of the uniquely flavoured mutton; vegetarians can cut out the middleman and munch on the seaweed themselves.

And I still haven't mentioned that

Crafts in Orkney

I've said plenty about Orkney writers, and also mentioned the galleries and festivals where you can see the work of some of the many painters and sculptors who live here. But I haven't given much information on the craft side of things. My excuse is that there are so many fine craftworkers that if I'd started listing them under their individual areas, I wouldn't have had room for anything else. I will attempt to make remedy now by listing a few of the outstanding products and producers – but remember that there are many more that I don't have space to mention even now.

Beautiful silverwork and other jewellery is made by Ola Gorie and sold at her shop The Longship in Broad Street, Kirkwall (☎0856 873251). Almost as attractive is the jewellery made by Ortak, who have a shop on Kirkwall's Albert Street (☎0856 873536), and by Sheila Fleet whose workshop in Tankerness is open to visitors (☎085 686 203). Also in Broad Street, Kirkwall, is Judith Glue's knitwear shop; you can buy arty and crafty things made by many different folk here, too (☎0856 874225). (Jane Glue's Shorelines Gallery is part of the same premises.) I don't know if this counts as a craft or not, but I'd just like to put on record that Lobban the butcher in Victoria Street, Kirkwall, makes the best black pudding I've ever eaten. Designer Ingrid Tait makes beautiful scarves, wraps and other felted fabric goods at the Tait & Style workshop in Stromness (☎0856 851186). Her namesake Helga Tait makes knitwear and runs a craft shop at the pierhead in Rousay (☎085 682 293). Stephanne Jaeger of Burray runs handspinning courses, as well as making and selling knitwear (☎085 673 228). Fursbreck Pottery in Harray is open for visitors, interested in seeing Andrew Appleby throwing his wide range of contemporary and Roman reproduction work (☎085 677 419). Seeing as I mentioned black pudding above, I think I should also be allowed to bring in oatcakes. Controversy rages as to which are better: Garden's thick oatcakes, or Stockan's thin ones. I think they're both wonderful. And ideal accompaniments to the various farm-made cheeses available: Swannay, Grimbister, and How are all excellent. Keep an eye out for more in various butchers, fish shops and grocers and get it while it's fresh and moist: it should squeak as you slice it. There's an Orkney word to describe this noise: just listen out for the neester of the How as you dig your knife in! As old as the tradition of cheese-making is the construction of woven straw-backed chairs. These keep out the draughts, with their high backs and hoods, but they also don't call for large quantities of that precious commodity, wood. From being an everyday piece of furniture found in every croft, these chairs have become much sought after, and rather expensive. But they are beautiful. Several shops take orders for them, or have them on display; some of the best ones are said to be made in Westray: contact the makers there direct on ☎08577 323. Finally, a word about two more good crafty/arty shops, which have a wide range of items on sale. They are both in Stromness this time, and both on Victoria Street: the Quernstone and the Waterfront.

Linklet Bay on the east side of the island has one of the outstanding beaches in Orkney! Even worse, I haven't mentioned that, as well as multitudinous birds permanently in residence, North Ronaldsay is famous for the regular dropping-in of exotic and exhausted migrants, off-course on their flights to or from North America, Russia, South Africa. Very rare, even unique sightings are made here every year. The staff at the bird observatory are always friendly and helpful, even if you're not a fanatical twitcher.

It's easy for a summer visitor to be bewitched by the atmosphere of North Ronaldsay. But before deciding to give up island-hopping and settle down, read Mary Scot's *Island Saga* or Christine Muir's *Orkney Days* for more realistic and rounded pictures of life here – including the days when the wind blows away everything that isn't tied down, and the waves smash down the sheep-dyke and flood the fields inside.

All of these islands are at the mercy of the sea and the weather, but here the power of the elements is even more obvious and awesome than everywhere else. As in so many ways, North Ronaldsay provides the ultimate Orkney experience.

How to get there

By boat (passengers only) with the Orkney Isles Shipping Company from Kirkwall; once a week, usually Fridays.

Always check if weather permits a sailing (☎0856 872044). By Loganair plane from Kirkwall twice a day, six days a week. There's a special reduced fare at the moment, which makes flying definitely affordable. Bookings (☎0856 872494).

Accommodation

Mrs Muir at Garso No 1 (☎08573 244), and Mr Ogilvie at Roadside (☎08573 221) each run both B&B and self-catering accommodation; the Muirs also run a taxi service. The Bird Observatory (☎08573 267) has a dormitory as well as private rooms for rent (and is currently building an extension to fit in more visitors). Check with Tourist Board for others.

Nearest Tourist Information Centre: Kirkwall (☎0856 87856).

Shetland

Shetland

In the summer and autumn of 1814, the author was invited to join a party of Commissioners for the Northern Lighthouse Service, who proposed making a voyage round the coast of Scotland, and through its various groups of islands, chiefly for the purpose of seeing the condition of the many lighthouses under their direction –

The nature of the important business which was the principal purpose of the voyage, was connected with the amusement of visiting the leading objects of a traveller's curiosity; for the wild cape, or formidable shelve, which requires to be marked out by a lighthouse, is generally at no great distance from the most magnificent scenery of rocks, caves, and billows. Our time, too was at our own disposal, and, as most of us were very fresh-water sailors, we could at any time make a fair wind out of a foul one, and run before the gale in quest of some object of curiosity which lay under our lee.

With these purposes of public utility, and some personal amusement in view, we left the port of Leith on the 26th July, 1814, ran along the east coast of Scotland, viewing its different curiosities, stood over to Zetland and Orkney, where we were detained by the wonders of a country which displayed so much that was new to us; and having seen what was curious in the Ultima Thule of the ancients, where the sun hardly thought it worth while to go to bed, since his rising was at this season so early, we doubled the extreme northern termination of Scotland and took a rapid survey of the Hebrides, where we found many kind friends.

Sir Walter Scott, from the 1831 introduction to *The Pirate*.

A Peerie Scar O Backgrund

The north Atlantic is a place of dramatic change, and weathers pass over Shetland at a rate of knots, as the maritime climate dictates. Low-lying mists transform in minutes to startling views, and sudden storms blow up from flat blue calm. The seasons too exact a polar pull. Daylight in the summer stretches eighteen hours and never really fades at all, while in the winter gloom six hours of light slip past and then the night returns.

No wonder then that such extremes of viewpoint as we find regarding Shetland should exist. There are those for whom it is the heart of a romantic vision, sublimely wild, often intemperate; their relationship a passionate affair where love and hate may alternate. Others who have been and looked have left, little the wiser. I once spent a week showing some friends a blanket of sea fog, so shrouded in mystery the islands remained.

Shetlanders have an affectionate name for their islands – 'the Old Rock'. A first glance at the treeless landscape might suggest there's little other than stone, in constant conflict with water and the whistling gales of air. But take the trouble to turn a stone over and you'll find amazing forms of life – crack the Shetland atom and you'll find, if not quarks, then certainly *Quarff*, strangeness and charm!

The oldest parts of Shetlandic history are as misty as the land itself can be, yet the remains are everywhere. The absence of intense cultivation and the sparse population has meant that the past isn't simply swallowed up or remade in the present, but is left in many cases virtually untouched: 'the best archaeology visible in Britain', it is claimed. But mysteries prevail, never more engaging than in the case of the brochs, the 'Pictish Towers' of old maps. Like the Picts themselves, the brochs continue to puzzle today – were they really the work of the Picts, or of another unknown Iron Age people? The shared mystery is perhaps the strongest link between the two.

Shetland is often bracketed along with Orkney, yet the traveller coming north from the southern archipelago will enter a different landscape and accordingly a different culture. If the green fields, dykes and low lands of Caithness are to Orkney, then the heathery 'moonscapes' and lochans of Sutherland are to Shetland, though Hoy in Orkney and Dunrossness in the Sooth End of Shetland are the exceptions to prove the rule. History also wrongly harnesses the two in a single yoke. Although Shetland was a part of the Orkney Earldom at the height of Norse ascendancy in the north, King Sverre Sigurdsson removed Shetland to direct rule from Norway in the late twelfth century, after an uprising by the 'island beardies'. From this it became natural for Shetlanders to look north to Faroe or east to Bergen, rather than southwards to Orkney. But the waning of Norwegian power in the fourteenth century left Shetland open to Scots invasion. In 1379 a dispute over succession to the Orkney Earldom was settled in favour of Henry Sinclair, a member of the Scottish family whose seat is now at Rosslyn outside Edinburgh, and although it is unclear whether Shetland rejoined the earldom in 1379, the influence of the Orkney earl increased. The crisis was exacerbated when the kingdom of Norway lost its sovereignty when united with Denmark in 1397. In the 15th century King Christian the First was faced with trying to hold together a vast Norse empire including not only Norway and Denmark, but Sweden too. Constant rebellions put a great strain on his treasury and he no doubt thought Shetland and Orkney distant lands, the least part of his worries. Unable to pay the dowry for the marriage of his daughter to the Scottish king, he mortgaged first Orkney in 1468, then Shetland the following year. It is perhaps telling that the sums involved were 50,000 crowns in the first instance and 8,000 in the latter.

The pledge was intended to be redeemed, and numerous attempts were made, as late as 1667. But Scotland seemed in no ways inclined to give up what she had got. The Sinclair family rose to a clan-like centrality, and were trailed by Scots merchants and necessary professions. The 16th century saw the consolidation of Scots power, till it became a political pawn, a little empire of bastardy, dastardy and intrigue in the north. In 1560, a 'velvet' reformation of the Church; in 1564, Mary Queen of Scots gave her half-brother Robert Stewart both Orkney and Shetland.

The struggle for power in the Scottish kingdom following the death of James V saw Mary involved in great intrigues with her father's 'natural' or illegitimate sons. Most famous is Lord James Stewart, later Earl of Murray and Regent of Scotland. Lord Robert was another. It's said that David Rizzio, the Italian Secretary who inspired so much jealousy in Mary's court at Holyrood at that time, 'was warned to beware of a bastard' by a French priest who dabbled in astrology, in reference to Murray. These words may illustrate the thinking that brought Robert Orkney and Shetland, granted to him in perpetual feu.

As far as the national picture went, Lord Robert stayed out of trouble during the turbulent politics of the 1560s and 70s. He quietly set about building a power base in the northern isles, moving in his own people. With Scotland in the grip of political instability, he made himself Chief Magistrate and operated a kangaroo-court with his half-brother Laurence Bruce, which had the main aim of confiscating as much land as possible, whatever the charge. A Royal Commission investigated complaints against them and Bruce was jailed, but held on to his profits. In 1581, whether to win his loyalty back after the investigation or to reward him for keeping his nose clean, James VI gave Robert the title Earl of Orkney.

Lord Robert was a minor branch of the royal Stewart tree, able to exercise a short-lived despotic power in a time of uncertainty – someone who took what he could while the going was good, knowing he wasn't really entitled to it. But his son Patrick grew up there, the vain son of a despot: a proud Stewart with a streak of Viking *berserker* mixed in. Under his rule, the ancient Law-Book of the islands disappeared. He tried to undermine the landowning families who had established themselves in his father's time, to take more power to himself, till it appeared he came to see himself as more than a mere Earl, with the audacity to resist the King's Men by force of arms. He restricted movement in and out of the islands on the pretext of preventing the spread of 'the pest' (plague). He overstretched the meagre island resources, taxed and fined to feed his vanity and ended up paying the full price, executed for high treason in Edinburgh in 1615.

Though Patrick denied few of the accusations made against him, and deserved what he got no doubt, one wonders if King James VI, in eliminating Patrick, rid himself not so much of a political threat, as a family embarrassment, an unpleasant rumour that started here in Shetland, and reached the court by the Thames, the full extent of Stewart influence in Britain.

In 1603, James VI of Scotland became king of England and the two kingdoms were united. James was anxious to impress the English court by his civilised, cultured kingly air – he was succeeding the great Queen Bess, after all. Patrick was the family's wild-oats offshoot, the man who had repeated Lord Robert's offensive Latin 'error': the inscription at his palace in Birsay which suggests that Robert actually *was* King of Scotland. As Walter Scott says, high treason was 'a rather severe punishment for false Latin'.

In 1633, the islands were granted to the Earl of Morton. Around this time, the

Dutch herring *busses* became regular visitors to Bressay Sound, buying fresh food and other wares from the islanders to sustain them while they fished, a process which saw Lerwick begin to grow as a centre. This trade was enough to worry the British government that the Dutch had designs of the Northern archipelago, and troops were garrisoned to defend the British interest. Despite skirmishes and three 'Dutch Wars', herring continued to bring the *Dutchies* north till the early years of this century.

Not so constant were the Hanseatic League merchants, who had been a part of the Shetland economy since the Middle Ages, buying fish direct from the folk, and bringing in other goods to exchange. In 1712, a punitive salt tax forced them out of the game.

Under the Norse law, the *udallers* held a number of rights and were largely free in their actions: according to Edmonston, *udal* land was held '*by uninterrupted succession without any original charter and without subjection to feudal service or the acknowledgement of any superior*'. Under Scottish rule they became tenants, but were able to trade freely with the merchants who came to their shores. The demise of the Scots landowning class in the early 18th century changed that. The new lairds, such as the Giffords of Busta, were merchants themselves, and they wanted the fish trade under their control. This meant a further loss of liberty and rights for the tenants, under the infamous *truck* system.

This was a total trade monopoly, with the *haaf* fishermen forced to fish up to sixty miles offshore in small six-oared open boats, *sixareens*, in exchange for goods from the laird's own store. Needless to say, folk often lived in perpetual hock to their landowner, without security of tenure. Throughout Shetland, there are many of these Lairds' substantial *Haa* houses, as distinctive a feature of the place as the many brochs.

The 19th century saw change. The

Napoleonic Wars brought the Press Gang and a third of the island men served, valued because of their skill at sea. The veterans returning brought new ideas with them. With the establishment of a regular shipping service, a greater number of visitors came north and trade became easier. The iniquity of the *truck* system was recognised and Arthur Anderson attempted to break the landowner's stranglehold on the fishing industry. The hardships of this period were severe, with famine and emigration, loss and deprivation at the back of every forward step, but Anderson was a genuine folk hero, who was as important as a symbol of the independent, successful man o' the world, a figure of hope, as for his many charitable acts.

The Crofters' Act of 1886 finally broke the landlord's grip, and the herring boom around the turn of the century brought considerable wealth to the island. By the outbreak of the First World War, a decline had begun but the heavy losses the island population suffered overshadowed the death knell of the herring. Shetland's strategic importance in blockading the Atlantic from German shipping led to the use of Swarbacks Minn as a base for a Cruiser Squadron.

The years between the wars were extremely difficult and when the Second World War broke out, the 'war in the sky' saw Shetland become the base of the RAF's northern defence. After the fall of Norway in 1940, it seemed that the massed German forces would next invade Shetland – the first air attack came within two months of the outbreak of war. But the onslaught didn't materialise, and the forces in Shetland instead struck back across the water into Norway by means of the *Shetland Bus* – an operation involving free Norwegians and fishing boats, which helped reawaken the old sense of kinship with the country to the east.

The post-war years have seen a great many developments. The widespread provision of utilities, the improvement of the housing stock and the establishment of a good road system has meant that the country areas are much less 'cut-off' or 'backward'. The North Sea oil era which began in the 1970s has contributed largely to this, although the 1960s had already brought a new sense of endeavour in the traditional industries. Today, Shetland stands at the beginning of a new era. Having benefited from the oil around its shores, it must now find long-term, sustainable answers to economic puzzles that are, perhaps for the first time, within its own hands. The many salmon-cages sited in the Shetland voes represent a major new investment that people hope will carry the present health of the economy into the 21st century.

Shetland has had as long a period of Scottish/British domination as it previously had Norwegian/Norse. Added to that are the long-standing contacts with Dutch and German merchants. The British influence is most prominent, but poking through the holes in that fabric you find the Norse is still there, underneath, like a layer in a complex archaeological site. The blend is unique.

Travel to Shetland: General

Ferries
P&O Scottish Ferries: Nightly service – Aberdeen (Scotland) 14 hrs.
Twice weekly (summer) – Stromness (Orkney) 8 hrs.
Summer service – Bergen (Nor.) 13 hrs.

Smyril Line:
Summer ser. – Torshavn (Faroe) 14 hrs.

Strandfaraskip Landsins: Summer service – Hantsholm (Denmark) 23 hrs.

Details of all services:
P&O Scottish Ferries
P.O. Box 5,
Jamieson's Quay
Aberdeen AB9 8DL (☎0224 572615)

Air
British Airways: Aberdeen to Sumburgh 1 hr. (Coach to Lerwick) (☎0224 722331)

Mon-Fri: 4 flights a day; Sat-Sun: 2 flights a day
Kirkwall to Sumburgh 35 mins. (Coach to Lerwick)
Loganair: Glasgow to Sumburgh 1½ hrs. (Coach to Lerwick)
Edinburgh to Sumburgh 1½ hrs. (Coach to Lerwick)
2 flights a day, reduced service at weekends.

There's one Tourist Information Centre in Lerwick (☎0595 3434).

The Sunday sailing from Stromness in Orkney is probably the easiest route to Shetland. It avoids both the stresses of the daily overnight voyage from Aberdeen and the sometimes turbulent descent to Sumburgh Airport over the headland lighthouse, which has been known to make even the hardiest flier gulp air in rapidly. Sailing northwards from Orkney, the continuity of land on the horizon is a comforting thing.

Armed with a map and a pair of binoculars the traveller has a clear sense of where he or she is all the time. Though it is fifty miles from North Ronaldsay to the southern tip of Shetland, the renowned bird-watching island of Fair Isle links the two. It stands like a fortress surrounded by the swirling race of ocean water passing between the open Atlantic and the North Sea, both a sanctuary for those creatures able to make landfall on its plateau, and a place of death for the many ships that have come to grief on its rocks – most famously, remnants of the Spanish Armada, trying to sail home round the north of Britain, against the prevailing winds. But on the journey north, Fair Isle is a pleasure to be investigated later, an elusive glimpse of what's to come.

Off Sumburgh Head, whichever route you've taken north, you get your first impression of the islands proper. Even if you've chosen the overnighter from Aberdeen, consider getting up with the daylight to see this southern approach. There is something defiant about the position of the lighthouse high above,

almost Gothic in its builders' aspiration, and if you wait until the ferry slips into shelter of the eastern coast before you rise, you'll miss that first important view.

Once in the shelter of land, the ferry still has quite a distance to go, north past the broch island of Mousa, and the rounded hilltops of the southern stretch of the main island. The cliffs of Bressay and Noss that appear on the starboard bow mark the south mouth of Lerwick harbour, with Bressay lighthouse low on the starboard as the entry is made, the stark cliff faces of the Ord and the Bard rising sharply behind.

Lerwick, Bressay and Noss

Lerwick is a fast-growing town which had no great importance in the Norse age, but grew out of the fishing trade with the Dutch, who began to use its fine natural deep-water harbour in the 17th century. A map of the town dated 1766 by William Aberdeen carries the following legend. *Every year betwixt eight or nine hunder vessels makes their rendivous here before they go to the fishing and was it not for this Dutchmen, the town of Lerwick would soon decay. the Dutch leaves Peas Barly Cheas, and Money for Stokings.* Growth was slow until the Napoleonic Wars, and speeded rapidly when the town boomed in the late 19th century when it was known as Herringopolis.

Lerwick retains that air of a busy trading place today, where the internal economic activity of the island meets the external. In the last twenty years it is North Sea oil that has extended its boundaries. The original main street is aptly named Commercial Street, or *da street* as it is still called, from when it was the only one, but the trading places have spread northwards round the coast, and over the hill to Dales Voe.

It is in this new Lerwick that the roll-on/roll-off ferry docks, a straggly industrial expanse in contrast to the tight windings of the old centre, where the ferry berthed until 1977. With some nostalgia, folk recall being able to sit in one of the centres of Shetlandic culture – The Lounge Bar in Mounthooly Street – and watch till the dockers made ready to shift the gangway, before rushing down to the pier a minute or two before sailing. The walk *in owre* from the new terminal is one of the less inspiring landfalls – all the more reason to make sure you see Sumburgh Head. But north a bit from the terminal, in among pipeyard and power station stands *Da Rød o' Gremista*, restored as a museum. This was the birthplace of Shetland's great Victorian benefactor, Arthur Anderson, co-founder of P&O Ferries – originally the Pacific and Orient – besides establishing Shetland's first all-year-round ferry service, first newspaper, a school and a home for widows – and being the first Shetlander to represent the constituency in Parliament. A familiar, kindly patron for islanders, whose own greatness synchronised with the expansion of his birthplace, Lerwick.

The bulk of Fort Charlotte, an unfinished pentagonal fortification built in 1665-7 during the war with the Dutch, at one time stood on the cliff edge and dominated the harbour. Nevertheless it was burned by the 'Hollander' in 1673. Now it is absorbed into the heart of Lerwick where reclamation of land and new piers have distanced the twisting of Commercial Street from the shore. Closely sheltered by buildings of various ages, arriving on *da street* is like stepping indoors – a feeling magnified by the light of the street lamps. Despite many changes, da street represents a constant in Shetland. Here you'll

glimpse a social life which goes beyond the commercial, not unlike that of the very American concept of the mall, but utterly different from it, in that this is an organic structure, created over many centuries. At the Market Cross, folk gather for the public event – the posting of the Up-Helly-Aa 'Bill', the New Year knees-up, the evangelising sing-along, the Saturday afternoon hang-out. Though not entirely traffic-free, at busy times the sheer weight of numbers means that it is the pedestrian who calls the shots.

It's worth spending a bit of time walking around the old centre, not just because it's the best place to shop, but because here you'll find that the islands you have come to see come to meet you. You'll hear the local tongue, *Shetlan* or *Shetlandic*, in a number of varieties, and get a sense of the distinctiveness of contemporary culture – which, while assimilating much of the global village, retains a fiercely determined sense of locality. The folk tradition is alive and well, and not confined to Aly Bain's latest CD. Perhaps inspired by his achievements, a younger generation of Shetland musicians are at the front of a new folk wave. The more academic Shetland Fiddlers Society meets every Wednesday during the summer, May to August, while in nearby Tingwall, a folklore society has regular Tuesday meetings.

It's easy to spot the waves of history in Lerwick's development. The town seems almost to have climbed out the sea at the old Sooth End where the *lodberries* rise directly out of the harbour water, designed to function as dwelling, store and pier. Smugglers' tales and secret passages spark the imagination walking through this part of town, while the narrow lanes that run up from the seafront to the top of the hill above the shore – the *closses* – represent the town's initial expansion.

If you follow the old main street southwards, the road takes you to a walk round the *Knab*, a sharp sloping headland opposite Bressay Lighthouse (1858), one of the many designed by the Stevenson family. Though fairly tame in comparison with the cliff scenery to be seen elsewhere, nevertheless it is an exhilarating walk with the wind sweeping over, and leads you back over the hill to the newer Lerwick: villas of late 19th and early 20th-century construction, symbols of wealth for a new merchant class; and further west again, a band of 20th-century council housing. Keep to the coastal path for a mile or so and in the distance you'll run up against Shetland's ancient history for the first time at Sound, there alongside its most recent phase.

Once a separate settlement, Sound is now part of Lerwick's reach. An award-winning 1970s housing scheme which quickly lost favour stands across the road from the Broch of Clickhimin. This visual anachronism is compounded by the view across Clickhimin loch to the new oil-age leisure centre which shares its name. The leisure centre is a good-looking building which seems to fit the landscape's low sweeping curves, an all-purpose hall that has accommodated a wide range of events, in much the way that the village halls in the country areas do. By day a sports centre, it has housed symphony orchestras and folk festivals, while the 80s cult band, The Smiths, were its first visitors in 1985. For those who remember the land beside the loch as the town dump, where seabirds fought over scraps, the transformation is remarkable.

But looking across the loch or the road to the new, it's hard not to wonder whether anything built in the here and now will last as long as the broch. These strange stone towers scattered across the northern isles and coasts of Scotland, so similar in design that some people have suggested that the one 'architect' is behind them all, have been around for a couple of millennia now. The Clickhimin Broch is among the best preserved in Shetland. At one time it stood on a small holm but a lowering of the water level in 1874 left it high and

dry on its present peninsula. An early undocumented 19th-century excavation left the site exposed and some loss resulted. Drawings dating from soon after show higher walls and more 'furniture' than are visible now, but enough remains for the visitor to get a sense of a substantial if primitive fortification.

In the 1950s, a fuller investigation was carried out, showing how the site had developed over the years from its first occupation by Bronze Age farmers around 700 BC. An Iron Age ring fort followed before the broch was built inside it. But the broch was not the end of the site's use – later, inside it, a 'wheelhouse' was built, a circular stone house divided into sections by stone pillars which served to support the roof. So the present-day height of the walls isn't a guide to what it might once have been. Stones would be used from earlier structures by those who came after, so that one layer of history not only lies on top of another, but reuses the material of the previous.

Having absorbed this first site of island history, a visit to the Shetland Museum in the heart of Lerwick is a good idea, where detailed information on the broch can be gathered. But on the way you can take in another of Lerwick's attractions. So skirt round the loch to the Leisure Centre, up Hayfield Lane opposite, to Gilbertson Road, turn left then first right into St Sunniva Street.

Here you'll find the hive of industry that generates the centre piece of the famous January fire festival of *Up Helly Aa* – the Galley Shed, with a permanent exhibition including a film and a replica of the Viking longship that's burned at the festival each year. Much has been said about the Victorian origins of the modern-day festival, in 19th-century fascination with things Nordic, but there can be no denying that the festival is now a vital community celebration, bringing together all aspects of Lerwick society, and representing as close to a show of nationalism as you're liable to find in Shetland. Accused of being sexist by virtue of its men-only rule on *guizers*, or bourgeois because of its tameness compared to the riotous round of dockboys with flaming tarbarrels that it superseded, Up Helly Aa seems only to shrug and grow even larger. For those visitors who want the thrill of sailing in a longship, in summer a 40ft replica the *Dim Riv* does trips around Lerwick harbour.

Although it isn't a particularly old building, the Shetland Museum in the Hillhead is far from adequate for the size of its current collection, especially as it must share the space with the local library and gives over one section of its limited area to various exhibitions. A long-running debate over the need for new premises is ongoing. But even so, there's enough on display to capture the visitor's curiosity, from the artefacts gathered over the years from the Shetland terrain, to items salvaged from the many shipwrecks round the coast, like the huge brass propeller outside the entrance, brought up from the *Oceanic*, 'the other Titanic' which sank off Foula in 1914.

For those investigating the literature of the islands, the Shetland Library holds a fine collection in its Shetland Room. While there is little remaining of the Norn language in text form, the last two hundred years have seen a number of writers try their hand in English, as well as in that distinctively Shetlandic Scot/English/Norse mix that is the present local tongue.

Over the Hillhead past the Victorian Town Hall (1884) and the swimming pool, down one of the steep lanes and you're back on *da street,* cosy on a fine day, comforting on a not so fine one. Carry on down the lane below to the foreshore, the small boat harbour and the pier. Here Shetland's northern cosmopolitanism is evidenced by the many flags and languages to be heard, and from this small harbour you can go direct to Denmark, Norway, Faroe and Scotland – or Bressay.

Three Shetland women rowed us over the Sound and handled the oars splendidly. The minister, a plump jolly bespectacled gentleman, who has not 'perpetrated matrimony', declared with a sign that he was an unprotected male, and on our arrival at the Bressay beach, he called aloud to the oarswomen to lift him out of the boat. These muscular dames shrieked with laughter and proceeded to unship their oars as if to buffet him: he, thereupon, leaped lightly enough on the strand and, turning round, would have improved the occasion by a word in season had not the tittering Nereids begun to splash him as he stood on the shingle.

Our first inter-island hop in Shetland takes you across the harbour on the short ferry crossing from the heart of Lerwick though not perhaps in the style enjoyed by D.T. Holmes, B.A. of Paisley in 1909. It's a rapid passage on the hourly car-ferry, with the substantial Laird's Haa at Gardie prominent as it approaches. Here Walter Scott dined with the father of an old school friend.

Once across on the other side there's a postbus service from the local PO at nine in the morning, but seats are limited so phone ahead. Even without transport there's plenty of good walking. The Ward, where the television transmitters are, is a healthy 'pech' (742ft) and the view of Lerwick and Bressay can't be bettered. From there, you see how they lie together, forming the sheltered harbour between them. What is not so obvious is the forced demographic shift in the area, when the then more densely populated east side of Bressay made way for sheep in the 1870s. On a clear day, the seventy-mile north-to-south stretch of the archipelago lies before you.

The cliffs at the south end of Bressay, the Ord and the Bard, are absolutely dramatic, as are those of the island to the east, Noss, a national nature reserve. These are worth exploring by sea, and a choice of trip is available from Lerwick, one with the writer Jonathan Wills as your captain/guide. While on Bressay, if it's in season (May-August) you can cross Noss Sound by inflatable dinghy to the reserve, 'one of Britain's most spectacular breeding bird colonies'. Weather is liable to be a problem though, so pick your day to see it.

At the southern end of the island was 'one of the wonders of the northern world' in the time of Scott's northern forays: the Cradle of Noss, a small wooden box on two cables stretched between the cliff top and the top of Cradle Holm, by which it was possible to pass across the gap between the two, at a height of 'a hundred fathoms at least'. The original purpose is said to have been the grazing of a few sheep on the Holm, but the contraption captured the Romantic imagination. The story goes that a Foulaman climbed the Holm from the sea to fix the cradle some time in the 17th century, and fell to his death trying to get back to his boat, though instinct suggests this was a device that myth grew rapidly around.

Back on Bressay, at Grimsetter there's an Iron Age *souterrain*, or underearth house, which might be a Tolkienesque hobbit-hole, while the north end of Bressay has a fine, deserted beach beyond Beosetter loch, a much quieter place than the screaming cliffs. Again there's birds to be seen, but then that's the case throughout the islands, so it goes without saying. And if it's nesting time, prepare for attack. Arctic terns are small, but have sharp beaks and like to dive-bomb intruders. Not that you should be disturbing them at their nests anyway, but if you do run into unexpected trouble, the trick is to carry something above your head so they bomb that. A general rule. And be warned also: on the Bressay side of the 'nort mooth' at Heogan is one of the most easily distinguished harbour characters – the fish meal factory, which has a skunk of a scent when it vents. But like many of the seafront characters, it knows a few right good stories.

But don't leave Bressay and Noss with that image; picture the cliffs as if from a ship approaching from the east, a 9th-century longship, whose crew have left their 'vik' (cf. Lier-vik – 'muddy bay') in the spring, on a prevailing easterly wind. They know that if they trust the pattern of the seasons, the open ocean and the open boat, somewhere along this ragged coast they'll make a landfall. Picture then, the sudden, glimpsed sight of Noss on the horizon, and hear the lookout shout – 'Hjalt land!' – the 'hild-land', it's said, though it isn't easy to see the simile. Unless you consider the venture southwards as a sword, and Shetland the part of it you grasp. From here, there's visible land to guide you all the way to Dublin.

By the middle of the 10th century, the Irish Sea was a Norse sea, and Shetland the first and last step in a trade route that boomed, with a Norse power base at Papa Stour on the west-side. What were the Scandinavians trading? Slaves, taken on their raids? Furs from the far north? In exchange for spices, for silver, for semi-precious stones? Whatever, a sudden end was brought to the flow of traffic by this route when the Normans conquered Ireland in 1169. Dublin, previously in the hands of tolerant Irish kings, was now closed to them.

Following this, Viking power in the west began to wane. It's said that King Hakon Hakonsson's sea-bound army en route to battle at Largs in 1263 anchored in Bressay Sound, That defeat was the death knell for one of history's great, if brutal, commercial ventures. The longship trip in the *Dim Riv*, through Bressay Sound, gets more attractive by the moment, doesn't it? Skol!

How to get there

Ferry
Car Ferry from Lerwick to Bressay: hourly (5 mins. crossing)
Shetland Islands Council: ☎0595 2024
Dinghy from Bressay to Noss: (May-August: not Mon or Thurs)
Scottish National Heritage: ☎0595 3345

Road
Bressay Post Bus: daily – 9.00am ☎059 582 200

Accommodation

Hotels
Grand Hotel, Commercial Street (☎0595 2826)
Queens Hotel, Commercial Street (☎0595 2826)
Kveldsro House Hotel (☎0595 2195)
Lerwick Hotel, 15 South Road (☎0595 2166)
Shetland Hotel, Holmsgarth Road (☎0595 5515)

Youth Hostel
Lerwick Youth Hostel, Islesburgh House (☎0595 2114)

Campsite
Clickhimin Caravan and Camp Site (☎0595 4555)

Where to eat

Restaurants
Noost Restaurant, 86 Commercial Street
Golden Coach, Hillhead
Candlestick Maker, 33 Commercial Road
Skipidock Inn, North Road
Maryfield, Bressay

Cafes
Central Bakery, 124 Commercial Street
Clickhimin Centre, Lochside
Islesburgh Community Centre, King Harald Street
Puffins, Mounthooly Street
Fort Café, 2 Commercial Road
Holmsgarth Café, P & O Terminal, Holmsgarth
Viking Café, Commercial Road
D & G Leslie, Ellesmere Stores
Fishermen's Mission, Harbour Street
Solotti's, Commercial Street

Pubs
Douglas Arms, Commercial Road
Thule Bar, Esplanade
Excelsior, Harbour Street
The Lounge, Mounthooly Street

Things to do and see

Centres and Activities
Clickhimin Broch
Fort Charlotte
Lerwick Town Hall
Shetland Museum, Lower Hillhead
Bød of Gremista
Islesburgh Summer Exhibition inc. Shetland Fiddlers Society, King Harald Street
Up Helly Aa Exhibition, St Sunniva Street
Shetland Sea Charters, Noss Boat Trips
Dim Riv (Longship replica) Boat Trips
Bressay Boat Trips
Leask's Coach Tours, Esplanade
Shetland Association of Sea Anglers (May to October)
Skolla Diving Centre, Gulberwick
Puffin Bike Hire, Mounthooly Street
Lerwick Boating Club (temporary membership available)
Dale Golf Course
Recommended walk: Ward o' Bressay and cliffs

Recreational Activities
Clickhimin Leisure Centre, Lochside
Lerwick Swimming Pool, Hillhead

Events and festivals
Lerwick Up Helly Aa (last Tuesday in January)
Shetland Folk Festival (late April/early May)
Shetland Accordion and Fiddle Festival (October)
Town Carnival (summer)
Viking Sea Angling Festival (Sept/Oct)
Regattas (summer)

Craft Shops
Commercial Street has a number of these, particularly: Shetland Workshop Gallery (original art work)
Spider's Web (hand-spinning exhibitions/lessons)

Tourist Information Centre
Market Cross, Lerwick (☎0595 3434)

General Information: *Shetland Times* (pub. Friday); BBC Radio Shetland (nightly)

Scalloway, Burra and Trondra

Approaching the old capital of Scalloway by road from Lerwick the view from *Da Scord* is potentially stunning. A sharp hairpin on the shoulder of the hill has a viewpoint with a visual display board. From here you see across the town and out over Trondra to Burra, with Papa and Oxna beyond.

The view west over Scalloway Castle to the setting sun has made it a favourite picture postcard shot for many years. Yet it is a structure that was little loved in old Shetland, built by forced labour for Earl Patrick Stewart at the end of the sixteenth century. Patrick, who ended up with his head in his hands – literally – forced the *udallers* to work without reward, to build this northern fortress. As a symbol of power, the building must have been impressive, but the castle is cursed, as tyrants' efforts often are.

But enough history, You're here to experience the now, not dwell on the wrongs of the past. Walk around Scalloway, explore Patrick's ruin if you will, but go to the new fish market to the east of the castle as well, and the new Fisheries College with restaurant in house to the west. You'll see that Scalloway can absorb change and grow without losing its identity. Not so long ago, Scalloway seemed like a village lost in a time-warp but these recent initiatives have brought it back to life. Still, you're hardly likely to be flattened by the hordes of shoppers on the main street. The close proximity of Lerwick has killed its trade, but there is a small local museum, detailing among other things the exploits of the Second World War *Shetland Bus*, which moved its base to Scalloway in 1942. For the walkers, the Gallows Hill above the town is a pleasant stroll, with fine views to the west side of the mainland.

In the summer football season, Fraser Park has seen many a passionate battle.

Shetland has a long record of sporting competition with both Orkney and Faroe and the pitch at the heart of Scalloway has its place in contemporary folklore.

The opening of *da Burra brig* in 1971 threatened to change the nature of these island communities. Burra, which had previously been an independent, fishing-based community close to the Burra *haaf*, found itself within easy commuting distance of Lerwick while Trondra, which was sorely depopulated, came alive with a few new houses. But despite predictions of doom, the modern high-tech Burra fleet has managed to keep ahead of the wave of change so far, and the new harbour facilities in Scalloway have provided an ideal base for their activities, though the difficulties faced by the fishing industry because of unsympathetic EEC bureaucrats and Westminster politicians are a constant worry.

Notwithstanding this, the village of Hamnavoe is a beautiful spot, quite distinctive from other Shetland hamlets, with rows of fisher cottages tightly packed above the harbour, which reflects the emphasis on fishing rather than crofting as the main industry. The Hamnavoe folk have a creative way with porches, and the great variety of paint used originated from the excess after the boats had got their coat!

At Papil, to the south, the old church site dedicated to St Laurens has turned up two sculptured Pictish stone slabs. The earlier find (1877) now resides in the Museum of Antiquities in Edinburgh, while the Monks Stone (1943) is in the Shetland Museum.

East Burra is a quiet spot, but the view across Clift Sound to the barren steep on the west coast of the southern mainland is striking. South of the township of Houss, the now deserted island of South Havra lies a couple of miles offshore. In 1909, there were twenty-five folk living there.

How to get there

By road

Shalder Coaches ☎059 588 217
Bus from Lerwick – Scalloway: (Mon-Sat) 11 times a day
Bus from Scalloway to Hamnavoe: (Mon-Sat) 5 times a day
Bus from Lerwick to Hamnavoe: (Mon-Sat) 5 times a day
Note: early closing Thursday

Accommodation

No hotels, hostels or campsites, but:
Brylyn Guest House (☎059 588 407)
Broch Guest House (☎059 588 767)
Recommended self catering:
Easterhouse Chalets (☎059 588 376)
Thatched Cottage, Papil, Burra (☎059 588388).

Where to eat

Restaurant: Da Haaf Restaurant, Fisheries College, Scalloway
Cafe: Castle Cafe, New Street, Scalloway
Pub: Fishermen's Arms, Scalloway
The Kilm Bar, Scalloway

Things to do and see

Centres and Activities
Scalloway Castle
Shetland Woollen Co., Castle Street, Scalloway
Scalloway Museum
Croft Trail, Burland, Trondra
Recommended walks: Gallows Hill to Burwick
Scalloway to Wester Quarff
West Burra (Papil to Kettla Ness)

Recreational
Scalloway Golf Course

Events and festivals

Scalloway Up Helly Aa (Jan)
Regattas (summer)

Tingwall, Whiteness and Weisdale

Back on the mainland, the Tingwall road from Scalloway passes through a pleasant green valley. The holm in the middle of Tingwall Loch was the site of the great Norse era assembly or *ting*, a week-long affair that would have filled the shores of the lochs with its retinue. So in travelling the short distance between Lerwick, Scalloway and Tingwall, you have moved back from the British phase of Shetlandic history, to the short but transformative Scottish phase, to the Norse. The islet no doubt provided a naturally charmed arena for the settling of disputes, land in a ring of water, a clearly defined area in which fair play should reign. But it was not always so, for here in Tingwall too is the stone said to mark the place where Marise Spella, a pretender to Earl Henry Sinclair's seat, was murdered with seven of his men in 1390, after a dispute at one of these *tings*.

Tingwall was also the site of the centre of the early Shetlandic pre-Reformation church, established through the archdiocese of Norway in 1215, though the original spired building is lost. Its stones were reassembled in the more restrained 18th-century manner a few metres away.

Beyond the crossroads in the heart of the valley, on the road west to Sandness is Tingwall Airport. This is a centre for flights to the outlying islands, with regular services to Unst, Fair Isle, Foula, Out Skerries and Papa Stour. It's also possible to charter an eight-seater Islander aircraft to the above, and additionally to Fetlar, Scatsta, Sumburgh and Whalsay. Beyond this, depending on aircraft availability, air-borne island hoppers can charter their own plane to Faroe, Orkney, Norway and Scotland. For those who want to keep their feet firmly on the rolling hills, we'll continue our journey westward, over Wirmiedale into Whiteness and Weisdale.

Above the road at Wirmiedale, on the summit of the hill is an enclosure of stones, and in Whiteness, there's a *bød* on the very extremity of the land at Nesbister, which is available for let, though facilities are basic. The Loch o' Strom has the ruins of a medieval castle (so-called) on an isle in the loch, and at the roadside is a stone-polishing company, Hjaltasteyn, which welcomes visitors.

In Weisdale there's a silvercraft shop, again by the road at Kalliness, a modern development of housing around a few older buildings. At the head of the voe, the road splits. A little up the valley is a refurbished mill, now an arts centre with a permanent exhibition dedicated to traditional knitwear. Beyond is the best established plantation of trees in Shetland, at Kergord. From here the road curls east, to join the main route north at the old *halfway hoose* or inn at lonely Sandwater, from there through the hills of *da Long Kames* to Voe. This central area around Weisdale is the location of two fine novels by John J. Graham, which focus on Shetland society during the era of the Lairds in the 18th century.

The road west climbs the side of Weisdale valley, with an essential photostop to take the view over the swarm of little islands that lie off Scalloway. These are all now uninhabited, though larger ones like Oxna supported a population of thirty-six at the turn of the century. Hildasay was quarried for a prize granite in the 19th century.

Crossing the shoulder of the hill, the view switches west to Sandness Hill and Foula, as the road dips sharply down the Scord a' Tresta into the sheltered land around Bixter Voe at the village of Tresta, from where the road to Sandsound branches. But before leaving Weisdale you should know that the westside is 'dry' and the Norseman's Inn is your last *howff* for quite a distance.

How to get there

Road

On the bus route from Lerwick to Walls: Mon/Friday/Sat 3 times a day, otherwise twice (not Sun).
Shalder coaches (☎059 588 217).
On the bus route from Lerwick to Culswick: Daily, departing evening, times vary.
J. Watt & Sons: Reawick (☎059 588 208).

Air

Flights to Tingwall Airport from Unst, Out Skerries, Fair Isle, Foula, Papa Stour: Charter service available.
Loganair, Tingwall (☎059 584 306).

Accommodation

Hotel: Westings Hotel, Whiteness (☎059 584 242).
Camping Bød: The Bød of Nesbister, Whiteness

Where to eat

Restaurants:
Herrislea House, Tingwall
Norseman's Inn, Weisdale
Cafes:
Hjaltasteyn Tearoom, Whiteness

Things to do and see

Visitor Centres

Tingwall Agricultural Museum, Veensgarth
Tingwall Folklore Evenings (check with Tourist Office)
Hjaltasteyn Stone Polishing, Whiteness
Weisdale Mill Arts Centre
Shetland Silvercraft, Weisdale

Recommended Walks

Strom Ness, south from Whiteness
Weisdale to Sandsound, by Weisdale Voe
East over hills from Weisdale to East Burrafirth

Foula

Along the western coast, you may see Foula, bold as you like on the horizon when the weather's clear, then suddenly no more when the visibility worsens, an intermittent presence in *da wast'airt*. From the Foula end, this infrequency parallels a long-running worry: whether or not the weather will allow the boat to get in. 29km from Walls, and not blessed with a natural harbour at Ham, at times Foula has been cut off for weeks on end. Recent attempts to improve the boat service haven't been without their setbacks. An expensive new vessel proved inadequate for the crossing, but an air service from Tingwall eases the problem. An aerogenerator/hydro-turbine in the south of the island produces the miracle of elecricity. Although the population has dropped drastically from 230 in 1909, it seems to have stabilised of late at about forty. All this is put in perspective by the fact that the Scottish Office refused to help finance a 'water scheme' in 1961, on the grounds that it would be empty in ten years.

The green arable land is all on the east side. On the west are some of the most spectacular cliffs you'll come across anywhere, barring perhaps St Kilda. Da Kame is 372m high. Of particular interest is the natural arch at Gaada Stack and the strange geological crack in the rock face on the west of the island, *de Sneck o de Smallie*: a name to play around your tongue, that shows the intermixture of the Norn language with Lowland Scots, registering in both, according to the 19th-century Faroese philologist, Jakob Jakobsen: 'the cleft in the rock of the small (undersized) one'. It's a squeeze for a large body!

Jakobsen is a vital figure in Shetland culture, and Foula is central to his story. Setting out to discover what remained of the Norse language, Norn, he gathered 40,000 words and phrases, causing a substantial reaction in island attitude. His extensive research, most spectacu-larly successful in Foula and Unst during the 1890s, was a feature of the period in Shetland. The establishment of the modern Up Helly Aa was part of a general move towards the loss of Norse culture, a loss that Shetlanders were well aware of as the century closed.

Jakobsen knew J.J. Haldane Burgess, the blind Shetland poet who penned the anthem for the all-new Victorian Viking Festival in empire-English, although Burgess wrote fine Shetlandic poetry, and was fluent in the Scandinavian tongues – perhaps if he had used Shetlandic for his lyric, it might now seem less of a bourgeois pose. If you're interested in the language, his best work is *Scranna*, ranking along with *Auld Mansie's Crø* by Basil R. Anderson as one of the classic Shetlandic poems. Of the present generation, Rhoda Bulter is outstanding for her fluency and breadth of knowledge.

Foula's isolation has meant that it has been less changed by the fluctuations of whichever people claimed Shetland as their property. In fact, Foula folk talk about going to Shetland! It held onto the Norn language and culture much longer than most parts of the main island. As if in accordance with Einsteinian theory, time seems to move more slowly here. Maybe it has something to do with the fact that the Foula folk still use the old Julian calendar, or maybe it's a matter of temperament. There's an old story that a visitor came upon an old Foula man just beyond the hill dyke of the community, lying on his back, staring up into the sky. When the visitor asked what he was doing, the old fella laughed and said 'Tinkin!'; telling us, maybe, that Foula is the kind of place which inspires reflection; a place to look back at the world from, an ultimate destination.

Relax and ponder being the owner of an island like this, like Ian Holbourn, an English professor who bought it at auction in London in 1901 after spotting it from a yacht. Since then the Holbourns have become an integral part of Foula life, and are to be credited with a major role in helping to save it from depopulation. Or perhaps you'd prefer to imagine yourself the last of the old Norse, a powerful medieval matron, 'the Queen of Foula', Katherine Asmunder, whose romantic story of love lost and subsequent spinsterhood echoes the isolated setting. But better that than being driven by famine from it, across the wild Atlantic, due west from here, to a Nova Scotia. While on Foula, you can abandon yourself to the wildness of the locality.

Foula is now home to the largest colony of Great Skuas in Britain, a large warrior bird known as *bunksi* in Shetlandic and a centuries-old enemy of the shepherd. At one time these were the natural enemies of the predatory sea-eagles but now they have no governance. They are aggressive, particularly if you stray into nesting territory, so carry a stick above your head, as with *tirricks*. On my last trip a hulking security guard from Essex was flattened, not once but twice.

How to get there

Ferries
Passenger ferry from Walls, sometimes West Burrafirth.
May to September: Tues/Thurs/Sat.
October to April: Tuesday (open sea crossing – be warned).

Air
Mon/Wed/Fri/Sat from Tingwall Airport (March to October).
Accommodation to be booked in advance.

Accommodation
Self-catering available.
B&B available.
Ristie Hostel (☎039 333 233).

You must arrange your journey well beforehand – have your accommodation arranged and food for your expedition. You are, after all, going to the edge of the world!

Wastside

From Weisdale west, the land has a common identity, *da wastside*. The central land is heathery and fairly flat, with sizeable voes cutting in from the exposed south, and a network of burns and lochs on the north: among these the walking is never dramatic as with the cliff scenery, but it is always interesting.

Travelling west through Bixter, at the peculiar house of Parkhall, the road to Reawick continues the coastal route into Sandsting, while the main road cuts through the peat hills past good fishing lochs in da Hulmalees. Following the coast, Sand is worth investigating. There's a fine example of a Haa house, a ruined chapel by a fine sheltered sandy beach, with a good walk on the ness beyond. Reawick is as its name suggests, a red sandstone bay, the colour quite startling in sunlight, after the more muted colours of Tingwall and Weisdale. The cliffs at Westerwick are natural sculptures. Here the poet *Vagaland* (T.A. Robertson) was born. He took his pen-name from the land around Walls and his poetry became a regular feature of the *New Shetlander* magazine, from its inception following the Second World War, until his death in 1973.

From Culswick, broch baggers can do one of the most interesting approaches, over hill and down dale to one of the finest settings of any broch, though not much of the structure itself remains. The Broch o Culswick's situation looks out over the water directly to Foula and guards the entrance to the sheltered water of Gruting Voe.

From the broch at Culswick you see the back of Vaila, an island with a story besides being beautiful. It was the site of the first struggle against the stranglehold of the lairds on the fishing industry, when Arthur Anderson established a fishing station there to give the workers their due wage in the 1830s. He leased the island from the troubled estate of the Scotts of Melby, and the venture met with great success at first, till Anderson himself seemed to turn away from it because of other commitments. The estate was sold in 1888 to a wealthy Yorkshire mill-owner, Herbert Anderton, in whose family it remained till a year or two ago. New owners seem intent on repeating the first Anderton's scale of investment.

But from Culswick you only see the sea-worn side of the island. Back on the coastal route through Selivoe and Gruting toward Brig o' Waas, there's an extensive neolithic site at Staneydale and at Brouster. Waas (Walls) itself is a far-spread community centred around a fine natural harbour, with good land and an agricultural show in August that's a local institution. At one time Waas was an important fishing centre, but no more. There's a small, independent museum at Burnside, and a number of sideroads to explore.

From the old Haa house at Burrastow (now a hotel/restaurant) we see the other side of Vaila – its baronial mansion, built by Herbert Anderton in the late 19th century. Here, like or not, I am forcibly transported back to my boyhood, aged five: *my family have been invited by the then Vaila shepherd to look around the island. It is the first time I have glimpsed anything amounting to material, capitalist grandeur: this baronial mansion, with its ornamental balcony, staircase and stuffed animals. And at the end of a walk across the island to Ham, a door on a small boathouse opened cautiously by the shepherd reveals a beautiful Buddhist shrine.* It was my first experience of the alien, face to face, and the word *Buddhist* resonated in my mind for many years. Sadly the shrine is no more, nor indeed is the island of Vaila part of the tourist route at present.

Continuing along the exposed west edge of the mainland, Foula haunts the horizon, with views from Mid Waas, Watsness, scene of WW1 fortification, and Dale o' Waas. The latter was a site

of a haaf fishing station, but is largely deserted now. A new road inland towards Sandness has opened its frontier slightly. This meets the road from the Brig o' Waas at the shore of Lungawatter, a small peaty loch famous for its show of white water lilies. From here the road snakes down Tronascord to Sandness, spread on a flat stretch of arable land, on the outmost south-westerly edge of broad St Magnus's Bay: to quote a much earlier traveller: *a beautiful flat of Corn, Grass, and Meadow ground, facing the west,* though the 'corn' is hard to find these days. Above it the bulk of Sandness Hill (817ft) rises sharply and the views across the Eshaness in the north are panoramic. Having scaled the north face of the hill, the steep cliffs south around Deepdale are magnificent.

The road branches at the public hall. East towards Bousta, a haven for seals, there's a riding centre specialising in horse-drawn carriages with a leather workshop and other attractions, while at Cratoon, a path leads to the Ness of Garth, a promontory fort. The road west to Huxter has another 'broch at the loch' for the Baggers, and shows an example of living archaeology: a *toun*, or group of croft-houses built back to back, a modern version of the wheelhouse idea of sharing sheltered space. Here too are three water-mills on the burn beyond the road end, still intact.

From Huxter, Papa Stour is only fifteen hundred metres offshore, but Papa Sound is notorious for its tidal rush. Beyond Papa Stour, you may glimpse the Ve Skerries, a graveyard of ships. Although Melby, where the renovated Scott's haa is inhabited, was the long-term ferry point for Papa Stour, a well-intentioned plan to improve the pier facility had the opposite effect, with the result that the Papa boat now goes to West Burrafirth, deeper in the confines of the bay.

But before leaving Sandness, let me, as a boy who grew up there, hesitate a moment to commend the beaches, cliffs and lochs most highly as places where imagination can find room to roam. And family loyalty aside (!) the story of the Sandness Spinning Company's new mill is evidence that industry and ingenuity can thrive in the most out-of-the-way places, and that, most crucially for similar communities, depopulation isn't necessarily the rule. Visitors are very welcome.

The walk from Bousta round by Snarraness to the rock-strewn hills of West Burrafirth is the shortest route. By road from Sandness, we must go back through the peat hills and lochs (another broch in a loch at Burgawater) to Da Brig o' Waas for the ferry to Papa Stour, 'the large island of the fathers'. The name refers to the Irish monks who settled there before the Norsefolk came. From their toleration of these monastic retreats, it seems that the Norse respected their devotion. And no wonder – some of the sites chosen for their 'hermitages' are almost beyond belief, and one wonders if sometimes intention rather than continual habitation was sufficient to create the myth.

Approaching the pier in Housa Voe, on the port side is Maiden Stack, one of these sublime retreats, though in this case it supposedly takes its name from the tale of the Norse Lord who imprisoned his daughter there to stop her running off with her suitor, not a heavenly devotion. All around the deeply indented coast, marvels prevail, with Kirstan's Hol the best known of many sea caves on its west side. It's possible to find a boat to take you round these locally, but the weather may rule against it. The sea-sculpture of Akers Geo has been likened to a natural cathedral, though unfortunately da Horn o' Papa as celebrated in Vagaland's *Sang o da Papamen* collapsed during a great storm in 1953. Recently fears have been expressed that erosion of the narrow isthmus between West Voe and Hamna Voe, and connecting the western part with the harbour in the east, may cut the island in two.

Once a centre of the Norwegian Crown's power in Shetland, Papa is now better known as the 'hippy' island, which advertised in the 1970s for settlers and met the whole Woodstock generation heading out of the cities on their way 'back to nature'. A few of them ended up in Papa. Some didn't realise how 'back' that trip was to be – the peat supply having been exhausted in the 1870s. At one point an evacuation to Fetlar on the east side of Shetland was discussed. From 272 in 1909, the population has fallen to thirty-two, despite the attempt to attract incomers.

Papa is a wonderful location for romantic adventurers, no question, whether as an early Celtic-Christian hermit, or new age-of-Aquarius traveller. Its archaeology is emerging by the year, thanks largely to Dr Barbara Crawford of St Andrews' University. Recent digs have uncovered the base of a substantial early medieval house, which may have been the residence of the 13th-century Norwegian Duke, later King, Haakon. In Norse times, the Papa Stour estate included large parts of da Wastside and Nortmaven, and it remained in Norwegian hands long after Shetland was pledged to Scotland.

Perhaps this accounts for the continuation of the Norse tradition of the Sword Dance here in Papa long after it was forgotten in other places. In notes to his novel *The Pirate*, written after a visit to the Shetland in 1814 with the Commisioners of the Northern Lighthouse Service, Walter Scott reprints a text of 'Words Used as a Prelude to the Sword Dance, A Danish or Norwegian Ballet, composed some centuries ago and preserved in Papa Stour, Zetland' with a description of the dance, which he claims to have taken from 'a very old' document. George P.S. Peterson, a Papa-born poet and scholar, has kept alive this dance, which is still performed at traditional folk gatherings.

Moving from the extremity of Papa Stour into the heart of St Magnus Bay, through the hills and the fine fishing lochs of the west-side between West

Burrafirth (don't forget the broch at Helister, baggers) and Clousta, we find three islands close together, protecting the sheltered waters of Eid Voe, Olna Firth and Busta Voe, where the villages of Eid, Voe and Brae lie respectively.

Eid is a bonny voehead village with a great lifeboat tradition. A road leads meandering towards the substantial farm of Vementry and the island that shares its name, home to the 18th-century strongman Christie Brown who, it was said, could outrow a fully crewed sixareen single-handed in a four-oar boat and lived a proud, free life at a time when the Laird had the folk as little better than truck-slaves.

In World War 1, two six-inch bore guns were stationed on the island's north side, guarding the entrance to Swarbacks Minn, where the naval force charged with maintaining a blockade on German shipping was based. The guns had to be winched up from the sea below, and when the Kaiser's threat was gone, the Vementry Guns were left to rust away.

The island has a further older intrigue: a strange structure called a heel cairn, because of its shape, which seems to have been a burial chamber with its door now sealed, and concealed. Even if it were found, who would dare risk a Vementry curse? Though there is no regular ferry, boat trips are available by contacting Vementry Farm.

Papa Little, in the middle of the Minn, is also uninhabited since the latter part of the last century, and its name relates to Papa Stour: more reclusive Irish monks seeking to get closer to God by hiding away from the tempting splendour of his Creation. In its day it seems to have been a successful enterprise, with reasonable arable land and its own small mill, an independent little place, with a good supply of peat. Here the Papa Stour people came when their own banks ran out.

WASTSIDE
How to get there
Road
Bus from Lerwick to Walls (feeder service to Sandness) Mon/Fri/Sat three times a day, otherwise twice (not Sun). Shalder coaches (☎059 588 217).
Bus from Lerwick to Culswick: Daily, departing evening, times vary.
J. Watt & Sons: Reawick (☎059 586 208).

Accommodation
Hotel
Burrastow House, Walls.
Self-catering/B&B widely available.
No hostels or campsites. Wild camping freely available.

Things to do and see

Visitor Centres/Sites
Staneydale Neolithic Settlement.
Scord o'Brouster, Bridge of Walls.
Walls Museum and Knitting Museum.
Jamieson's Spinning Mill, Sandness.
Shetland Leather & Angora Centre, Sandness.
Shetland Carriage Driving, Sandness.
Walls Swimming Pool.
Recommended Walks
From Culswick to broch.
Overhill from Dale o'Waas to Sandness.
Crafts
T.A. Nicolson, Shetland Sheepskins, Aith.
Events
Walls Regatta (July).
Walls Agricultural Show (August).

PAPA STOUR
How to get there
Ferries
Ferry from West Burrafirth: May to September – weather permitting.
Early ferries: Mon/Wed/Fri/Sat.
Late ferries: Fri/Sat/Sun.
Bookings: T. Gray (☎0595 873 227).
Air
Tuesdays: Return flight from Tingwall Airport (☎059 584 306).

Accommodation

Dinner, B&B from Mrs Holtbrook (☎059 573 238).

Things to do and see

Boat trip around sea caves
Coastal walk around island

Delting, Nortmaven and North Roe

To get to Muckle Røe by sea from Papa Little is a short crossing. By road from Eid, by way of Gonfirth and the villages of Voe and Brae, it is almost twenty miles. From the voe head at East Burrafirth, by following the burn you will find your way to the slopes of Scallafield (921ft.), and the central hills of the mainland.

Perhaps this area of Shetland more than any other shows how the building of roads changed the dynamics of the Shetland society. Before 1841, there were only five miles of road in Shetland, around Lerwick. The great famines of the 1840s, when the potato crop failed due to blight, led to an outcry for government assistance. This came in the form of subsidised employment in the making of what became known as the *Meal Roads*, so called because the workers were paid in the form of a bag of *meal* a day.

Though the distances between Eid, Voe and Brae are not great, the land is hilly and arduous walking. By comparison, the relatively sheltered waters of the Minn make easy sailing. So the community travelled about by boat. Places on the water but difficult to get to by land, which had previously lain between the three villages, found themselves isolated when road travel took over.

Grobsness is one of these forgotten places, a small nipple of land at the foot of a steep hill, marking the opening of Olna Firth. The approach by road is dramatic, with a steep drop in the left hand side, and must be a trial in winter. With the old derelict laird's Haa on the slope above the now abandoned crofts, symbolically overseeing, Grubsness seems a monument to a sea-based social structure now long gone.

Voe is often described as a little bit of Norway in Shetland and its secluded setting is beautiful, at the joining of five roads. This is the natural centre of Shetland, equidistant between north and south, east and west, but it's a sleepy place. The oil era passed Voe by, though some new houses were built at Tagon across the voe. Voe prospered in the 19th century during the era of the sail-powered smack, which fished cod as far away as Iceland and the Davis Straits. It was also a base for the woollen trade – one of T.M. Adie's jumpers went to the top of Everest in 1953, on the torso of Edmund Hillary!

Down in the old village, the 19th century seems to slumber untroubled – except that the laird's house now belongs to an oil company. If you're looking for a taste of times past, try the Old Sail Loft on the shore which has been converted for basic rented accommodation.

From Voe, the road round Olna Firth hugs the shore. On the far side you might glimpse the remains of the croft of Kjurkigirt, tucked under the hill, where it is said folk only saw the sun during three months of the year. Past Waddersti is Brae, drastically changed in the last twenty oil years. Now it is a sprawling community of old and new randomly juxtaposed, with the new tending to swallow the old. It is like the embryo of a town with many organs still to evolve, though there are facilities enough to make it a profitable stop. Whether it continues to develop, or halts when the oil is over, time will tell.

The setting of Busta across the voe is perfect, tucked away among a mature garden that defies the impression of barrenness the land around it gives. This was the power base of Thomas Gifford, one of the greatest of the merchant-lairds. The Giffords had a chequered history, with no little intrigue and tragedy surrounding them. The progenitor was a churchman who decided that land-owning was the better occupation. Thomas Gifford became the most powerful man in Shetland in the early 18th century, but in 1748, his four sons disappeared one night, while sailing in perfect conditions on the voe. A long-running wrangle over inheritance brought the once proud estate to penury.

Busta House is now one of Shetland's premier hotels and worth a visit simply to absorb the atmosphere. If the old village of Voe is a bit of Norway, here in this sheltered corner you might be anywhere in Scotland.

The island of Muckle Røe is as its name suggests, a 'big red', consisting of red granite. The channel between it and the mainland is narrow and a crossing was just about possible before the bridge. When a man died in the attempt, a narrow structure was erected, which led to the widespread popularity of the tiny Austin A7 with Muckle Røe folk, as it was the only car able to cross! The present bridge dates from the 1950s. All the houses are on the east, but the pink cliffs on the west side are stunning in the light of the setting sun and worth the trek. Muckle Røe is little known and out of the way, a fine place to wander free.

Nortmaven, the north-western part of the Shetland mainland, is almost an island itself, connected only by a narrow neck at Mavis Grind, where supposedly you can throw a stone from the Atlantic to the North Sea. The Norsemen had a more purposeful use for the isthmus, hauling their ships across it and so saving a long sea voyage round the north tip of Fedeland. Some say that the massive quarry has spoilt the area forever, but speaking personally the ravaged cliff face adds to the drama of the place.

Travelling north on the main road through a watery land of peaty lochs like the Wastside, we pass the place where the *Gunnister Man* was pulled from a bog in 1951. Three late 17th-century coins were found in a purse and all his clothing was well-preserved. Like that other great find of the 1950s, the St. Ninian's Isle treasure, the Gunnister man went south to the Museum of Antiquities in Edinburgh, where he remains. Over the hills to the east and west are interesting road ends into Nibon and Sullom, the latter lying over the voe from the oil terminal.

As with Muckle Røe, Nortmaven is a red granite land, and as you will notice travelling north, it is dominated by the bald head of Rønes Hill (450m), the highest in Shetland, with a heel-shaped burial cairn at the summit. In its shadow, hidden until you are upon it, the serpent-shaped voe that shares its name coils inland, virtually deserted, though around Heylor the remains of fishing and whaling stations slowly decay. Here is a bleak, blasted beauty under a stormy sky, but a place of safe haven compared with the land further north, though the adventurous will find some good fishing among the many small lochs. The walking is this area is well worth the effort.

The road branches before the lock of Eela Water, west into Hillswick, once a port of call for the islands' steamer. The road drops sharply down to Urafirth, then runs around the voe to the rudimentary harbour. Two buildings break the skyline: a wooden hotel imported from Norway at the turn of the century and the imposing bulk of an early 18th-century Scottish kirk, while by the shore, Hillswick House shelters the oldest of Shetland's pubs, *Da Bød*, established by a Hamburger in 1685. Recently its owner has created a sanctuary for seals in the beer garden, so you can enjoy a flippered floorshow. South from the harbour, Hillswick Ness is a worthwhile walk, for the view to the needle-like Drongs. The mineral wealth around these coasts makes raking through the pebbly beaches great fun, and all sorts of little semi-precious treasures can be pocketed.

Beyond Hillswick to the west is the flat land of Eshaness, poking out into the Atlantic, like the weather-beaten head of some ancient mariner. The sea sculpture rivals that of Papa Stour, which lies directly south, but has the advantage of being remarkably accessible: the road take the traveller right to the edge, at the sheer cliff-top setting of Eshaness lighthouse. What it lacks in elevation, the short tower makes up for by its dramatic location. It is doubtful if a better place exists to watch the sun go down. Before the last incline to the lighthouse, is the site of the old Cross Kirk, and once a place of pilgrimage.

From the lighthouse, the walk north along the coast has much to offer. Da Hols a'Scraada is a blowhole up through the cliff, and there's an unexcavated 'broch in the loch' at Houlland. A couple of miles north, Da Grind o da Navir is like a gateway in the cliff from land to sea, with a hinterland of volcanic ignimbrite that echoes the Giant's Causeway. Southwards at Stenness are the ruins of a haaf fishing station, while offshore the arched rock of Dore Holm appears like a huge petrified dinosaur drinking from the ocean.

Eshaness is associated with two of the best-loved Shetlanders. It was the stomping ground or *bon hoga* of the late Tammie Anderson, whose work in rescuing the island's fiddle music is already legendary, and in the 18th century, a Hamnavoe man known as Joannie Notions administered the first known inoculations against smallpox. Entirely self-educated, John Williamson spent many years developing his serum, though the medical profession of the time vilified him. No doubt the fact that it worked diminished the status of the doctor in the community. The house that stands on the stead of his original

dwelling is now available to let, through the Shetland Tourist Organisation's *Bed down in a Bød* initiative.

North of Rønas Voe, the road hugs close to the sea at Colla Firth, then cuts inland past Lochend to Nort Røe, the landscape greener along this eastern side. North of the road end at Isbister lies the peninsula of Fedeland, where the largest of the haaf fishing stations was sited, though the area is now completely deserted. To the west of the fine beach at Sandvoe is a similarly deserted place, Øea, a green place which once supported a community of 100 folk.

Having reached this northern point, the only option is to return to Mavis Grind and Brae, to head up the other side of Sullom Voe. On the way, a detour into Ollaberry and Gluss will compete the picture. Ollaberry is a former fishing station with a solid 19th-century pier and a forbidding Haa, while Gluss has an interesting new restaurant, surrounded by the gnarled remains of a coppice. From here the giant oil-terminal across the water looms like a lost city, its Olympic flame flaring on the hill above.

North of Brae, at Voxter, a converted Haa now operates as a hostel and a little further on at Graven are the remains of the WW2 air base, from where 'flying boats' patrolled the North Sea, crewed by servicemen referred to by Lord Haw-Haw as 'that nest of vipers in Shetland'. Where the RAF settled briefly in mid-century, now the multinational oil industry rules its own autonomous mini-state. The terminal is closed to all visitors so no more than a studied look across the water is possible. The years of its construction, when the number of incoming workers made the war influx seem few in comparison, are now just a folk memory. The great workcamps housing thousands at Firth and Toft have largely been flattened, although the sports centre at Firth is now open to the community.

The ferry to Da Nort Isles leaves from Toft, where one or two of the oil-age buildings still stand, sorry-looking places whose broken windows seem to make a mockery of the not-so-distant grand plans, for a Northern University or a technological centre.

How to get there

Ferry
N/A
Road
Bus service from Scalloway/Lerwick to Sullom Voe: morning and evening.
Bus service from Lerwick to Brae, Hillswick: 4/5 times daily.
Bus service from Lerwick to Hillswick Nort Røe: Mon/Tues/Thurs/Friday.
Air
No scheduled service: charter available from Tingwall/Sumburgh/Unst to Scatsta.

Accommodation

Hotels
Brae Hotel.
St Magnus Bay Hotel, Hillswick.
Busta House Hotel, Brae.
Valleyfield Guest House, Brae.
Youth Hostels
Voxter House, Delting.
Campsites
Valleyfield camp site, Brae.
Johnnie Notions, Hamnavoe, Eshaness.
The Sail Loft, Voe.

Where to eat

Restaurants
Mid Brae Inn
Ayre Crofthouse Restaurant, Gluss, Ollaberry (☎236).
Pubs:
Da Bød, Hillswick.
Crofters Arms, Ollaberry.
Mossbank Inn.
Club Bar, Voe.

Things to do and see

Activities Centres
Tangwick Haa Museum, Eshaness.
Coastal Walk, Eshaness.
Coastal Walk to Fedeland from Isbister Rønies Hill (1476ft).

Recreational Facilities
Brae swimming pool.
Fraser Peterson Leisure Centre, Firth, Mossbank.

Events and festivals
Brae and Hillswick, Ollaberry Up Helly Aas.
Regattas (summer).
Voe Show (July/Aug).

Crafts
Shetland Crafts, Hillswick.

Yell, Unst and Fetlar

The island of Yell has attracted a lot of bad press, generally from those who haven't bothered to explore it fully: *so uncouth a place that no creature can live therein unless he be born there,* runs one infamous quote from George Buchanan. Certainly its very name suggests a state of desperation and its central southern landmass is peat and more peat. But round the coast there are many beautiful fringes. Another view has it that Yell: *stands for kindliness and remoteness, for wildness and yet for peace.*

Arriving on the ferry at Ulsta from Toft, the road splits east and west. It's best to choose one and save the other for the return journey. The western option has fine views over to Northmaven, and the bonny community of West Sandwick with a substantial 'twinned' Haa now a restaurant. Just before the two roads join at the island's waist, a road runs west to Da Herra, perched above Whalfirth, a long elbowed, cliff-lined voe which makes a spectacular walk.

The eastern road from Ulsta twists and turns to Burravoe, the main centre in the south. Here the Haa of Brough (1672) is open as a visitor centre, with a display on local history and wildlife. Also worth a visit is St Colman's Episcopal church, built at the turn of the century and a perfect example of the Arts and Crafts movement, somehow incongruous in Yell's open landscape. At Gossabrough there's a fine beach with two ruined Haas, one at either end, like two giants slain in a combat to the death, while Otterswick at Queyon, the figurehead of a ship, the Bohus, which was wrecked in 1924, looks out to sea. Known locally as *Da Widden Wife*, she was recently restored and is now resplendent in a white dress, holding her black Bible, head upraised in solemn prayer.

The two roads meet at Mid Yell which is, with an oil-age leisure centre and high school, the focal point of the island. A scattered community on the slope of the hill above the harbour, an inchoate town without sufficient industry to fill the spaces between the houses, the pierhead is its main attraction and the sheltered waters of the voe are ideal for sailing. As Bressay protects Lerwick, so Mid Yell has Hascosay, once believed to have hallowed soil, but now uninhabited. The eminent naturalist, Bobby Tulloch, whose heartland this territory is, runs boat trips to Hascosay by arrangement.

A mile to the west of Mid Yell is the 'haunted' *Windhoose*, which is eerie whether ghosts inhabit it or not. High on the hill above the road, it's out of Emily Brontë by way of *The House with the Green Shutters*. Not the best place to book in for the night, but if you like that sort of thing, watch for the ruined lodge by the roadside.

North again from Mid Yell, the road traverses the peat hill to Sellafirth on Basta Voe, famed for its otters, thanks to a BBC documentary filmed there. A dead-end track along the voe to Kirkabister will provide your best opportunity for viewing them, but they're elusive creatures so be patient. There are RSPB reserves on either side of Basta Voe, and the walk past the lochs

of Lumbister to the steep *daal* at the mouth of the Whalfirth is recommended. Among the birds breeding here are red throated divers, merlin and twite.

Over the hill from Sellafirth on Basta Voe is Gutcher, the ferry terminal for Unst and Fetlar. But if you cross straight over, you'll miss the fine scenery on the north-east coast of Yell, around Cullivoe, where a new pier has enlivened the coastal activity. At Brekkin on the north side, the white sand beach sweeps over a wide area of land, including the medieval Kirk a' Ness, a pre-Reformation church dedicated to St Olaf but abandoned in the mid-18th century. This seems to have been a sacred place in many ages, and some folk think there may be a Jarlshof-like complex of settlement somewhere in the shifting sand. Skeletons have been found here, so you never know what goodies the kids may turn up.

Beyond Brekkin, the township of Gloup marks the end of the road. In the great storm of July 1881, the 19th-century haaf station lost six boats and it's said the community never recovered. Today a sturdy stone woman holding a child scans the ocean from the hill, perpetually watching for the drowned. It's recorded that a characteristic of Shetland women in the days of the haaf was to go to the place where they thought their men would come ashore and watch the sea. The site of the station itself is over the hill from the monument, on Gloup Voe.

Unst, the furthest north of the isles, is a fertile green place after the dark peat hills of Yell, split by a fault line running north to south through Burra Firth and the Loch of Cliff. The eastern side is famous for serpentine, while the west is mainly gneiss and schist, containing various embedded minerals. Robert Louis Stevenson visited Unst while his uncle David Stevenson was engaged in the construction of Muckle Flugga lighthouse, and a quick comparison of Billy Bones' map of *Treasure Island* with that of Unst shows a curious resemblance.

The ferry from Gutcher lands at Belmont (another broch at Hoga Ness to the west) from where the road heads inland, before branching east to Uyeasound, and west to Westing.

The Uyeasound road passes by the shore with views to Skeleton island (sorry, Uyea), to Muness Castle, which dates from the era of the Stewart Lords and is probably to the design of Andrew Crawford, the architect of Scalloway Castle. A striking feature is the number of decorative shotholes in the stonework, suggesting that its owner Laurence Bruce was not the 'worthy man' that the panel above the door claims. History records him as a tyrant, with good reason to consider his defence important. According to legend, the castle was burned out in the seventeenth century by Hakki of Dikkerim. Beyond the road end at Muness, there is a superb beach at Sandwick.

The Westing road has a number of points of interest. At Boardstubble is the largest of Shetland's standing stones, while the remains of St Olaf's Chapel date from around 1200. At Underhoull (another broch), a Norse longhouse recently excavated has revealed an earlier Pictish site below, while the Westing Watermill is still in working order.

Back on the road north, we pass the trout-fishing Loch of Watlee with an ancient wishing well, *Helia Brun*, at its south end, and arrive in Baltasound, the main township in Unst. Once a great herring port, with hundreds of boats and thousands of workers, it is a quieter place now, though the airport has benefited from traffic to the North Sea oilrigs. Like Mid Yell, Baltasound now boasts a new leisure centre.

Over the hill, the Keen of Hamar Nature Reserve is a small area of land where the serpentine rock litters the ground, surrounded by unique native flora. At nearby Hagdale are the remains of the long-standing chromite mines, while

talc, a particular variety of serpentine, is still mined at Clibberswick. Here too the Unst Heritage Centre presents a surprisingly detailed account of local life.

By this time your northern journey is nearing an end. Now you are entering the land of tourist 'records' – 'the most northerly post office' at Haraldswick, 'the most northerly house' at Skaw and so on. The bonny beaches here are good places to contemplate the end of your road, in the shadow of the huge RAF radar station on Saxa Ford. But there's still a way to go, back to the Burrafirth turn and out to the real 'ultima thule' of Muckle Flugga. The nearby Loch of Cliff is a good fishing loch, and from here, the final trek through the national nature reserve of Hermaness begins, with over 100,000 birds and ubiquitous sheep for company.

The final northern view to the 200ft tower of Muckle Flugga lighthouse raises wonderment at Victorian engineering skill. Finished in 1858, it cost the then vast sum of £32,000, and is manned by three keepers. Beyond it is the last speck of rock, Ootsta, where the wife of Sir John Franklin, an explorer who went off in search of the north-west passage never to return, went to pray for her husband's safety in 1849. Here too, according to folklore, a beautiful mermaid lived, the object of the desire of two giants, Saxi and Herman, who guarded the mouth of Burra Firth. Such romance is somehow entirely appropriate here, at the end of the road north.

Returning to the ferry terminal at Belmont, set your compass for the one-time 'garden of Shetland', the island of Fetlar. The name in the Norse means 'fat lands', and Fetlar had at one time 900 folk living off that land. Now the number is nearer 100, thanks to the 19th-century clearances under the guidance of Sir Arthur Nicolson. Despite recent initiatives to bring the people back, including the aborted idea of transporting the peatless Papa Stour folk over from the Wastside, Fetlar remains an echo of its former green self, though it still has the potential for growth. Nicolson's great 'gothick' lodge at Brough (1820), near the ferry terminal at Oddsta on the west of the island, seems the same kind of monument to the suffering of the poor folk as is Patrick Stewart's castle in Scalloway. Now fallen into decay, its crenellated round tower folly was built using stone from the crofthouses of families given just forty days' notice to quit.

Over the long hill of Lamb Hoga, the 'fatland' lies before you, with a beautiful sandy beach at Tresta, while the nearby loch of Papil Water is good for both sea and brown trout. Further on, at Houbie there's a visitors' centre and tearoom and the imposing Leagarth House, a state-of-the-art construction around 1900 for another of Fetlar's knighted residents. In front of the house is the Ripple Stane, a standing monolith.

Fetlar's more recent famous inhabitants are feathered, the Snowy Owls which raised twenty chicks in the North Fetlar reserve between 1967 and 1975. Although they haven't nested since then, there are usually one or two females around. Access to the reserve is restricted and the warden at Bealance should be contacted for advice. Within this restricted area are a Neolithic chambered cairn and a ring of stones around two central ones, said to be dancing trolls circling a fiddler and his wife, but probably the remains of a Bronze Age cairn.

Further east, on Funzie Ness, there is an RSPB hide for viewing the rare Red Necked Phalarope, while on the north east tip of the island at Standibrough is a monastic site. The land around the bay to the west shows the remains of Sir Arthur Nicolson's clearance.

From Fetlar, the ferry takes you back to Gutcher. On the trip south, you can see the side of Yell not seen on your northward jaunt. At Ulsta, the Toft ferry brings you across to the mainland once

more, passing the RSPB islands of Samphrey and Fish Holm. Over the hill from Toft, take a short detour into Mossbank, the old ferry point for Yell. Of all Shetland, this is perhaps the place most affected by oil development, with estates of houses stretching along the side of the voe.

From Firth, take the road east to Voe again, and see the magnificent glacial valley of Dales Voe in the east of Delting, where the road climbs the 'fjordside' with fine views east towards Lunna. Collafirth is strangely unaffected by the development around it. Just south of Voe, the road to Laxo take you to the ferry for *da bonny isle* of Whalsay.

Y E L L

How to get there

Ferries
Car ferry from mainland: Half-hourly, Tel: Burravoe (☎095 782 259/268).
Car ferry from Unst: Half-hourly, Tel: Burravoe (☎095 782 259/268).
Car ferry from Fetlar: Eight times a day, Tel: Burravoe (☎095 782 259/268).
Road
Bus from Lerwick twice daily: J. Leask, Esplanade, Lerwick (☎0595 3162). (Sat-Sun once daily).
Bus from Baltasound (Unst): Mon/Tues/Thurs/Fri: Nicebus (☎095 781 224).

Accommodation

Hotels
North Isles Motel, Sellafirth, (☎095 784 294).
Pinwood Guest House, South Aywick, (☎0957 2077).

Where to eat

Restaurants
North Isles Motel, Sellafirth, (095 784 294).
Cafés and Tearooms
Seaview Cafe, Gutcher
Old Tearoom, Burravoe
Pubs
Hilltop Bar, Mid Yell

Things to do and see

Old Haa Visitor Centre, Burravoe..
RSPB Bird Reserve, Limbister
Boat trips to Hascosay with Bobby Tulloch, prize-winning author/naturalist, Mid Yell, (☎0957 2226).
RSPB Black Park Reserve
Mid Yell Leisure Centre and Swimming Pool.
Whalfirth Walk from the Herra.
Sellafirth Walk to Cullivoe (Old road from Voehead).

UNST

How to get there

Ferries
Car ferry from Gutcher (Yell): Half-hourly (☎095 782 259/268).
Air
Daily Service from Tingwall.
Daily Service from Sumburgh.
Road
Bus/Ferry twice daily from Lerwick: S. Leask, Lerwick (☎0595 3162).
Bus around Unst daily: P. Mills, Baltasound (☎098 781 666/379).

Accommodation

Hotels
Baltasound Hotel, Baltasound (☎095 781 334).
Clingera Guest House, Baltasound (☎095 781 579).
Youth Hostels
Gardies Fauld, Uyeasound (☎095 785 298/311).
Pubs
Magdale Lodge.

Things to do and see

Unst Heritage Centre.
Keen of Hamar National Nature Reserve.
Hermaness National Nature Reserve.
Muness Castle.
Baltasound Leisure Centre – includes swimming pool.
Norvova Knitwear.

Events and festivals

Regatta – summer.
Up Helly Aa – February.
Dony Sales – October.

FETLAR

How to get there

Ferries
Car ferry from Gutcher (Yell): Eight times a day, Burravoe (☎095 782 259/268).
Air
Charter available from Tingwall Airport.

Accommodation

Self-catering available on the island.
Garths Campsite, Velzie (☎095 783 269).

Where to eat

Fetlar Interpretive Centre, Houbie.

Things to do and see

Fetlar Interpretive Centre, Houbie.
RSPB North Fetlar Reserve, Warden (☎095 783 246).

Lunnasting and Nesting, Whalsay and Oot Skerries

No thanks to North Sea oil, Whalsay is a prosperous island with a highly equipped fishing fleet and factory. Despite the lack of a good natural harbour, the endeavour of the Whalsay folk has provided an example for isolated communities far beyond Shetland. This self-reliance has led to mistaken accusations of unfriendliness, due to the fact that islanders don't sit around waiting for visiting wealth but actively generate their own. Anthony Cohen's study of island society, *Belonging*, is recommended.

At Symbister harbour is the restored Pier Hoose, a booth or *bød* used by the Hanseatic traders from medieval times

to the 18th century, with a hoist for lifting goods from boats below. The *bod*
contains an exhibition on island life
generally. Overlooking the harbour is
Shetland's 'outstanding Georgian building', built for the Bruce lairds in 1830,
and now the local school. Symbister too
has a new leisure centre.

The road that circles the southern part
of the island takes you to da Loch o
Huxter, a good fishing spot with the
remains of an Iron Age blockhouse fort
and causeway. Other archaeological sites
of interest are north of Isbister, where a
large oval house has been excavated.

A more recent dwelling worthy of a visit
is the poet Hugh MacDiarmid's house at
Sodom: the reroofed Grieve Hoose is
available for let, though facilities are
basic. MacDiarmid, real name Christopher Grieve, arrived in Whalsay in 1933
with his wife Valda and young son,
Michael, his meteoric Scots-Modernist
rise to fame having burnt out in London.
Here, for nine years, the family lived a
difficult, isolated existence, though
memoirs by Michael Grieve see the
more idyllic side of Whalsay life. The
hardship which Grieve endured gave
rise to some of his finest poems: *On a
Raised Beach* has been called 'one of the
great poems of the century'. Always a
man of contradiction, Grieve's philosophy and politics were tested to the
extreme during his time on Whalsay, as
his sympathies lay with the folk, while
his interest, perhaps naturally enough,
wandered to the extensive library put
at his disposal by the laird. A recent
book edited by Brian Smith and
Laurence Graham, *MacDiarmid in Shetland*, contains some fascinating essays.

East of the Whalsay ferry terminal at
Laxo, the township of Vidlin scattered
round a voehead offers a number of
roads: the 'garden' of Swinnin, which
shows what can be achieved in the
Shetland climate; the long peninsula of
Lunna Ness, where the so-called *Shetland Bus* had its first base. David
Howarth's best-selling book tells the
story of this remarkable enterprise,

which ran great risks during WW2 in
keeping the Nazi-occupied Norwegian
coast open to refugees, while carrying
out spying and guerrilla attacks using
Norwegian crews and fishing boats.

Lunna House (1660) surveys its former
estates from the hill above the old kirk,
a beautiful little building with a 'leper's
squint', through which the sufferers
could take part in the service without
coming into contact with the rest of the
congregation. It is hard to credit that
this peaceful spot is the landfall for the
giant Ninian pipeline, through which
crude oil passes on its way to Sullom
Voe. Beyond Lunna House, the road
carries on along the ness, where you've
a good chance of seeing otters. Here too
are the glacially deposited Stones of
Stofast.

From Vidlin, a ferry to the Oot Skerries
leaves Friday to Sunday. It's possible to
return direct to Lerwick from da Skerries on Tuesdays and Thursdays, so
you may want to stay a couple of nights
in this rocky outpost. The sea route to
Lerwick is a fine one, entering the
harbour through the *north mooth*.

Like Whalsay, Skerries is a fishing
community, as the islands offer only a
little arable land. In compensation, the
natural harbour is one of the finest in
the islands, formed by three islands,
Housay, Bruray and Grunay. The first
two are linked by a bridge and Grunay
is now uninhabited, since the lighthouse (Stevenson again) was auto-
mated. The walking is easy as there are
no peat bogs, the climate as varied as the
scenery, while the community is famed
for its 'togetherness'.

Assuming you want to see as much of
Shetland as possible, you will take the
short ferry back to Vidlin, thenceforth
to Laxo, turning south on the Nesting,
road. This eastern side of Shetland
between Laxo and Lerwick is off the
main route and fine for exploration on
foot or by bike, with seals and otters
along the shore. Important in Norse
times, there is much excavation still to

be done in this area. At Newing, there's a prehistoric settlement of four houses, cairns and a burnt mound, while Eswick was the location of the ancient estate of Borg. The view from Gletness south to Bressay is a worthwhile diversion.

The Nesting road rejoins the main route north at Catfirth, another WW2 base, before the Loch o' Girlsta, named after a Norse woman, Geirhilda, who is said to have drowned here. Her father, Floki Vilgerdarsson, the first prospective Norse settler in Iceland, passed through Shetland in AD 865. Girlsta mill, dating from 1861, is still largely intact. Detouring through Wadbister along the shores of Laxfirth, the road arrives back at Tingwall valley. Here there's a privately run agricultural museum, which predates much of the later public research work on island history.

In Tingwall, the roads from the *airts* reconvene. Over the hill in Dale is the island's main golf course, with Lerwick and Scalloway a couple of miles distant.

How to get there

Ferries
Car-ferry from Whalsay-Laxo. Journey time is approx. 45 minutes. There is a reduced service on Sundays. Car-ferry from Lerwick to the Out Skerries, twice a week. Car-ferry from Vidlin to Out Skerries at the weekend.
By Air
Loganair fly to Out Skerries from Tingwall airport, 4 times a week. (☎0595 84306). Charter flights from Tingwall to Whalsay.
By Road
Bus service from Lerwick to Laxo. 2/3 times daily. Bus service from Lerwick to Vidlin.

Accommodation
Lingavec Guest House, Symbister, Whalsay (☎080 66 489).
Knowes Guest House, Skellister, Nesting (☎059 589 204).
Campsites
The Grieve House, Whalsay.
Lunna House, Lunna
Bremen Cafe, Symbister

Things to do and see
Pier House Museum, Symbister.
Walking: recommended – Lunnaness and Gletness.
Whalsay Leisure Centre.

Events and festivals.
Regattas (summer).
Nesting Up Helly Aa.

South Mainland

The southern arm of Shetland stretches some twenty miles from Lerwick. At first the road hugs the eastern side through Gulberwick, where there's a well-equipped diving centre, to a glacial break in the hill at Quarff (from the Norse *hvarf*, a place where boats could be dragged across land as at Mavis Grind).

The church here was designed by Thomas Telford. At Fladdabister, the old township system of crofts and outhouses is sadly neglected, though its structure is beautifully intact and shows the characteristic careful organisation of space and facility. Cunningsburgh, an area of good arable land, is the victim of a speedy oil-age road, cutting through the middle of it rather than bypassing, but the side roads are well worth exploring. The harbour at Aiths Voe shows the signs of herring fishing.

Leaving Cunningsburgh, stop to take the view back from the cliffs to the south, with Bressay and Noss beyond. At the head of the cliff road to Sandwick, turn off for Leebitten. The best-preserved of all the brochs is before you, a short summer boat trip from Sand Lodge.

Approaching the island of Mousa by sea, the size of the tower strikes home slowly. No doubt its situation helped prevent the common reuse of stone for other later buildings, as happened elsewhere. The walls are over 13m high, almost as high as its base is broad. Here the imagination can't help but wander, back indeed as far as the time of Christ, when this marvellously simple, integral structure was built. What kind of warring society existed here then, to necessitate such an impregnable fortress? What sort of enemy might have threatened, so long before the Viking raiders appeared over the horizon? Did word reach the far north of Roman legions invading the southern reaches of the land of the Picti? It hardly seems credible. Fear, rather than the actuality of an enemy, may well be at the heart of it.

Consider the primitive mind at the mercy of all kinds of supernatural fear, existing here in the north where the winter darkness dominated two-thirds of the day. Think of how these towers must have allayed those fears, how secure and cosy life inside them must have been when the natural enemy of the climate turned aggressive, the fierce biting gale sweeping overhead while the fire burned warm and the people slept safe in their tiny chambers. Maybe the origin of the brochs, which after all occur largely in these windswept northern places, are not so mysterious after all.

Back ashore in Sandwick, as in Cunningsburgh there's a network of little side-roads to be explored, with the Shetland Knitwear Co. in Hoswick where you can see the industry at first hand. At Channerwick, which lies below the road, the road splits, with an offshoot west to Bigton, while the east road passes on, high on the hill above Levenwick, where there's a fine beach and the remains of yet another broch. Further on towards Boddam is the Crofthouse Museum, which gives a genuine glimpse of 19th-century life for the ordinary folk.

The escarpment of the western coast ends dramatically at Maywick, south of which a strip of good farm land runs to bonny Bigton. Here, connected to the mainland by a narrow strip of white sand (a tombolo) lies St Ninian's Isle, where in 1958 a local schoolboy helping a party excavate the 12th-century Norse church uncovered what has been described as the finest Pictish trove ever found – twenty-eight pieces of silver, with the inexplicable addition of the jawbone of a porpoise! Ninian was the first Christian missionary to Scotland, in the fifth century. It's thought that the treasure of 1958 was concealed from Viking raiders in the 8th century.

Southwards round Mossy Hill, through Scousburgh, the 'hand' of the southern arm flattens out into some of the best arable land in Shetland. This is Dunrossness, where the houses and dykes have an Orcadian look to them, and there are records of settlers from the southern archipelago. This was the boyhood home of Tom Henderson, who did so much in the mid-years of the century to awaken interest in local history and establish the Shetland Museum.

The RSPB Loch of Spiggie is renowned for its fishing, and the road around its shores a delight. On the loch all sorts of wildfowl winter. On beyond the loch, the road heads south to Quendale, thrust unwillingly into the media spotlight in January 1993, as the scene of the wreck of the tanker *Braer*. Writing now, less than a year on, it is difficult to believe that the 'disaster' ever took place. On the surface at least, it seems that the predictions of doom were overdone. Today, the mile-long stretch of white sand in Quendale Bay seems as pure as it ever was. Perhaps it is ironic that Shetland, which has suffered often at the hands of wild storms, has also to thank the ferocity of the weather for dispersing the cargo of the *Braer*. Similarly ironic, for unspoilt walking the immense bulk of Fitful Head, above the carcass of the 'stricken' tanker, cannot be bettered.

Returning to the east via Boddam, a centre for the Shetland pony trade, the road passes over the hill to the village of Virkie, where the Pool o'Virkie is a haven for waders – including a few years ago, spectacularly, a slightly disoriented flamingo! At Sumburgh the airport governs, a massive new oil-age terminal with runways jutting out into the sea. Above it, the lighthouse on Sumburgh Head which the early risers spotted from the ferry north, another Stevenson job, dating from 1821. South from the village, the road to the Ness of Burgi points towards an Iron Age fort on the tip. Offshore lies Horse Island, said to have a thriving population of black rats, the survivors of an old shipwreck.

At the other side of West Voe's white sand beach is Jarlshof, so named by Walter Scott in his novel *The Pirate*. Scott could not have known, though perhaps his choice demonstrated the artist's intuitive gift, that a violent storm in 1905 would uncover the many layers of civilisation that underlay the medieval farmhouse he selected as his location, so turning it into one of the wonders of the northern world. Jarlshof is a place to spend the day, to wander through its maze of tunnels and walls, to explore the beaches round about. In many ways it bring together all the different eras of Shetlandic history you have seen in your travels, from the modern-day respect and care for archaeological sites back to Viking times and on through 3,000 years of continuous habitation. Well-maintained and eminently well covered by the on-site interpretative centre, no more need be said of it here.

How to get there
Ferries
Ferry to Mousa (summer only) from Sandwick.
By Air
Flights to Sumburgh from Orkney and the Scottish mainland.
By Road
Bus service from Lerwick to Sandwick, 5 times daily.

Accommodation
Barclay Arms Hotel, Hoswick, Sandwick.
The Swan Hotel, Levenwick.
Sumburgh Hotel, Sumburgh.
Meadowvale Hotel, Virkie.
Campsites
Levenwick campsite.

Where to eat
Mainland's Shop, Boddam.
Wilsness Terminal, Sumburgh Airport.

Things to do and see
Diving:
Skolla Diving Centre, Gulberwick

Boat trips to Mousa
Crofthouse Museum, Dunrossness
Jarlshof.
St Ninian's Isle.
Spiggie Loch RSPB Reserve.

Events and festivals
Cunningsburgh Agricultural Show (August)

Crafts
Barbara Isbister Knitwear, Meadows, Cunningsburgh.
Shetland Woollen Co., Sandwick.

Fair Isle

So we have come to the end of the road. All that remains is that final pleasure which you passed coming north, if come north you did – the MV *Good Shepherd* to fortress Fair Isle, which might be said to be neither a part of Shetland nor of Orkney, but a tiny world of its own, equidistant between the two. The ferry from Grutness in Dunrosness has an eccentric schedule due to the poor harbour on Fair Isle, so check ahead.

Internationally known for its knitwear and bird-watching, Fair Isle has no natural harbour, so the importance of crofting is accentuated. The ferry boat has to be pulled out of the water for safety. It's all very much a community effort and visitors can be helpers during the summer months, staying at the Puffinn, getting real experience of island life. The north side of the island is mostly common grazing, with the arable land to the south. Both ends of the island have a Stevenson lighthouse, dating from 1891. Unfortunately the keepers' houses at the North light were demolished after automation in 1980. A new technological landmark is the 65kw aerogenerator, which not only provides for the islanders' needs but also produces a surplus supply.

The myth that the famous Fair Isle knitwear owes its origins to the wreck of *El Gran Grifon*, the flagship of the troop transporters in the Spanish Armada, no longer has any real credibility. It might be fun to think that complex Moorish patterns found their way by sheer chance to the simple people of the far north, but it's a rather Mediterracentric conceit that fails to give due credence to the native civilisation of the north. Whatever, the wreck itself looms large in Fair Isle history even yet. 300 men were billeted on the 1000 islanders for six weeks, during which time some fifty of the soldiers died. Their graves are in the south of the island.

What they really made of each other, if they weren't sitting around swopping knitting patterns, is hinted at here, and there. One Spanish diarist calls the natives dirty savages, neither Christian nor heretic, which would seem to be contradicted by the local story that folk believed the Day of Judgement had come when they saw the bold Spaniards in their armour. The wreck was located in 1970. It had carried thirty-eight guns, one preserved, still loaded.

The other mark of Fair Isle fame, its Bird Observatory, was the brainchild of George Waterston, an ornithologist who bought the island in 1948 and used the old naval station at North Haven as his base. These huts were replaced in 1970 by the present structure. Fair Isle lies at the joining of two streams of migration, one from Greenland via Iceland and Faroe, the other south along the Norwegian coast. Over 340 different species of birds have been recorded.

In the 1950s, like many other isolated northern islands, Fair Isle's population was very low, to the point where the communal nature of life was threatened – there simply weren't enough people to do the necessary work, like pulling the ferry boat ashore. Evacuation loomed, but the then Zetland Islands Council and the National Trust managed to come up with a rescue plan, which has seen the number of residents rise from forty-four to over seventy.

As a staging post between Orkney and Shetland, Fair Isle was important in Norse times and there are various stories associated with it. During the 12th-century internecine struggle for the Earldom of Orkney, one unfortunate Fair Isle beacon-lighter, Dagfinn, was tricked by a fleet of small boats with large sails and was 'axed by Thorstein of North Ronaldsay' for his mistake. It can be more than uncomfortable being the one in the middle!

Leaving Fair Isle does not mean goodbye to Shetland. You'll have to return north, either to Grutness, Tingwall Airport, or by direct summer ferry to Lerwick, before the islands let you go. A last day or two in the town will give you a chance to reflect on all that you've seen, perhaps to pick up the souvenir you forgot. Wherever you're headed, whether north to Faroe and Iceland, east to Norway, south to Scotland or Denmark, *gying du in paece.*

How to get there

Ferries
Passenger ferry from Grutness, Sumburgh, to Fair Isle (☎03512 222). In summer, crossings are made twice a week; in winter, once a week. Passenger ferry from Lerwick, twice a month, in summer only (☎03512 222).

By Air
Loganair fly from Tingwall airport (☎0595 84306). Fair Isle Airstrip (☎03512 224). Charters are also available.

Accommodation

Hotels
Fair Isle Lodge and Bird Observatory (includes a museum)
Hostels
Puffinn (for volunteer workers)

Things to do

Explore!

Crafts

Knitting demonstrations in community hall.

The Islands of the Clyde

Bute

Bute is part of the Argyll and Bute district. The North end of the island resembles much of Argyll but the South end has quite a different character. This is because Bute is bisected by the Highland Boundary Fault which runs from Rothesay to Scalpsie Bay. South of the fault the rocks are old red sandstone, the land is pastoral and fertile, resembling Ayrshire, and there are still many Ayrshire cattle to be seen. North of the fault, which is marked by the Loch Fad/Loch Quien valley, the rocks are metamorphic and the land infertile moor. A large area of the north end of Bute has now been planted with forestry and there are raised beaches with an ancient shoreline at the fifteen-metre level.

The island is a little over twenty-three kms long and over seven kms wide at its broadest point. It is separated from Argyll by the Kyles of Bute which is about 600 metres wide at the Colintraive-Rhubodach narrows. The area of the Kyles has been listed nationally as an Area of Outstanding Natural Beauty and is world-famous. The climate is equable with the temperature seldom rising above 70°F in summer with little frost or snow in winter.

There are two towns, Rothesay and Port Bannatyne and a biggish village, Kilchattan Bay. The majority of the 7500 inhabitants live in Rothesay which is the shopping and administrative centre. Most of the hotels, restaurants and cafes are in Rothesay although it would not be untruthful to say that Bute is not famed for gastronomic weekends. Rothesay is also the centre for most of the leisure activities.

The Rothesay of today is largely a creation of the 19th century and was perhaps the most popular of the Clyde resorts until the early 1950s. Paddle steamers brought the citizens of Glasgow directly from the Broomielaw by the boatload and at Glasgow Fair the town was bursting at the seams. The steamer pier has been restored to a resemblance of its Edwardian grandeur with a pagoda-roofed pier building which replaces the previous shoe box, happily gone and unlamented. Of the former Edwardian building destroyed by fire in 1962 only the cast-iron cabbies' shelter and public toilet remain. Both are splendid examples of a vanished era and the toilets have now been restored to their former glory. Since the war Rothesay's holiday clientele has gone to Majorca and the Costa Brava and the town had gone into a decline from which it is now recovering thanks to both local effort and inward investment.

Having said that it is a Victorian and Edwardian town it has however a very ancient history. The castle, which is now in the centre of the town but was once on the shore, the area between it and the present shoreline being made-up ground, was attacked by the Vikings in 1228. This, the first of several battles, culminated in the Castle being burnt by the Duke of Argyll in 1685. Since then it has been a ruin. The family of the Stewarts of Bute have been keepers of the castle since the 15th century as is the present Lord Bute. The 3rd Marquess was responsible for the restoration of the Gatehouse in 1900. The castle is a courtyard castle, unique in Scotland, circular in plan with four round towers and surrounded by a moat. Within the castle is the ruined 14th-century chapel of St Michael. The complex is in the guardianship of Historic Scotland.

Of the other interesting buildings in Rothesay, St Mary's church is a roofless shell of probably the 14th century in the churchyard of the present High Kirk. It contains two recessed tombs. The Bute Estate Office is in the High St in what was a town mansion of 1681 built for a businessman from the mainland and subsequently the town house of the Butes. The Winter Garden on the Esplanade built in 1923-4 is a very typical creation of McFarlane's Saracen

Foundry. It has now been restored for us to enjoy after a decade of neglect thanks to the leadership of Lady Bute and in spite of the opposition of one or two not entirely disinterested individuals on the island. At 30 Columshill St there is what is reputed to be the smallest house in Scotland. The Bute Fabrics Mill is a long, white harled building, originally an orphanage. It now specialises in the weaving of upholstery fabrics. Finally on Ascog Point there is a circular structure with a concrete dome which occasions much curiosity and is no more than a sewage screening chamber.

Mount Stuart, the home of the Marquess of Bute, is on the east side of the island between Rothesay and Kilchattan Bay. It was designed by Sir Robert Rowand Anderson and built in 1879. It resembles a great medieval palace which would not be out of place in Italy but is somewhat surprising on Bute. It is understood that it will be open to the public from time to time on a restricted basis from 1995.

Port Bannatyne was originally called Kamesburgh and the name was changed by the Marquess of Bute in the middle of the 19th century to commemorate the Bannatyne family who held Kames Castle. This is one of the oldest continuously occupied houses in Scotland and is a tower house which may date from the 14th century. Wester Kames Castle is also a good example of a Scottish tower house and was extensively restored by the fourth Lord Bute in 1905. The present town is a row of buildings and shops of the 19th century on the east side of the bay with later developments on the west.

Both Rothesay and Port Bannatyne were naval bases from 1939 until several years after the end of the war. The submarine attack training school was at Port Bannatyne and was still in use until the 1960s.

Kilchattan Bay on the south-east coast of the island is a product of the holiday boom of the late 19th century. It consists of a row of buildings strung along the shore which would not look out of place in Glasgow but are a little incongruous here.

The hamlet of Kerrycroy is a creation of the second Lady Bute and consists of a cluster of white half-timbered houses clustered round a village green complete with maypole. It was the original terminal of the ferry from Largs.

The island has many remains of times past. The chambered cairns at Dunagoil, Glenvoidean, Glecknabae and Lenihuline have been excavated and dated to the third millennium BC and there are other important Neolithic sites. The Bronze Age is well represented by burial cairns of which a good example can be seen beside the road at Scalpsie car park. Grave goods have been found on excavation and many examples can be seen in the Museum in Rothesay. The vitrified fort at Dunagoil is one of the best-known Iron Age forts in Scotland and a great deal of material was recovered when it was excavated between 1915 and 1925. The vitrification, which was a result of the burning of the timber-laced wall, is particularly striking.

There are Early Christian sites of which the most important are on Inchmarnock, an island off the west side of Bute, at St Ninians Bay and at St Blanes on the south end of the island. St Blanes was an early monastic site but the present ruined church dates from the 12th century. It lies in the centre of the monastic complex which contains structures which may date back to the sixth century. It is a particularly beautiful and peaceful group of ruins and is well worth a visit. All these sites are very well described in the booklet on the History of Bute by Dorothy Marshall which is on sale in the Rothesay Museum.

The cotton industry in Rothesay dates from 1779 and the mill was the second oldest in Scotland. It was water-powered and the remains of the water cuts, constructed by Robert Thom in the

1820s to bring water to the mill, are one of the features of the island.

Bute has benefited greatly from the generosity of succeeding Marquesses of Bute who have not only donated much to the island but have stimulated others to develop its potential. The gardens at Mount Stuart, the home of the Marquess, are open to the public on selected days in the summer and should be visited by all garden-lovers.

The principal present day industry of Rothesay is tourism which has suffered, as have all the Clyde resorts, from the change in the holiday destinations of its main clientele. Bute has been particularly badly affected thanks to the stranglehold of a grossly inefficient ferry operator which abuses its monopoly and also a somewhat unimaginative town council. In spite of this, Bute is a beautiful island, full of interest, and one hopes that it will regain its rightful place as one of the jewels of the Clyde.

How to get there

Ferries

Ferry from Wemyss Bay to Rothesay. Approx 14 ferries per day in summer, 12 in winter. Time on passage ½ hour. First ferry at 7.10am. Last ferry in summer 8.40pm, in winter 7.30pm. Takes 36 cars and up to 650 passengers. Does not necessarily connect with the trains to Glasgow or the buses on Bute and is notorious for leaving intending travellers on the pier both at Wemyss Bay and Rothesay.

Ferry from Colintraive to Rhubodach. Continuously from 6 am until 9 pm in summer and 6 pm in winter. Time on passage about 3 minutes. Takes 12 cars and about 200 passengers.

Both ferries are operated by Caledonian MacBrayne. (Telephone nos: Head office, Gourock ☎0475 33755; Wemyss Bay ☎0475 520521; Rothesay ☎0700 502 707; Colintraive ☎0700 84235).
As this company has a monopoly the

fare will surprise you. The Colintraive ferry is certainly one of the most expensive ferries in Europe for the distance run. It costs 14 times more per yard than the Cal-Mac Gourock-Cowal ferry where there is a competing company.

Accommodation

There are too many hotels to list them all. Here is a selection:

St. Blanes Hotel, Kilchattan Bay (☎0700 33224).
Kingarth Hotel (☎0700 83662).
Crown Hotel, 54 Marine Rd, Port Bannatyne (☎0700 504158).
Alamein House Hotel, 28 Battery Place, Rothesay (☎0700 502 395).
Ardbeg Lodge Hotel, 23 Marine Pl., Rothesay (☎0700 505 448).
Bayview Hotel, 21-22 Mountstuart Rd, Rothesay (☎0700 502 339).
The Commodore, 12 Battery Place, Rothesay (☎0700 502 178).
Glenburn Hotel, Glenburn Rd, Rothesay (☎0700 502 500).
The Glen Royal Hotel, Glenburn Rd, Rothesay (☎0700 505 575).
Invercraig Hotel, 39 Mountstuart Rd, Rothesay (☎0700 502 323).
Regent Hotel, 23 Battery Place, Rothesay (☎0700 502 411).
Waverley, 37 Argyle St, Rothesay (☎0700 502 390).

Camping and Caravan Parks
Rothesay
Lanarly Garth, Rothesay (☎0700 502 048).
Roseland Chalet Park (☎0700 504 027)
G. Morrison, 'Braeside', Loch Ascog. (☎0700 505 457).

Where to eat

Rothesay
Ardencraig Tea Room, Ardencraig Lane.
Coffee Stop, 29 High St.
Copper Kettle, 17 Victoria St.
Craigmore Tearoom, 67 Mountstuart Rd.
Ettrick Bay Tearoom, Ettrick Bay.
India Pavilion, 7 Argyle St.
Pavilion Cafe, The Pavilion, Argyle St.
The Winter Garden Bistro, Victoria Street.

The West End Cafe, 3 Gallowgate.
Zavaroni's Cafe, 20 Argyle St.

Cycle Hire
Bute Electrical Centre, 5 East Princes
St., Rothesay.
Calder Bros. 7 Bridge St., Rothesay.

Craft Shops

Isle of Bute Candle Shop.
Isle of Bute Jewellery Shop.
Rothesay Creamery, Townhead.
Tourist Information Centre: Bute &
Cowal Tourist Board, 15 Victoria St.,
Rothesay (☎0700 502 151).

Things to do and see

The Front Gardens & Ardencraig Gardens
The Castle
Dabbles, Old Kingarth School, Kingarth.
(Spinning & Weaving Courses)
Kingarth Trekking Centre, Kingarth Old
School, Kingarth. (Pony Trekking)
Rothesay Riding Centre, Ardbrannan,
Canada Hill, Rothesay.(Pony Trekking)
The Winter Garden, Victoria St., Rothe-
say. (Cinema, Exhibition, Visitor Centre
& restaurant)
Rothesay Golf Club, Canada Hill, Rothe-
say. (☎0700 502244)
Port Bannatyne Golf Club.
Kingarth Golf Club.
Bute Museum, Stuart Street, Rothesay
(Important collection of archaeological
finds, natural history displays and
memorabilia)
Rothesay Creamery, Townhead, Rothe-
say. (Demonstration of cheese-making)
Bute Outdoor Activities, c/o The Pavil-
ion, Rothesay, Outdoor Activities.
Bute Sub-Aqua Centre, Ascog. (☎0700
505271)
The Swimming Pool, High St., Rothe-
say. 25-metre pool and tearoom .
The Moat Centre. Community Education
Centre with indoor Recreational Facili-
ties.

Both the PS *Waverley*, the last sea-going
paddle steamer in the world, and the
Second Snark; operate pleasure cruises
in the summer from Rothesay Pier.

Sailing
Bute Berthing Co., 15, Watergate, Rothe-
say. Berthing for 30 yachts on pontoons
and 45 on moorings.
Isle of Bute Sailing Club.
Angling
The island is unique in providing game,
coarse and seafishing.
Loch Fad: Rainbow & brown trout. 23
boats available.
Loch Ascog: Pike.
Loch Quein: Brown trout.Greenan
Loch: Carp, Roach, Tench.
Sea Fishing: Boats available locally.

Events and festivals

Jazz Festival (Last weekend in May)
Folk Festival (Middle Weekend of Glas-
gow Fair).
Bowling Week 16th-22nd August. (Provi-
sional).
Bute Highland Games 22nd August.
Agricultural Show 12th August.
Horticultural Show 5th-6th September.

Great Cumbrae

The Cumbrae (sometimes known by the
name of the town, Millport) is a children's holiday island. Millport Bay has
a beautiful and completely safe sandy
beach with two islets, the Eileans, in the
middle, perfectly situated for Viking
raids by ten-year-olds. Fintray Bay, on
the west side of the island, is another
completely safe and sandy bay. The
island itself, being only five kms long by
three kms at its widest point is a perfect
size for children to cycle round and the
shore road, being on the ancient fifteen-
metre beach platform, is completely
level. The popularity of bicycles is
acknowledged by the ferry operators,
Cal-Mac, who charge twice as much to
take a bicycle on the ten-minute journey
from Largs as on any other of their ferry

routes including the 5¼ hour journey to Barra. The hill road provides superb views from its highest point. Unhappily the view of the Ayrshire coast has been ruined by the now redundant ore terminal and building yard at Hunterston and the nuclear power station.

Geologically the island is old red sandstone which breaks down into good farming land. There is a swarm of basalt dykes which break through the sandstone to outcrop on the east side of the island. The most obvious of them is the Lion Rock 300 metres north of the Marine Station. The sandstone has eroded into fantastic shapes one of which has been painted to resemble a crocodile and another, near Fintray Bay, a giant.

Millport boasts the Cathedral of the Isles, Britain's smallest cathedral. Completed in 1886, it was designed by William Butterfield.

The Marine Station is the furthest outpost of London University and has an international reputation for research into marine life. The aquarium is well worth a visit.

Little Cumbrae

This island is privately owned and landing without permission is strictly forbidden. It has the second oldest lighthouse in Scotland and the ruins of an early chapel. There is a ruined tower house on an islet off the east coast which was a royal residence at the time of Robert II and which was burnt by Cromwell.

How to get there

Ferry from Largs approximately hourly in winter from 6.45 am until 6.45 pm with an extra sailing at 7.15 pm on Fridays and Saturdays. In summer, sailings are half-hourly until 8.15 pm with extra sailings on Fridays, Saturdays and peak periods. Time on passage 10 minutes. Takes 13 cars and 160 passengers. Ferry is operated by Caledonian MacBrayne (☎0475 674 134). An island bus meets every ferry.

Accommodation

Hotels

The Islands Hotel, 11-13 Barend St (☎0475 530 397).
Millerston Hotel, 29 West Bay Rd (☎0475 530 480).
Craig-Ard Guest House, 1-3 Craig St (☎0475 530 532).
Glencoe House, 1 Kames Bay (☎0475 530 350).
St Clair, 2 St Clair Gardens ☎0475 530 402).
Royal George Hotel, 1 Quayhead St (☎0475 530 301).

Caravan Park & Chalets

Isle of Cumbrae Caravans, Kirkton Caravan Park, Golf Rd (☎0475 530 370).

Cycle Hire

Bremners Cycle Hire, 17 Cardiff St (☎0475 530 309/530 707).
Mapes of Millport, 3-5 Guildford St (☎0475 530 444).
A.T. Morton, Mount Stuart St (☎0475 530 089).

Where to eat

The Newton Bar, 1/2, Glasgow St., Millport
Fintray Bay Tearoom, Fintray Bay.

Things to see and do

Robertson Museum & Aquarium, University Marine & Biological Station, Millport (☎0475 530 581).
Museum of the Cumbraes, Garrison House, Millport.
Scottish National Sports Centre, Burnside Rd., Largs (☎0475 674 666). Sailing and water sports tuition.
Millport Riding School, Upper Kirkton Stables, Golf Rd, Millport (☎0475 530 689)

Sailaway Sea School & Yacht Charters, Fairhaven (☎0475 530 040).
Millport Golf Club (☎0475 530 311).

Festivals

June Cumbrae Week, Millport.
Mid. June to end of August: Monday evenings: Summer Playhouse, Millport.
July; Fancy dress parade, Gala Days and raft race, Millport.
September: Illuminations and firework display, Millport.
Tourist Information Centre: 28 Stuart St, Millport (☎0475 530 753), or the Promenade, Largs (☎0475 673765).

Arran

The big attraction of Arran is its accessibility: a short drive from Edinburgh or Glasgow and a fifty-five-minute ferry trip and you're there. Just enough time to make you feel that you're going somewhere different but not such a long journey that you couldn't face it on a Friday afternoon. The island has a sense of remoteness and unspoiltness that is usually associated with the Western Isles. Often described as 'Scotland in miniature' Arran boasts rugged mountains, beautiful glens and small coastal villages, mapped out on an island mass twenty miles long and ten miles wide.

A narrow twisty road takes you around the island in about two and a half hours. This is well worth doing for the changes in landscape Arran is famous for.

Brodick is the main ferry port on the island and this bustling village offers a number of hotels and recreational activities to the visitor. Goatfell (2866ft) supplies a spectacular back-drop, standing over the bay with majestic splendour, and is best tackled by a path near

Brodick Castle. The Arran Heritage Museum is on the outskirts to the village and displays island life through the ages. Further along the road stands Brodick Castle and the adjoining Country Park. Built out of the local red sandstone, the castle can be seen from the arriving Ardrossan ferry. Originally the home of the Dukes of Hamilton, this impressive building now belongs to the National Trust of Scotland. The surrounding gardens are well stocked with exotic and rare plants and the tracks and walks through the Country Park make for an energetic afternoon.

The road north follows the rocky coast to the picturesque village of Corrie. On the way you should look out for seals basking on the rocks along the shore line. Corrie is one of the least spoilt villages on the island and washed cottages are scenically set against the hillside. The road continues on through North Sannox to Lochranza, a charming village where the houses nestle into the surrounding hills. The views are spectacular, across the Kilbrannan Sound to Kintyre. On a promontory jutting into the loch stands the ruins of Lochranza Castle dating from the 13th century. A seasonal ferry runs from Lochranza to Claonaig and is popular with travellers who want to go to other islands. Seals, stags and golden eagles can be spotted from the village but only if you're very lucky! There are a number of sandy, secluded beaches along this stretch of coast.

Further down the west coast is the peaceful village of Machrie, the ideal place to delve into the island's mystical past. A group of seven stone circles, dating from the Bronze Age, stand on Machrie Moor and give the area an almost spooky atmosphere. There is a small, sandy beach a short walk from the main road not far from the entrance to the route to the standing stones.

In between Machrie and the village of Blackwaterfoot is the King's Cave where Robert Bruce had his famous encounter with the spider. A gentle coastal walk will take you to the cave and offer spectacular views of the coast. The String Road leaves from Blackwaterfoot and crosses the middle of the island to Brodick. It moves up the valley for about two miles and passes through the village of Shiskine.

The coastal road passes through Kilmory and Kildonan and continues on to Whiting Bay. This is the holiday resort on the island with a number of hotels, restaurants, craft shops and outdoor activities. It has a marvellous sandy beach at Sandbraes with playing fields and swing parks close by. The spectacular Glenashdale Falls are near by and are well worth a visit.

In the next bay lies the village of Lamlash with the Holy Isle and its 1000ft peak dominating the view. Ferry trips can take you round the Holy Isle but these depend on the weather. The island's hospital, Council Offices and High School are all situated in Lamlash. From the village there is the single-track Ross road which takes you through the beautiful Monamore Glen to Sliddery.

How to get there

Ferries
Roll-on/roll off ferry between Ardrossan and Brodick. Duration – 55 minutes. Contact Caledonian MacBrayne, Gourock (☎0475 33755) for further details and sailing times.

By Air
No direct flight. From Glasgow Airport catch the ferry train at nearby Paisley.

Road
The ferry at Ardrossan on the Ayrshire coast, south-west of Glasgow, is an easy drive from Glasgow, Edinburgh and the south via Carlisle.

Trains
High-speed electric train service from Glasgow Central direct to Ardrossan harbour. Duration – one hour.

Accommodation

Hotels
Too many to list them all. Here is a selection:
Blackwaterfoot Hotel, Blackwaterfoot, ☎0770 860 202.
Greannan Country House, Hotel, Blackwaterfoot
☎0770 860 200.
Kinloch Hotel, Blackwaterfoot
☎0770 860 444.
Arran Hotel, Brodick
☎0770 302 265.
Auchrannie Country House Hotel, Brodick
☎0770 302 234/302 235.
Carrick Lodge, Brodick
☎0770 302 550.
Kilmichael House, Hotel, Brodick
☎0770 302 219.
Kingsley Hotel, Brodick
☎0770 302 226.
Hotel Ormidale, Brodick
– ☎0770 302 293.
Catacol Bay Hotel, Catacol
☎0770 830 231
Corrie Hotel, Corrie
☎0770 810 273.
Drimla Lodge, Kildonan
☎0770 820 296.
Lagg Hotel, Lagg, Isle of Arran
☎0770 870 255.
Glenisle Hotel, Lamlash
☎0770 600 258/559.
Marine House Hotel, Lamlash
☎0770 600 298.
Apple Lodge Hotel, Lochranza
☎0770 830 229.
Lochranza Hotel, Lochranza
☎0770 830 223.
Ingledene Hotel, Sannox
☎0770 810 225.
Cameronia Hotel, Whiting Bay,
☎0770 700 254.
Grange House Hotel, Whiting Bay
☎0770 700 263.

Youth Hostels
Lochranza Youth Hostel, Lochranza
☎0770 830 631
Whiting Bay Youth Hostel, Whiting Bay
☎0770 700 339

Campsites

Glen Rosa Campsite, Brodick
☎0770 30 2380
Breadalbane Lodge Campsite, Kildonan
☎0770 820 210
Middleton's Caravan Park, Lamlash
☎0770 600 255/251
Glenscorrodale Farm Site, Lamlash
☎0770 870 241
Lochranza Golf Caravan and Camping Site, Lochranza
☎0770 830 273

Where to eat

Most of the hotels listed above have restaurants open to non-residents as well as offering bar meals. It is a good idea to look out for the Taste of Scotland sign which indicates the use of traditional local produce. Below is a selection of restaurants and cafes:

Creelers Seafood Restaurant, Shop and Smokehouse, Brodick – ☎0770 302 810. Specialises in locally caught fresh fish and shellfish though meat and vegetarian dishes are also featured, Taste of Scotland member.
The Pantry. Whiting Bay – ☎0770 700 489. Unlicensed bistro. Offers morning coffee, lunches and afternoon teas as well as evening meals.
Trafalgar Restaurant, Whiting Bay, Isle of Arran – ☎0770 700 396. A licensed restaurant where 'A la Carte' dinner is served every evening. Advisable to book your table.
Coffee Pot, Whiting Bay – ☎0770 700 382. Specialises in home baking.
Glenisle Hotel Restaurant, Lamlash – ☎0770 600 559. A Taste of Scotland member well worth a visit for their delicious home-cooked meals.
Pirates' Cove Restaurant, Brodick – ☎0770 302 438. Specialises in local seafood.
Andy's Place, Lamlash. Local pub which offers folk music and loads of atmosphere.

Things to do and see

Fishing

A popular place to fish on Arran is Loch Garbad which is regularly stocked with brown trout by the Arran Angling Association. They also administer the rivers such as the Sliddery and the Sannox burns, both easy and accessible places to fish. Other places to fish are Iorsa River Fishing, contact: Dougarie Estate, Machrie ☎0770 840 229/259, Machrie River Fishing, contact: Water Bailiff ☎0770 84 241, Rosaburn Fishing, Contact: ☎0770 302 203 (permits available from Arran Estate). Tidetables and tackle are available from Johnston's Marine Stores, Lamlash. Tackle is also available from Bay News, Whiting Bay. Permits can be obtained from: The Tourist Office, Brodick, Shiphouse, Lamlash, Bay News, Whiting Bay, Lagg Post Office, Lagg, Corrie tearoom, and the Good Food Shop, Brodick.

Golf

Golf is certainly a popular pursuit on Arran with a total of six courses on the island. They are as follows: Blackwaterfoot (12 holes), Brodick (18 holes), Lochranza (9 greens and 18 tees), Machrie Bay (9 holes), Lamlash (18 holes), Whiting Bay (18 holes). Green fee prices are available from the Tourist Information Centre, Brodick.

Boat Hire/Charter

There are a number of places where you can either hire a boat or learn how to sail one. Whiting Bay Boat Hire (☎0770 700 382) offers ferry trips around the Holy Isle as does Lamlash Boat Hires (☎0770 600 349). Sailing tuition can be obtained from Kings Cross Dinghy Sailing Tuition (☎0770 700 442). Regular boat hire is available from Brodick Boat and Cycle Hire, The Beach, Brodick (☎0770 302 388).

Pony Trekking

Cairnhouse Riding Centre, Blackwaterfoot, ☎0770 860 466 offers novice treks and two-hour hacks for the experienced rider. Advisable to book in advance.
Cloyburn Trekking Centre, Brodick, ☎0770 302 108 and North Sannox Trekking Centre, Sannox, ☎0770 810 222 offer treks through the surrounding countryside.

Cycle Hire
Brodick Cycles, ☎0770 302 460, has Mountain Bikes and Speed Cycles for hire throughout the season. They also have a shop that stocks a wide range of spares and accessories and operates a repair service.

Mini Golf Cycle Hire, Brodick, ☎0770 302 272, offers reduced rates for parties and group hires can be delivered and collected from your accommodation. At no extra charge, you are supplied with a rider's helmet, small rucksack, basic tools, repair kit and lock.

You can also hire bikes from Spinning Wheels, the Trossachs, Corrie, ☎0770 810 640 and Whiting Bay Cycle Hire, Whiting Bay, ☎0770 700 382.

Walking
Arran is definitely the island for outdoor pursuits and there is a wide variety of walks ranging from strenuous hill-walking to gentler low-level forest and coastal walks. A few are mentioned below and for further information contact the Tourist Information Office, Brodick or the Ranger Service, Brodick Country Park, ☎0770 302 462.

Goatfell is one of the most striking features of the island. At 2866 ft it is the highest of Arran's peaks and falls just short of a Munro. On a good day it is an easy and enjoyable climb and you are rewarded with panoramic views over Argyll and Ayrshire and surrounding islands. You should allow six hours and always inform someone where you are going and when you will be back.

The path to the impressive Glenashdale Falls, near Whiting Bay is a spectacular low-level forest walk. A fairly gentle walk, it will take about two hours.

The coastal path to the Kings Cave near Blackwaterfoot offers superb views of the west coast of the island.

Brodick Castle
An impressive museum and castle, originally owned by the Dukes of Hamilton and now administered by the National Trust of Scotland. There are a number of walks and trails in the grounds of the castle together with the standard National Trust tearoom and shop (☎0770 302 202). Open Easter to September. Entry fee charged.

Machrie Moor Standing Stones
Near Blackwaterfoot, these standing stone circles date from the Bronze Age and give the place an air of magical mystery.

Arran Heritage Museum
Situated near Brodick, this museum provides an intriguing glimpse of island life over the centuries. Open April to September. Entry fee charged.

Arran Aromatics, Home Farm, Brodick
A wide selection of personal care products made on the island.